Diary of a
Pigeon Watcher

Diary of a Pigeon Watcher

By DORIS SCHWERIN

WILLIAM MORROW AND COMPANY, INC.
NEW YORK   1976

Printed in the United States of America.

1 2 3 4 5 80 79 78 77 76

Library of Congress Cataloging in Publication Data

Schwerin, Doris.
  Diary of a pigeon watcher.

  Autobiographical.
  1. Schwerin, Doris. I. Title.
ML410.S433A3   362.1'9'6994490924   [B]   75-38849
ISBN 0-688-03019-X

BOOK DESIGN: HELEN ROBERTS

For my son, Chuck, and my nephew, Peter

For their help in making it possible to re-create certain places and events, I would like to thank Dr. Benjamin Salata, Dr. Joseph Irgon, Evelyn Gay, Dr. Gerson Lesnick, Dorothy Richmond, Celia Patterson Salata, Dorothy Silverstein, Lois Berman, Alice Gilman Ellis, Zachariah Polivnick, Mrs. Tillie Israel, Mrs. Ruth Copeland, Pauline Bakeman, Geraldine and Charles Schlein, and most importantly, my sister, Elizabeth Gilbert. I would also like to thank Sherry Arden for her unusual gifts of joy and validation, and the editor of this book, Hillel Black, who from the beginning understood the song.

A special thank you to Dr. Robert Simonds, who carefully and lovingly steered me through the steamy archipelagoes of past time with the touch of a master pilot. And to my husband, Jules, "my glorious friend." Without his love I would not have sailed at all.

Introduction

IT was five years, almost to the day, that a tragic sense of impermanence was leaving me—that feeling of rush and futility I had grown to accept as myself, an inability to accept Time, for Time was of no use without a definite assurance of future Time. It occurred to me, much after the fact, that my pigeon watching had some connection with my cancer operation. I had always been profligate with Time, with or without the sword of termination hanging over my head. Before the cancer, Time was what I chose to waste. After the cancer, it nagged at me constantly, that to be profligate with Time was the ultimate degeneracy. Only a fool would not change under the circumstances.

So, I waited for instant purification. I watched to see a change in me, a feeling of blessedness for each moment, a new way of greeting day, swallowing hours, embracing friends and work—as I waited to learn what my cells would do, grow obscenely, or recede into normalcy.

Instead, a new, undefined anger became superimposed on all the old angers. Nothing had changed. It just became worse, and more, and there was a new blindness. It was not enough that I asked questions all my life and learned very little from the asking. Now, I knew something was wrong and couldn't even see it or feel it. For I knew as little about my bloodstream and cells as I knew about the galaxies. Would the cells run riot, or would they behave? Could they be controlled by my mind, or was that nonsense? Should I go and sit under a tree and get cosmically quiet? Should I try to forget that something had maimed me and made me unequal? Should I try to work as I never had before, with assured and deadly passion? For there would be no other time. Being maimed, was I now marked to "know" the trueness of everything, the best of beauty that there was? There being only "one time around," was I one of the lucky ones who could finally understand Time?

Each morning, the questions asked themselves, remained unanswered, got pushed onto the back burners, and cooked quietly all through the day, giving off a constant, low heat—a pot always too hot to touch, never eaten, never even tasted. Just there. Cooking away. A cancer pot of beans, God, it might burn, blacken, set the house on fire, make itself irrevocably known to me, once and for all. What other people cook occasionally and eat surreptitiously in Stygian, midnight moments of panic, I cooked constantly. The fear of death.

Sometimes, there was a devilish sense of elation, that I was cooking something most people never cooked. It was a perverse and illicit excitement. And if one was supposed to be born to joy, redemption, humility, love, grace, industry, piety, I, on the other hand had none of that, was here for none of those. I had something special. Shadows. And I would revel outrageously in all that was opposite of light. Those were the bad days, when I treated gloom with Dionysian delight, licked my wounds and loved the taste, rose to greet the day with a "Hell, you!" danced a pas de deux with depression in the matinee, and sang barbershop quartets with the Furies in the evening. A cornucopia.

Then, something most unexpected happened. I took refuge in someone else's Time, so as not to watch my own, dumbly. It was in the middle of my five-year wait (the magic five years they give cancer patients to see whether they'll make it or not) that I shifted my attention from my own mortality to the more mysterious one of another of God's creatures. Of all things, pigeons! Dirty, ubiquitous, lowly pigeons. The meeting, greeting, flying, love making, mating, birthing, tending, talking, resting, sleeping, cooing; the storms, the wars, the victories and defeats, the devotions, the laughter—the fight for life and joy of flight—pushed me back into the center of myself. I rode their waves in slow recognition and was reminded of many forgotten things in this cold, stone city.

Diary of a
Pigeon Watcher

Gifts

GIFTS. That's how it started. My husband gave me a pre-Christmas gift of a lovely little round table and two bright yellow chairs for my study, which until then had only a desk, chair, bookcases, and typewriter, all set up in what we called "the green room." The walls are covered with memorabilia, and under the desk, in a place of honor, sits the cat's pan. I don't think I could write without a vague odor of ammonia in a room.

We set the new table and chairs next to the window that looks out on a narrow corridor adjoining the neighboring building, just a matter of eight or ten feet away. Being true New Yorkers, we never looked out the window. It would be indelicate with our neighbors so close. When we want to look out a window, we take a bus for four hours and look out a window in Vermont.

I put a gay, floral tablecloth on the table. The yellow chairs lit up the room as though it were summer, and we changed the name of the room from the "green room" to the "breakfast room."

The next morning, while breakfasting on my new acquisition, I looked out the window between marmalading toast and picking up my teacup . . . and *saw* the ledge of my neighbor. On the ledge was a huge flower pot and several smaller pots on either side of it. In the large pot sat a pigeon. ZOOM! I looked again. The pigeon had flown off, and there were two eggs, resting on dried grass and twigs, like large pearls laid on luxurious brown velvet cloth.

"Hey!" I yelled.

The sound of my voice made Jules, my husband, come running. "What, what, what?" he said.

"There are two eggs in that pot. Look!"

We both peered out the window. It was a cold day, and our breath steamed up the glass.

"Two hard-boiled eggs," he said.

"Don't be silly."

"Well, so a pigeon is sitting on two eggs," he said.

"Well, for heaven's sake," I said.

And, that was the beginning.

Who zeros in on anything in New York? There is so much not to see, to forget, in this town of noise, scrambled planes, dope, black-white fear, hatred, ominous quiet, smog, fog, accelerated heartbeat, garbage, pop, op, oops art, innovation, recession, depression, inspiration, tempo, bridges, traffic, steel and glass drums beating back the sun. You run home, close your door, bolt it tight, and try to remember your name.

And there was a ledge with two eggs, in the midst of it all, in the dead of winter.

I have to tell you about our cat, Miss Willow, known to her intimates as Willie. What can I say? She's a gray alley aristocrat, with illustrious markings, fit for show. She does somersaults when she feels all's right with the world, talks to our plants, has consumed three thousand dollars' worth of fresh kidneys, and looks out the many windows of her home, dreaming of garbage cans or Vermont woods and field mice. She has often felt, when pressed for an opinion, that she could easily turn in her velvet pillows and her silk chairs for a couple of mice. But she's too polite to say so out loud.

As I sat at my new breakfast nook, Willie jumped up on the table, touched my nose, gave me a long, full gaze, then looked at the two eggs, looked at me again, and said, "There, dummy. That's what I've been observing for three years, ever since we moved here. Pigeons, pigeons, pigeons. Fascinating, dirty, ubiquitous pigeons." Willie is an inveterate watcher of "Sesame Street." Her vocabulary has improved noticeably because of it.

Willie grew up on the Lower East Side, in our former house, which was situated at the east end of a quadrangle, facing a park. There, we could look out our windows, see the tops of trees, the clock of an insurance company, hear the batting of balls without end, wake to the sound of a trumpet breaking the air at 4 A.M. (a love child, far from home, and lonely), have Sunday brunch to the tune of Hari Krishna, as sung by ten runaways hypnotizing their souls on a cement sabbath. But there were no birds. Only human sounds. We found Willie in a garbage can when she was six months old, raped and pregnant. She knew all about the ghetto, and its sounds bored her. She inclined to aloofness and forgettery and ceased to find the struggles of the poor interesting. Her energies, now that she was "saved," were spent mainly in eating and fattening up her soul. She had given birth to four enchanting children. They were reared according to Spock and had four respectable homes found for them. She had her last big love affair on Fire Island, became pregnant and gave birth to another litter, had postpartum psychosis and refused to feed her babies. They all died. This was enough to make anyone totally self-involved. She refused therapy, marched around the house like deposed, middle-Europa royalty, indulged in short shrift, demanded total respect, and watched, with unconcealed disdain, the comings and goings of the household from her Riviera window seat.

Then one day, we moved "uptown," close to Riverside Drive and the west winds. It took her six months to adjust to the newness. She spent most of her time under a bed, coming out only at mealtime, with her tail high and her eyes casting sidelong glances of recrimination. She missed her past and couldn't find it.

The day the grand piano arrived, she came out from under the bed for good. It was too big an event not to notice. She had been used to upright pianos, and this instrument was something else. The horizontal strings were indeed an advance for a cat. One could lie on top of this thing and actually watch the production of tones, specifically Mozart, her favorite. The trills, appoggiaturas, ah, the "Turkish Rondo." She also let the overtones of Bach massage her stomach, and life had some compensation.

Not too long after the arrival of the piano, Willie discovered that her new home had many, many windows.

Birds in the morning. Birds at sundown.

"Willie, get out of the way. I'm closing the window!"

"What are you looking at, the rain?"

"Down, down," we'd scream at dawn, when she'd wake us with her bumping against the venetians. We had to put screens in all thirteen windows, for fear she would fall, doing this curious cat thing. In her twelfth year, she became frisky as a kitten. The big, green eyes lost their shadows. A deep, enduring wisdom took their place. She was motivated, needed, committed. We had no idea to what.

It finally dawned on me that moment when I sat at my new breakfast nook looking out the window at the two eggs, that Willie had been a pigeon watcher for almost three years, that she had tried to involve us in her theater-going, her

else would make someone run from one window to another,
all thirteen of them, hour after hour, but an all-consuming
passion for the dramatic event?

Why had we never looked? What was it she saw?

❧

I never knew that city pigeons mated all year round.
A bird fancier at a cocktail party told me city pigeons were
DDT crazed. It was a particularly warm, late fall. Then, the
rains and snow and sleet came. It was a lousy time to bring
forth life. Yet there they were. Two eggs in a flower pot,
sitting on the ledge of a neighboring apartment house, just
a matter of ten feet between windowsills, ours and theirs—
a narrow corridor, close enough, almost, to reach out and
touch. It was a very large flower pot, big enough for a huge
rubber plant. How clever of the parent pigeons. A perfect
home.

> "And God said, 'Let the waters bring forth
> abundantly the moving creature that hath
> life, and fowl that may fly above the earth
> in the open firmament of heaven.'"

In the winter? There was no snow in the Garden of
Eden. It was the underbelly of civilization, warm and moist.

> So, if the First Book of Moses is correct, then
> it must be that the pigeon did Become before
> Man. It all happened somewhere between
> the fourth and fifth day.

The way one says things to one's self, I did, looking at
the eggs, turned away, and forgot about it for the rest of
the day.

The next morning, it was raining, cold, almost snow-
rain. I sat at my new table having breakfast and reading
The New York Times, a mystifying addiction. What's new?

There's gonna be a lotta dyin'. Why should this day be any different from any other day, age, era, eon? I looked out the window. "Christ in concrete!" There was a tiny yellow head peeking out through its mother's feathers. (I learned later it *was* the mother bird, and I was right.) The eggs had hatched sometime in the cold, rainy night. Creation! A bonanza. Why?

"Hey, there's a baby in the pot." Jules came running. We both peered out the window. It was raining hard.

"Where's the father?" He was perched on another ledge to the right of the pot ledge, about two feet away. And he was watching. He saw us and didn't like it. He flew to the pot ledge and sat on top of the iron grillwork that surrounded it like a playpen.

"But there were two eggs, weren't there?"

"Yeah, there were two eggs," Jules answered, walking away to go back to his shaving.

I looked at the little yellow head, through its mother's feathers. I looked again. Not one head, but two! Two babies. Talk about female instinct. Some stranger in me wanted to strip to the waist like lightning, ready to nurse. Twins on a ledge, in a flower pot, under a mother, ten feet away, in the corridor, right outside our window on Eighty-third Street. Relax. Wrong species. You'll just have to watch. And it's raining.

The quality of the air? In my head it wasn't raining. It was clear and quiet, and the quiet was so bright, it was the color of amber in medieval religious paintings. The silence gave off a light that shimmered all about the ledge. Jesus, Mary, and Joseph! I went back to *The Times*. There was nothing in it *that* new, not as new as two yellow babies in the rain. I couldn't keep from looking out the window. *The Times* dropped to the floor.

Ma and Pa don't seem concerned about the wet.

I go back to *The Times*. The military-complex

dollbabies have venereal disease and wear dirty underwear. It says so right in The Times. The dinosaurian conglomerates swing their ten-ton tails in the money mud. The sounds are awesome. You can hear the people yelling. Everyone's wired up to a mike or a movie camera. Everyone knows the top of everything. You can smell it. The bottoms of the icebergs can now be imagined. A lot is happening. The fight is getting tougher every day.

I looked out at the two little yellow heads through their mother's feathers. Damn it, that's beautiful. It really is.

Back to The Times. Hey, you son of a bitch, what in hell do you think you're doing? Dissent, outrage, indignation. Something's coming. Everyone's swimming upstream, like millions of spermatozoa wriggling up a birth canal, looking for eggs to puncture. Wham! Looking for eggs to connect with, fertilize, settle in for a long, dark birth.

It can't be all bad. What's good? The moving creatures are good. The fowl that may fly are good. The great whales are good. And man? With his dominion over the fish of the sea, over the fowl of the air, and over the cattle, and over every creeping thing that creepeth over the earth? The New York Times makes your eyes very tired.

I prefer looking out the window. Pa has flown off. Ma nestles in, pushing the two yellow heads deep under her feathers. What on earth made me wonder about the rain? Safe. With a mother like that, how could you get wet? She pokes them gently into an even deeper trough, beneath her bosom. She plumps out her feathers, looking pretty pleased with herself, and closes her eyes. Safe. How clever of them to have chosen a flower pot on a ledge with an iron grill around it, facing east, away from the prevailing winds. Peace.

> Every night, just blocks away, girls in white boots and teased hair, white girls in black wigs, and black girls in yellow wigs and thin coats, lean against buildings, and cars go by slowly. And no one's where they should be or want to be. There's a lot of darkness around, as though the universe hadn't quite begun, as stipulated in the master plan. People sell it on corners. Other people buy it, and sniff it, and it knocks them down (the darkness) into sleep, and no one is around to warn anyone that you can sleep through your time of knowing.

Well, at least two little yellow heads were where they were supposed to be, in time, and place and history. How simple.

I turn on the radio. My tea is cold. Mozart. That's fortunate. Relief, order, sounds of light-footed hope. The rain is coming down heavily. A whoosh of sound outside. Pa is back, teetering on the grillwork. Ma moves over, and Pa takes her place. Just like the guard at Buckingham, neat as a trick, without one raindrop spilling on the two yellow heads.

Pa pushes one head back under him and feeds the other infinitesimal beak. The father and child are beak to beak. Regurgitate. Feed. Regurgitate. Feed.

The first seems stronger, more insistent. It pushes away the second little beak. Woops. Siblings. Pa, feed the second. I find my nose pressed against the window, my breathing shallow, my heart beating. Feed the second one. Don't neglect it. Please don't. For Christ's sake . . . who needs this! I storm off into another part of the house.

A Sense of Order

I BEGIN to keep a diary. I would contrive ways to be at the window in the breakfast room. I tried to do it obliquely, so as not to annoy my neighbors, on whose ledge, after all, had settled this tiny kingdom of birds. Even so, I was aware that my neighbors, shadowy figures, were casting offhand looks at me, looking out. Perhaps I was a deviate of some kind, peeking for a dark reason of my own. In large cities, there is a suspecting, cool attitude toward madness. We shrug and turn away, making believe that what we see is normal, unless it hits us with a great, wet-toweled paw.

There was much madness in the small, New England town where I was born. But it was so woven into the familiar patterns of everyday life, the numbers were so small, and the embrace of the madness so familial, the strange were simply named "odd."

There were two severely retarded boy-men who lived diagonally across the street from us. The older one would occasionally run screaming up the street, waving his hands in the face of some fantastic figure who talked to him. That was Julius. He was a citizen of the town. He belonged there. And, his brother Benny, who sat in front of his house, smiling the livelong day. He too, was a citizen. One said good day to him and he answered with a shake of his head and a smile. When Julius, the elder, went screaming up the street on certain, uncertain days, one smiled for him, knowing he would calm down as he reached the top of the hill. One never turned away. He was Julius, not a stick of dynamite. Julius never scared me, not even when I was little. That's because he belonged to us. We never made believe he was normal. We knew he was mad, and because he knew we knew, he was pleasantly, calmly mad.

Then there was the Turk, with the pockmarked face, who lived in a roominghouse on the red-light street in town. He came to America without a woman (Turks in our town never brought their women to the new land), and became mad, probably with loneliness, working all day in a leather factory, drinking all night in the little Turkish bar under his rooms. On his day off, he would loiter about the steps of the library, scaring the clean little girls who went in and out with books under their arms. He never hurt anyone. He was just the mad Turk who lived on Walnut Street, part of the scheme, the fabric of the place, with its immigrants who came to work in the leather factories, its Yankees who ran the town. He was part of us, the Irish, the Pole, the Russian, the Jew, the Greek. He was the Turk. And we weren't afraid of him, at least not in the way one is afraid in a big city, where a stranger lurches toward you, loaded with a history too vast and alien even to conceive.

In a large city, the light turns green, you run across the street to escape the strangeness of strangers. You're afraid, and the stranger is angry you're afraid. I don't think we were meant to "nest" in millions. We are surrounded by insanity that doesn't belong to us. Nothing is personal, familiar enough to embrace. We have turned inward, gray, grasping, growling. Cities have outlived the possibility of love.

But I? I had just been given a gift, the chance to look

microcosmically at something that was not manmade. My
eyes had been hooded with veils of poured cement.

Yes. That would explain it all, my finding any pretext
to be in the breakfast room and look out the window, casually, mind you, at my pigeon family hard at work, living out,
with a quiet intensity, a sense of order, as though they were
nesting on a prairie bush, a mountain tree, a dune shelter.

The parent pigeons were doing what they were programmed to do. It was enthralling, a television channel I
kept on, hour after hour. I contrived to pass the window trying to respect their privacy, not knowing how much they
wanted to be looked at, then, sitting down to look further.
The idea of excitement being free made me wonder where
I'd been—to be so grateful for natural things. There was that
city, stone-cold mind again.

The babies were being so protected, I hardly saw them
in those early days of "watching." Obviously, I was peeking
out at the wrong times, and missed the feedings. There was
always a parent bird in the pot, sometimes both, just sitting,
staring out into infinite pigeon space or gently pecking the
neck of the other or touching beaks or squirming delicately,
as life squirmed under them.

When I was lucky enough to catch a feeding show, I
was amazed by my naiveté. Didn't I know that baby birds
were nurtured by the regurgitation process? I knew, but had
never "seen"—unobserved, behind glass, close enough to note
special characteristics in what looked like two identical silly
yellow bodies. One was stronger, more insistent than the
other. Because of that insistence, one child pigeon was fed
first, the other second. Oh, that second one. There it is—
survival of the fittest in microcosm. And I, too, was programmed to admire the stronger, feel sad for the weaker.
You're watching fate, baby, I said to myself. My, wasn't I
getting hooked on something. It was like listening to a
simple line of melody and wondering what the component

parts of that melody were that gave it power, imbedding itself in the brain like a musical tick.

It was a sense of order that hooked me like a melody. Something about the nest, the family, the flow, the feeding, the air around the pigeons as the days passed, pigeon Sisyphuses starting to roll their stones up the mountain. The blessed dumbness of it. Who needed pigeons! And, yet, there they were—in perfect order.

One day, as I peeked out, it struck me what I was getting—a sense of peace. A relief from human things, a different way of rolling the rock up the mountain. I sat down and thought about the using of time to make one's own peace. Why had I never been able to do that? Quiet time has always been spent in adding up the injuries, old, new, anticipated. Then, surprise! The largest package of them all, wrapped in silver, with ribbon made of gold spikings, mailed from Hades—cancer, nature's joke. Was it any wonder I would want to peek at some semblance of nature's order. Cancer, of course, can be cured. I will be one of the lucky ones! I think about how my former days were the ringside encounters of a third-rate fighter, with the smell of old failures not yet cleaned up before the new ones intruded their musk. I think of ghosts, stalking, like beasts of prey out for play, not meat; a bloody gambol, not to swallow, just to tease and leave in the underbrush. But now, with such a handicap, who would not run like hell and try to win the prize—a sense of order.

When did I last feel it, that prize? Ah, yes. Was it reading Plato's *Apologia,* on a lounge chair, facing a brook, with a bright wind and a high, hot sun? Aware of a slowing up, watching the yellows and reds and evergreens of Fall, the trickle of a slow water, slow and deep enough to understand the *Apologia,* every word of it? Perhaps.

Was it when I tired of the brook and the *Apologia,* and

walked to the October pond, floating like a listening seal, smaller looking than in summer . . . drifting leaves over half of it . . . leaf pointillism on opaque water . . . everything drifting: trees, water, clouds, drifting into winter? Perhaps. Or was it when I tired of the pond, it was down to the Ingmar Bergman forest of pines, and I said, "What happened?" Who dared strew confetti on the palace floor? It was yellow from the birch, red from the maple. Oh, my, there'd been a party in the half-light of the giant pines. Someone had carried bags of color 'cross the brook. It made me laugh. Was the delight a sense of peace? Perhaps.

Once I felt peaceful after someone said, "Stop playing games." And I stopped, and we talked for the first time in a long time; and even when the words came tumbling down and the marriage looked like it was the side of a stone mountain caving in . . .

Sometimes, after nine or ten words have marched in decent step, one right after the other, and I light a cigarette to look at them in the typewriter, and oxygen and smoke surge down my throat into my lungs . . .

I remember Mama combing out her long hair in front of her dressing-table mirror, and I'm standing so still in the aura of my own jealousy that I think the stillness is peace.

Once I sat in a room that had a bed with someone in it, who had her red wig hanging on one of the bedposts. Her long white arms lay next to her. They didn't look like they were dying, but she did. She told me all about what she was like at nineteen, and it was very quiet in the room and peaceful. We both enjoyed the story, and I left before she had to take another morphine tablet. The branches and leaves of big chestnut trees had rubbed up against her windows like green pussycats as she talked. It was a beautiful spring day. Now I see she had been using Time to make her peace.

Another lady died, just today. She died all alone with her high blood pressure. But she wriggled on the end of her own line before she gave up. She'd wriggled most of her life, stumbling over her own shadow, as though it were made of concrete. She smashed into it with her slightest move. When she got up to answer a bell that never rang, she fell, as though someone had pushed her. She blew smoke rings that spelled "Help," but they dissolved into thin air like smoke rings do, and nobody could read a word, not even she. Did she give, or did she take, or did that all pass her by? Whatever is, was; she's dead now and at peace. That's not the kind of peace I'm talking about. No siree.

I must name those silly pigeons out there. Smith. That's it. The ubiquitous Smiths. His will be Heracles, and she'll be a Sarah. Heracles and Sarah Smith. It's too soon to "nomenclate" two tiny yellow heads. I haven't even seen the rest of them yet. My, have I been wasting time!

But I continue to look, and look, and look, and days go by. I close in for a look at infancy again, and my amazement with it amazed me. I had done it and done it well! Don't I remember? Of course I do. My son was born in twenty minutes, a natural-childbirth baby. Not an aspirin. I remember seeing green fields on the top of my head when the doctor said, "Bear down." It was not painful. It was apocalyptical. I was amazed and delighted that I was translating pain into green, rather than snakes and earthquake and horror. But then, why not, I thought later. It was the most exciting moment of my life, when my Time suspended itself and made way for the true order of what I am, a woman, in total use; and, what a gift at the end of that Time, a son!

Then, I called my father, a general practitioner in Massachusetts, and told him he was a grandfather to a boy again (my sister had beat me to it by four years), and that the baby (he) had come out without a blemish, easy, calm and free of drugs, that it was natural childbirth.

"That's not new," my father said. "That's normal."

"Well, not for me, in the middle of the twentieth century," I said. "I think I'm pretty terrific."

(Silence.)

"How much does he weigh?" my father asked.

"Enough," I said. "I guess I smoked too much. He's little, but he's long. Not red, just right. He came out sweet, and you know what?"

"What?"

"He grabbed my little finger the minute he was born."

(Silence.)

"Is it snowing in New York?" my father asked.

"No, Papa. It's clear and cold." I had lied. It *was* snowing in New York, but the falling down of the telephone conversation, was the only descent I wanted to acknowledge at that moment. Papa always froze in the joyful crunch. I should have remembered that and not allowed a smidgeon of anger to infect the lovely day when my son arrived. I didn't. I lay and watched the falling snow on the last day of that old year, and I let everything around me in the hospital room be hallelujah.

My hairdresser is a moribund, repellent individual. He barely acknowledges your presence when you walk in from the street, with your dirty hair and hopeful spirits—hopeful that, once again, he will make you clean, bouncy and feminine by some kind of magic. He is not involved one iota in your rumpled presence, not even to comment on the weather from which you came. He is holy in his reluctance to admit his importance in your life. Au contraire, he goes out of his way (absolving himself from all responsibility) to prove that you barely exist, if at all. I talk to him in a loud voice, because I think he's deaf. Again, on the contrary, let it be but a whisper from another operator in the salon, and his answer is alacrity itself. For his customers, he is earless. As he submits your hair to curlers—reducing you to the state of a plucked chicken—his eyes have a far-off gaze, and his little behind jiggles to the tunes of endless cries for Love, Lost Love, Punishing Love, oozing from a never-turned-off radio somewhere in the back where the tweezing goes on, the leg shaving practiced, and the dye is kept. I notice each week that he is, indeed, not earless, because as he jiggles while he curls, one of his ears sparkles from a diamond embedded in its lobe. I swear that proves he has an ear. Jamming your brains under a hot dryer, with your outer head haphazardly tied in a hair net that droops over half your forehead, and so reducing you to a sight that makes certain your I.Q. has suddenly dropped to zero, he runs to his drugstore-bought books on astrology and pores over them with the intensity and dedication of a rabbinical scholar in the late Renaissance. Then, you, under the dryer, are for all practical purposes dead until you're dry, at which point, he wrenches himself from his horoscope and summons you to be "combed out," as though you were the last survivor of the Industrial Revolution.

He has, my hairdresser, only once or twice, fulfilled my tonsorial dreams of being beautiful, too seductively shampooed and set, enough to drive the nearest person to hirsute madness. More often, *it* happens when I wash my own hair at home.

One is always short-changed when one has to *pay* for a laying on of hands. What makes me think that my nirvana lies in the hands of a diamond-eared, sad homosexual, of course, is my misconception.

What a blessing to run home from the Broadway of hairdressers, to sit at the breakfast table and stare out at the two tiny heads in their pot. That Broadway! With its buses going south and its buses going north, its helter-skelter he's and spaced-out she's. That Broadway, New York City, two and a half streets away from the Pigeon-Smiths on their ledge, in their pot that faces away from the prevailing winds, with their babies under their warm bosoms, existing, not for buying, selling, turning tricks, eating hamburgers in formica temples. Who knows whether the moon is full or the tides are high? You can only smell the air between the buildings that limit your perspective. A sense of order? Everything seems to be off its axis on Broadway, as though something had a temper tantrum and proceeded to tear the strings of order out of their pinnings, plick, pluck. The latitudes and longitudes, meridians and poles of the collective mind lie strewn like torn-out surgical stitches on the operating room floor. The doctor went mad on Broadway.

❦

Weeks go by, and all is order on the ledge on Eighty-third Street. The baby birds are growing through the rain and sleet and reluctant sunshine of early December. Their yellow baby color is turning into something more practical; hues, a harbinger of maturity. One of the babies is becoming blue-black with a tiny tip of white at his "end," which is not yet a tail. The other is curiously brown. His tail remained, stubbornly, not a tail for much too long.

The nest was pristine and cozy, no matter what the weather. Each parent flew off at prescribed times, down the corridor between the buildings, and turned west toward the Hudson River, no doubt to forage on the ground for whatever pigeons forage before checking out the streets for garbage. When one parent returned, it would feed the youngsters, and then the other parent would take off. There was tremendous excitement each time a parent returned. The little heads, now stronger, would push out with chirps and wrigglings and lift their beaks to receive the bounty.

Soon, their whole bodies were exposed during the feeding ritual, and so I saw the change of color as the days passed. The baby whose feathers were turning blue-black was insistently unmanageable. The one whose feathers were turning brown was always fed second, because he was never there in time to be the first. The situation cried out for them to finally receive names. And so I named the blue-black baby Plucky and the browning baby—Brownie! They became birth-certificated in my diary. As I named them, I realized how dangerous it was. They were mine, my pigeon babies, and all that *that* implied, the responsibility of a Godmother, for as long as it was necessary, through sleet and snow and rain, sickness and in health. I was furious with myself for having made such a commitment.

Not long after the naming, I was called into service. The first real snowstorm of the year arrived. It was a lulu. I ran to see how the Smiths were faring. There they sat, the two parents in the pot, Plucky and Brownie under them, nowhere to be seen. The snow was settling on the parent feathers, and the parent bodies were making themselves as fat as possible to keep the nest dry. It snowed and snowed, and it dawned on me that neither parent was flying off to look for food. There was much squirming underneath them because feeding times were coming and going without something to eat.

The first of my hysterias concerning my pigeon babies began to form. I tried to make light of it. I fed my own face. Willow the cat got a midday snack. The newscasters on the radio that sat on the sill of our breakfast room were wild with excitement, describing the tie-ups on all major arteries leading into and out of the city. The traffic reporters from the helicopters signed off with a chuckle, and the city secretly rejoiced with a slowing up and silencing of its daily dementia. The city always seems to sigh with relief when something bigger than it takes over. By late afternoon, the laughter of children was throwing snowballs down a fast-disappearing street, and I looked out the window to see that Heracles and Sarah Smith hadn't budged the entire day from their positions in the nest.

How were they going to get food? I saw white undulations forming down by the river, and the branches of trees getting heavy with ermine strips. Tough work for a pigeon to bring home the bacon. Slowly, it came to me that I could, if I wanted to, rectify the situation. Out came the wheat cereal and onto the ledge of our bathroom window, which was diagonally across from the nesting ledge. I ran to the breakfast room to see if either Ma or Pa would notice. At that point I didn't know which was Pa and which was Ma, but the bigger and more aggressive pigeon cocked its head, looked at me through my glass, and did nothing. I sat very still at my breakfast table, turned the lights off (it was now almost five o'clock) waited for what seemed like five minutes. Then, a flurry of movement. The bigger parent flew across the corridor and was on my bathroom window ledge, gobbling up the Total, vitamins, minerals, and whatever else they put into those prepared boondoggles. Just as quickly, he was back in the nest, feeding the babies. The other parent flew over to the bathroom ledge, back to the nest, and fed them too. The snow, by then, was coming down in half-inch stars. It was going to be a rough night for man and bird, for stalled subways and clogged highways. But one thing I did know. Plucky and Brownie had full stomachs. They had stopped squirming under their parents, and all was well. What I didn't know was that parent birds will go hungry to feed their babies and that Ma and Pa Smith went to bed without sustenance that night, because I didn't put out a second sprinkling for them. It took me weeks to understand that.

I'll never forget when I met my first fool. I was two years old, sitting at a breakfast table in a farmhouse in New Hampshire, where we used to summer as children. I remember the air, crackling sunny of an August morning. My mother sat opposite me and announced that I, by myself, would salt my cereal for the first time in my life. Someone was on my left. It probably was my sister, who was five years older. I was only aware of Mama, her being, a cameo, close to my face. I took the salt shaker and sprinkled, and sprinkled with unending dispatch, as shouts of "No, no, no!" finally made me stop. It was oatmeal, with butter and cream floating on the top and sugar and raisins. I brought the spoon, filled with newly baptized cereal to my mouth, as my mother watched my face screw up in horror. It was too salty. I put my spoon down.

"I don't want it."

"You'll have to eat it. We don't waste cereal." (There was that royal *we.*)

"I won't."

"You will, or you'll have it for supper!"

"I won't!"

And I didn't. I was dismissed from the table, ran out to the barn, where I was not allowed to go alone, and wept and wept, till Farmer Brailey appeared with pail slops for the pigs and cordially asked me if I would join him in their breakfast. He was a nice gentleman. That evening I was presented with the cereal for supper. I ate it. My mother was a fool because, as I remember, I was two, and she was thirty-five. So much for cereal, which, strangely, I love to this day; hot, healthy cereal with lots of sugar and cream and raisins, and very salty! The salt invigorates me and sends down tremors of freedom on my tongue, waves of bright mornings, the smell of hay, as new as I was.

Strange, that in my son's babyhood, no such thoughts of cereal and salt and fools came up. His babyhood was free-flow charm and wonder from me to him and him to me. I don't think I'm bragging. He laughed for the first two years of his life because of how we touched and loved him. Why, he could have salted the stars and back again, that's how free he read himself in the pupils of our eyes.

It seems to me I read somewhere that the pupil of the eye in some ancient tongue is the same word as *mother*. Even if not true, perhaps it should be. Where else might one look for validation but in those parental circles whose shape mirrors the earth?

How simple it was to be completely, only, a pigeon. Certainly, the symbiotic state of the nest must be to teach us something it's so easy to forget, something about that early brew of dependency, that natural state of things when attention flows back and forth between creatures, older to younger, with no thought of taxation. How unlike the higher order of creature, who, almost from the beginning abjures connection though dependent, rails against restriction though flat on his back, yells with his first quavering voice: I am not an entrail, appendage, windup toy. I am your rage, your love, but that gives you no right. Why are you deaf? Stop pulling me into your footfalls and belches. Help! I am real. Himself. Your child, in deep flight, traveling upward. Do you wish me free? If so, contain within yourself *your* pestilence, if you'll be so kind. How simple it was for Heracles and Sarah. Brave, yes, but ultimately, simple. How simple it was for Plucky and Brownie; food, to grow strong, to develop instinct, to fly. It had to do with use of Time. I knew there was a lesson there. I didn't know what it was, but it made me calm.

The snowstorm ended the next morning, and it took the city several days to come back to a muddy normal. Then, it was hit by astoundingly cold Canadian air. The temperatures were zero and below. A most unusual winter, my radio kept intoning all day long. The Smiths begin to count on my food. I thought about all the goodies I should be putting out on the bathroom ledge to make Brownie and Plucky grow bright and strong, but I fought against spoiling them and making the family too dependent. So it was always cereal or bread or pumpkin seeds. My concern for their culinary welfare made my husband tease me and suggest I go out and buy a pigeon cookbook. City pigeons must have sophisticated tastes, he said. "Cold quiche, a bit of leftover stuffed lamb, but remember, no squab," he warned me. "They'd never forgive you. Then they'd fly away, and you'd have nothing to look at except me and Willow."

"Very funny!"

First of all, they weren't about to fly away. By now, they were owners of a choice, three-room apartment on the Upper West Side. The Smiths were rich. The three rooms were the nesting ledge with its huge flower pot (the nursery); as the babies got bigger, the parents took over a ledge right next to the nursery for their bedroom; the dining room was our bathroom ledge. They even had a cook. Me! Leave? Never! So I rose at seven A.M., in time for their breakfast, and managed to be home around sundown, which was pigeon suppertime. They fended for themselves for lunch. Enough was enough. I would stick to this schedule until the weather became a little warmer. Not Plucky and Brownie, but Heracles and Sarah really looked annoyed and strung out, in spite of the protective coat of oil in their feathers. They were so plumped out against the freezing air, I thought they'd burst. Well, just another few days. I mean, really! This was becoming preposterous. My friends were laughing at me, and not only they. I was laughing at myself.

A theater director of great sensitivity and note with whom I worked, pinched me once in the dark as we were watching a production we had done together. In a whisper, he said to me, "Hear that silence? When there's not a cough in the house and all are sitting as one, but each separately?

Then you know you're right, and magic is being made. Those are the moments we work for, darling."

There were great silences for me as I watched Plucky and Brownie grow. Everything was so clear, so wondrous, so simple once I gave myself to their rhythms, their cocked heads, their flashing eyes. I began to be able to understand their vocabulary of ornithological gesture. I could tell when Ma and Pa were saying things to each other.

"I'm hungry, Sarah."

"So, go down to the Drive, Heracles."

"Look, sweetie, you've been sitting here long enough. You're restless. Go visit the stone wall at the end of the corridor. Maybe there's someone out there from another part of town. Someone interesting."

And sure enough, Pa Smith would fly off the nest and my eye would follow him to the stone wall at the end of our corridor, where all the birds of the neighborhood would gather for exchanges. Ma was the more stoic of the two. She accepted her role totally, I could see that. Pa was wanting his freedom again. The babies were growing into young pigeons. So Pa would be away from the nest for longer periods of time. And one day, even Ma decided to leave the nesting place, sit on the parent ledge a foot or so away, and watch her children in the pot all by themselves, uncovered. I noted how full their feathers were becoming and how elegantly she made her decision to leave them exposed to the weather, because she *knew*. Her knowing was simple and sure. It was like the silence in the theater the director had pinched me about.

I had a feeling Ma didn't approve of me. She never came of her own volition to eat the food I put out. She only came after Pa flew over. She seemed to have a healthy distrust of anything that wasn't pigeon. Pa was the cosmopolite. He took chances, he was that sure of himself.

The days passed. Plucky and Brownie were growing

bigger and bigger. One day I saw real, little wings! From then on I noted the parents, returning to the nest from their forays, would flap their wings furiously as they approached the iron grill that surrounded the nursery ledge. Brownie and Plucky would answer with an awkward moving about in the nest, and their wings lifted themselves up an inch or so. The lifting of wings became an hors d'oeuvre to the feeding, beak to beak, of parent to child. How clever, I thought. How dumb of me not to know that. Well, how would I know if I'd never seen it happen? So, before each meal, Plucky's and Brownie's wings got a good workout, and as the little wings grew, there was more and more bustle and pushing about of the air, as one parent or the other would return to the nest. There came a time when the parent, flying home, would not fly directly to the nest but rather light on the grillwork around the nest. This set up such a flurry of anticipation that the youngsters' wings would flap furiously and they would push each other about in the confusion. Once, little Brownie fell on his beak in the excitement and had to right himself, by which time, naturally, Plucky was already eating. Oh, Brownie. He was beginning to be a caution, growing into the sweetest brown bit of nonsense.

Some afternoons, the flapping and exercising of little wings was so great, a mythical beating of the air, so beautiful to behold, so loud, it would make me turn from my typewriter. And Brownie, he flapped so much and so hard when he got the gist of what was expected, I sat at the window roaring like a fool. His little wings were being stretched to their ultimate, and he was still, always, fed second.

And so, I had rightly named Plucky, Plucky, because he flew first, demanded to be fed first, because he was the stronger and more alert, aggressive. For all those reasons, the favorite child. A go-getter.

Brownie got his name because he was brown. A little brown, talking pigeon who complained and commented constantly. I watched this little underbird fight for his place and his just desserts. And I held back from loving him too much.

It seemed that Mozart was always on the radio the following days. With graceful arcs of classic simplicity, Plucky and Brownie were narrowing the distance between themselves and the world. The winter air giggled and sparkled around them. When difficult things were tackled, like hopping from the pot to the ledge, a matter of six inches, the music in the air would suspend itself in slow, loving, thoughtful drafts, only to return, jubilant, pure calls of pleasure—as they walked past each other, feathers touching in friendship and awkwardness. They were always bumping into each other. Their little clawed feet were getting used to the cold cement. They were conquering the ledge, making zero distance between them and it, with its bumps and frost. Sometimes, they would stop and just look, their beaks pointed skyward. Look, and look, and look, and the music would rise in careful tones, higher, higher, a soprano, climbing her way to unexpected surprise. All was candor, truthful as new beaks sniffing the possibility of flight. In the key of E major. Four sharps, bright, virile, not a cloud in sight.

The Marauders

ALL the other pigeons in the neighborhood respected the Smiths' three-ledge territory. Sometimes, out of curiosity and high spirits, unfamiliar birds would fly into the corridor for a quick look, light on a ledge, sniff about, and some brief stirring from Ma and Pa Smith would send them on their way.

Pa and Ma were conducting their life in the corridor with order and grace. The days came and went, and Plucky and Brownie were growing larger and stronger, as I checked them each morning, Plucky always a little ahead of Brownie. Brownie would watch and a few days later tentatively try the same tricks. Soon, they were both standing at the edge of their ledge to await the return of one parent or the other. One parent was always present, if not on the nursery ledge, then sitting over on the parent ledge a few feet away. As soon as the small ones sensed a parent rounding the corner at the end of the corridor, a great fluttering of little wings would start, and they would hop back into the pot to await the goodies given them beak to beak.

It occurred to me how difficult it must be for pigeons to find those goodies as the weather remained constantly frosty and bitter, which is why Ma and Pa might have looked so satisfied each time they returned, to be able to fill those determined, growing beaks and themselves. I noticed something else. While Brownie talked constantly, Plucky, more active and full of learning tricks, said nothing. Brownie was always raising a fuss. He had something to say about everything.

Whenever I became aware of a chirping that went on and on, with cadences sounding like talk, I would look out the window, and something was always happening, either a parent returning, Plucky doing something new, or Brownie himself trying to do something new. Brownie's voice was becoming my pigeon drum, telling me all the news as it happened.

As quickly as he told me, it went down in my diary, which, now that Brownie was talking, was becoming fuller and fuller. I felt absolutely ridiculous making believe I was Jane Goodall in Tanzania. Only I didn't have to go to Africa. I could sit in my bathrobe scribbling away at the table in my breakfast room, not knowing at all why I was recording the domestic life of four out of three trillion pigeons on this earth. Every time I observed, now that I was deeply in their rhythms, it felt like opening tiny Christmas boxes; something impelled me, and so I did it, as though I were the first. Somewhere in me I knew it was important to me, if to no one else, and that I would continue to do it, and then put it away in a drawer with other private papers. There was a dignity about the Smiths that prevented me from thinking my scribbling about them was totally ridiculous.

Plucky was looking more and more like an Olympic gymnast every day. He hopped down, and he hopped up. He flapped his wings, and he craned his neck, becoming each day more fine, more in tune with himself and all around him. He was even aware of me through the glass. His tail feathers were growing as long as the rest of him put to-

gether. Brownie was right behind him, almost by a week—
"Hey, wait for me"—when Plucky did something spectacular.
Brownie seemed to be growing in spite of, rather than because of. His brown color became rich and shiny, yet when
he hopped or flapped, it was accompanied with sigh and
wonderment that he had accomplished it.

They were intimate as two bugs on a leaf, Brownie and
Plucky. They shared every sound and movement. They ate
ravenously morning and night, and when the sun hit the
ledge for a half hour of winter heat, they looked especially
handsome and happy, pecking away at the ledge, encrusted
with ice, New York soot, and parents' droppings. Yummy. It
didn't bother me at all. The excrement of one's own is quite
tolerable. They looked as sweet to me as though they wore
clean diapers and had just been bathed!

Ma and Pa were fending for themselves very well. What
I was putting out on the feeding ledge was the whipped
cream. Soon, only one parent was sleeping through the night
in the nursery, the other on the parent ledge, and the kids
were on their own, in their pot, feathers big enough to keep
them warm. All was well. The weather was holding, clear
and cold.

Into the scene one morning came a stranger. He didn't
fly in and out of the corridor like the other curious birds but
arrived with a great swoop, settled on a ledge around the
corner from the nursery, and stayed there. That ledge had
a large pot on it too, and an air conditioner to the right of it.
It was an even larger ledge than the Smiths' but more exposed. Ma was on the parent ledge and the kids were parading about the nursery. Well, well. I had things to do.
Brownie's voice reached me in another room, and I came
back. The stranger bird swooped over the nursery, then flew
to our ledge to get a better look straight across the corridor.

I sat as still as I could, noting how much bigger and
fatter this pigeon was than Ma and Pa. He was huge, his

neck throbbing with feathers, every color under the blue-black of his surface feathers. His eye cocked with fire, and he certainly looked like someone you don't fool around with. Suddenly, he flew to the nursery and sat on the protective grillwork around it. How dare he! Plucky and Brownie hopped into the pot with such dispatch a few twigs from the nest were blown out by the concussion. Ma Smith rushed over from the parent ledge, and the stranger flew off, out of the corridor, into open space. Ma sat nervously on the grill-work, cocking her head down the corridor. Heavens to Betsy. Where on earth is Pa? She stayed on the grillwork until he came swooping home, and there was much pecking around the neck as the kids sat, still as mice, listening. Pa was being told all. That was for sure. He looked down the corridor, patroled about a few times, then settled on the parent ledge, where Ma joined him. Situation normal. The stranger must have made a mistake, walked into the wrong apartment. All is forgiven.

Fifteen minutes later, there he was again. Brownie be-gan to set up a howl. It was way past my lunch (it always seemed to be when something was about to happen). There was the stranger, a quarter larger than Pa, swooping about the corridor as though he owned it. He flew in, and he flew out, then, damn it, he flew in again. This time, he hovered over the nursery, and Pa flew at him like a shot. The stranger didn't budge, and Pa flew at him again. This time the un-invited visitor left. Ma went for a foray down at the river. Pa stood watch. The stranger came again. The two birds con-fronted each other again. The bigger bird had a loose, arro-gant, motorcycle-gang-leader air, but Pa was a feisty James Cagney, making sharp figure eight's around him, and the stranger left, repulsed.

Brownie and Plucky didn't leave the pot all afternoon. Ma came home with supper, and that night both parents slept in the pot with their children. At least they tried. There was hardly room for them all anymore. Just before my own bedtime, I checked the pigeon silhouette in the dark. Ma was in the pot with the children, and Pa was scrunched up at the foot of the pot.

What now? The next day, there he was again, the stranger, but accompanied by another pigeon, just as big and beefy, but of a lighter color, a blue-gray. He looked like a Khrushchev, and she, the spitting image of a Madame K., a placid, sweet, big, Russian housewife in a great fur coat. Pa Smith had the lean and hungry look of a 1920's expatriate poet in Paris, in comparison. Where on earth had those new pigeons been eating? They looked positively stuffed. They waddled about and flew like cargo planes. Something was up. It dawned on me. They were apartment hunting! And had found just the place, a three-room suite filled with charm and old-world atmosphere, working fireplace. The food on the Smith dining room ledge was irresistible.

The strangers settled on the ledge around the corner from the nursery and made believe they were welcomed guests. Pa and Ma joined forces and shooed them both away. They left with a shrug. In the afternoon, they were back again. It was becoming an eyeball-to-eyeball situation.

Look, said I to myself. Mind your own business. This is pigeon affairs of state. (But I had a sinking feeling that danger had slithered into the Smiths' Eden.) You know nothing about the normalcy of pigeon life. On the other hand, said I to myself—with a Talmudic lilt—it hasn't happened before, so it's not normal. Maybe it *is* the serpent. Since when is the serpent abnormal?

The hell with it. I have my own. I pulled down the shade of the "watching" window and went about my business. On the other hand, I couldn't help thinking as I prepared dinner—those birds, I can't call them strangers anymore. They were marauders! Big, fat, Russian marauders. Beefy, probably dumb, *and* cruel, *and* anti-Semites. The kind that made pogroms and raided Jewish homes. My Smiths were in jeopardy. My husband roared when I told him at dinner.

"You'd better intensify your watch," he said.

"You're damn right. I'll call the police," I said.

"Which? The czar's or the GPU! What century are you in, pussycat? What Russians do they remind you of, your father's or ours?"

"My own!"

"Your own what?"

"My own marauders."

My Own Marauders

ORDER is precariously maintained. Then something happens and throws it off. First comes danger, then marauders, then, dissolution of the norm. Anarchy takes over, if there is not a strong enough will to fight, if there is not a hero-leader, outside or within. And, if reason is not behind the fight, forget it. Anarchy will be the hero, and anarchy is the worst of all, for within it are the cancers that use it as host.

In what river was I dipped? Was I Amazon-ed, or Nile-ed? Surely, not Hell's, Mother! Unlike Achilles, my heel, I find, is made of steel. It's my heart, that in dipping, you forgot. Cancer appeared on my left breast over my heart. Outrageous? I prefer to think about it a little more, until I've beaten the rap.

When the breast was removed, I heard my heart beating as I never had before. It lay under the exposed ribs, shorn of its outer self. There it is, my God, my heart, exposed like a man's. Unpleasant things? They are facts, never not to *not* be, only truths with which I must make peace. And, all the ancient and now gods willing, might I find a way to inject humor into the aftermath of accident.

I had lived with lumps all my life. Cystic lumps make

full breasts, the sure sign of a femme-desirable. An artist friend still reminds me of a yellow bathing suit I used to wear, when we were on a twenty-year-ago Rockport beach. His eyes twinkle, and I'm sure he's forgotten he is talking to the now-me, who *now* has only one of what he liked so much, that most men like so much. I'll never forget the look on my husband's face when I said, "If I want to find a lover in this new state of mine, he'd have to be a man who'd lost one ball. Then neither of us would feel short-changed. There'd be a balance." No, the humor backfired. I guess I couldn't make believe I had slipped on a banana peel.

Two years before I acquired my very own physical cancer, I went to see a woman doctor, complaining of swollen breasts that hurt even after a period. She had been newly abandoned in the shady part of her life (middle age) by a husband who left her for a younger woman. I came in with my juices overflowing, full, cystic breasts, nervous, and with tales of a lover. She winced and could barely look at me. She put me on male hormones, and I came running back, horrified. My breasts had gone flat. She put me on female hormones, and they rose up again. That was more like it. I never went back to her. I could barely look at her! She made me feel guilty that I was moist and she, dry. My body was so vulgar in its retention of fluid and hers so flat with denial.

My lover was danger. Defining love was danger. Wanting to be hurt was danger. Wanting what I couldn't have was danger. If I had been less New England and more root-less as to background, less Calvin and Old Testament, I would have met "him" in London and destroyed my marriage. The good old Old Testament tied me to the nest. I chose the order I knew over the disorder I didn't know but smelled. The choice was searing. The ghosts of the writers of Deuteronomy hovered over my head like avenging angels. The deafening music of my Cabala ancestors shut out all other decibels. I was a Jewish wife and a Jewish mother. Amen.

When all is well, balance maintained, a sensible peace, the norm, I would bet my bottom dollar there is no cancer. When there is grief, denial, guilt, depression, I bet whosoever *is susceptible* will sequester cancerous cells, when one's life is most vulnerable.

"No. She got cancer because her mother had cancer, her sister had cancer, the doctor who prescribed hormones did not know these facts, for some wild reason, and so, she was fertile for the marauders, who, if successful, could brilliantly attack the Achilles heel of her structure, which was in an emotional uproar, which was a willing victim."

Which is just what I said. When there is peace, it is not possible. When there is no peace . . . anything is possible.

🍁

The night before the operation, I knew I was living through a Time as Greek as ever I would know. I was a tiny figure walking into an amphitheater in the not-yet-committed, pale morning sun. None of the featured players had arrived, just a few members of the chorus, a musician or two were going over their parts. A black lab technician with a soft Island accent took my blood, and we laughed when I told him most of it would be alcohol, and that I better not drive up to my room. I had decided to arrive "tight" at the hospital, to make light of the awesomeness of the theater, to make believe I was the jester, not the queen.

I wanted to meet the actor who would be lowered in the deus ex machina, but I knew that wouldn't be until the sun was high. What God would he be playing. Mercury? Was I important enough for Zeus or Hera herself to intervene? Had some minor deity made a mess of things, and they would set it straight? Had I done everything in my own behalf, and so could stand, clear, in front of them, worthy of divinely highest intercession?

Two friends, usually great drinkers, accompanied me to the hospital signing-in. They looked at me as though I had gotten my signals crossed. I was not behaving in a hospital manner, i.e. cowed, frightened, and giving myself completely to the air of fascism that runs such institutions. They didn't know I was busy in my head transforming the monolith into a pussycat nest that would be my own; that I was the central player of noble birth, having accepted the role of tragic queen, just for "kicks"; that I was giddily trying to fool the lesser participants, and only in the presence of Hera or Zeus would I face the "role" in all seriousness. There would be enough time for that. Twelve hours. Tomorrow. Tonight, I would have long, fat hours in which to go over the script, carefully apply makeup, do my breathing exercises, and watch the dawn come up. There was no need for sleep. This would be my most precious wake-Time.

I was prepared for the worst. Three doctors had told me they suspected the lump was not benign. All three were male. The first, when he saw the fright in my face, said: "Don't worry about it. It will save your life, and the worst thing will be, you won't be able to wear a bikini anymore." He looked at me straight and then added with a smile, "Anyway, you're not eighteen anymore. Leave the bikinis to the teen-agers." He winked at my husband, sitting next to me. We left his office and never went back.

Time was pressing, and we looked for another expert. We found a fine one. He was kind and gentle, but as he examined me, I broke into tears, because he had me lying on my side on his examining table the way I used to when Papa lanced the cysts I would get in adolescence behind my ears. And I felt trapped by Papa's fear as he held the little knife, because he really didn't want to be treating me and shouldn't have, but it saved money. I knew I would never fully trust this new doctor, as hard as he tried being tender with me. Then, I rationalized that his hospital affiliation was not "the best." Papa would have wanted the best. I needed to be more royal, gambol on the Riviera, not at a church supper.

We found a third doctor, whose front door was entwined with ivy and looked like Beacon Hill. On such things are decisions made. But he was also a "big" doctor. There were fine pictures and objects in his waiting room, and he approached me, handsome, graying, a bit severe, a master-craftsman-quality permeating his tall frame. His hands examined my breasts with cool agility, and fifteen minutes later, he ordered his nurse to book a room for me immediately. I was to "go in" for a biopsy, and further than that, nothing was said, but all was surmised. I didn't ask one question. His air was too serious.

My husband and I left the office, walked up Madison Avenue and went into a posh bar for a drink. We were like two children on probation.

"Life is *not* a fountain," I said. This doctor was "top man" at his hospital. I could go no higher, except to another "top man" at another hospital. But I'd heard about "him," that other doctor. He was cruel. The man I had chosen was not cruel. He was handsome and sure. What the hell. The Bloody Mary made it a little better. Wow! What a secret. Cancer! The only other time I felt *that* inevitable was when we got back the returns of a positive rabbit test. This time we'd get back the return which would also be positive, which would be negative. The Bloody Mary was not really working.

I could run to Boston, where, Papa felt, the best medicine was practiced. But Papa was dead, damn it, and I was full-grown, and the air of New York was where I breathed and married and procreated, and must stay for the outcome.

If ever I needed the Oedipus figure behind me, it was

now, and my husband would have to be "it." (The Bloody Mary was working again.) Papa, the doctor, was dead. What a magic package, Papa and doctor. I couldn't run home. There was no one there. There was no one's word to believe, in simple trust. I was on my own, and even my husband, playing Oedipus, was wrong. He could only be himself, and I had no right to fancy any other role for him. His silent weeping for my ordeal was enough for any man who loved me.

So, it must be—alone. In the fat hours, I would find that feeling and hang onto it for dear life. If I found it, it would be the first time in my life, and I would be flying in the *Spirit of Myself*, a jerry-built, two-engine plane that would get me across the ocean of tonight, to tomorrow.

Several days later, pleasantly tight, my friends and I rode the elevator to my new nest. It was fine. I had brought a thermos of orange juice and vodka, and we drank to ourselves, after we tested the bed, rolled it up, and rolled it down. I put two books on the table next to the roll-up, roll-down bed, Thoreau's *Walden*, and the plays of Aristophanes, one to make me quiet, the other to make me laugh. The room had a balcony. We stood in the night air, looked out at the New York skyline, a nurse arrived, and my friends left.

"Make believe you're a tourist. Observe everything with new interest," I said to myself. "Put on the hospital gown dutifully. Chat with the resident who is examining the offending breast. Treat him like a new friend. Watch the blood being taken, with wonder. It's so dark. Be alert and intelligent when you talk with the anesthesiologist. Tell him how allergic you are to everything. Put him on notice. Tell him your father was a dying breed, a country doctor. Pull yourself up from the sea of anonymity. Tell him a joke. Make him remember you, this Mr. Morpheus. He is the boatman who will row you over. Make it known he is being watched, not only by you, but by your father's ghost. And last of all, that you know more than is good for a citizen to know in a fascist state," I said to myself. And did.

It was ten-thirty. Everything was done that had to be done. I refused dope. There was too much for me to do, getting my plane ready. A fanatic-mystic friend, who was then "into" numerology, organic, Zen and the stars (and now irrevocably into Jesus), called. She asked me to contemplate my breast, its skin, its muscle, its cells. She asked me to concentrate on the cells in my lump, to talk to them one at a time, to calm them, to prepare them for hurt, if not to make them normal. I felt like laughing, but I did what she asked. Who knows! And her voice went on and on, that dear friend, over the phone that lay on my bed, and not on my ear. I thanked her for her love and said good night and realized she would be the last one I spoke to as my old self, except for my husband, who would arrive early in the morning to bid me well and hold my hand as far as the ubiquitous elevator to the operating floor.

I knew I had cancer and that what the biopsy would turn into was revolution for my favorite breast. I knew it, yet long after my mystic friend hung up, I lay there talking to my cells, sensing each one, strangers within me. I didn't know what else to do but stopped when I got bored, counting, isolating the bad from the good. Never did I understand bad and good, as well as I did then. My breast felt radiantly healthy. I decided to get dressed and go home. Instead, I turned on the television set and stood at the French windows overlooking my balcony. Not listening.

The "hour of lead" was starting. Choice, I thought. I concentrated on the word. Choice. Am I an amber salamander, clenched in the fist of a child, fishing in the bushes of his childhood? Choice. Am I a female pachyderm, floundering in my dry and dusty land, in search of separated young, scared from my side by gunshot? Choice. Am I a brilliant-breasted bird, caught off guard, in a downdraft, made by some Sunday pilot's wing machine? Choice. Am I lapdog to the countess of my psyche, clutched to the suffocating bosom of her loves and hates? Choice. Ah, I was getting closer. Or, am I prisoner of myself, sailing in the falling shadows of myself, Mark Twaining in the waters of my undiscovered islands, my breasts, my womanhood, crying out the shallows and the deep, with no one there but me to chart the course and decide the wisdom of my attitude?

I turned around and looked at the television set. The face of Elisabeth Schwartzkopf filled the screen. She was singing a German lied. Her hair glistened in a braid that crowned her head and reminded me of Mama, who wore her hair the same way. I stood listening, very quiet, and a sob came out of my mouth. A sob so large that it only pierced the air once. A single cry, and then, silence. Like the cry of Willow, when she was placed on the examining table of her veterinarian for the first time, a cry that shook her tiny frame, too small for such a sound. The cry of a lion in the frame of a pussycat.

"Well," I said to myself. "You're finding out, aren't you!"

So it went. A dialogue. And I realized I'd made a mistake. I should have brought Plato, not Aristophanes. Well, I would make my own.

"Listen here," I said to myself. "Allow the experts to do what they have to do. I *am* strong. Strength is a responsibility. Make the decision, and end the torture of two minds. The die is cast. How many times in one's life can one say that so definitely? There is nothing more to do but go with the tide, colored by die-cast. Wherever I am, home is not far away, for I am home. My self, my things [I touch the jet brooch I'm wearing over my hospital gown, with the picture of my son in it] my books, my wishes, my total self—are always where I am. This thing (the operation) must be done well."

I listen to the lieder filling the room with what I love. Music. There *is* something perfect, manmade. Schubert. Thank God. Why not try to do "it" that way! Anarchy is chaos, dispersion. To do something well, that's the task. Elisabeth's smile, as she sings, is fabulous.

When there is so little time, doubt is a disease, indecision a plague, confusion a sin. I *must*, too, be beautiful . . . in grace.

I must try to sew a sampler for my soul tonight. Let me begin, in petitpoint. Why not? I've got fat hours.

"You may walk to the edge of the grave, my dear. With luck, you may enter the light again! You may not rest on a rock above the water line. Find a dangerous rock. I don't like satin pillows. Do you? I slide on satin pillows. Yes, we are shredding memory like brittle lace. Needless to reiterate: the lizard leaves its skin to dry and crumble in the sun. We both know that. I did it yesterday. But there are always leaves to rake and purity to contemplate, only as a ghost. And formulas to formulate. Ah, yes. Bullshit! I'm scared. So what? Proceed to sew some more, so what!

"Seeds dig in for sleep. Milkweed rises up to kiss the wind. Never stay where you are," I say to myself, "neither here, nor there. Proceed, proceed, proceed. The lesson for today is: [say it after me] Anger is the broken clock, lying in the attic eave. No, let's change that before it's sewn. Fear is the broken clock, lying in the attic eave. Babyhood, youth, first love, welcome and godspeed. Notice how the dust accumulates across the road. Better find a place. Make a printing with your naked feet. Watch it fade, brown to black to whiteness, and away. No, don't sew that. Don't sew 'fade' tonight. Finish it with 'yes.' Three yeses. 'Yes. Yes. Yes.' "

That's how Elisabeth Schwartzkopf sounded. Yes, yes, yes.

"Well, are you finished with your petitpoint? Not yet? What else? What do I love? How do I love?" (The being of my son fills the room, and I wonder how he'll take it all, this real-life stuff, Mom in extremis, naked, vulnerable, in the face of cancer, but why deny him reality as it was denied me?)

"What do I love? I . . . love . . . Bach! Certainly! Fresh-cut flowers! I love glorious Mozart! I adore Rachmaninoff. Oh, yes I do, even though his lines soar nowhere but upward, downward, inward, outward, unabashed, unclassical, unchecked, like adolescence. Ha! You try to do it as well. I love the sun, sky, water, sea, trees, babies, eyes of lovers, friends. . . ."

(It's midnight.)

"Then, I can love myself, for am I not made of everything I love? I must lie on the operating table loving. Let me be lucky! Let the lump be benign."

Elisabeth Schwartzkopf stopped singing, and the station signed off. Schubert was my last visitor of the evening.

"Now, to frivolous things. Those were the practical things. I will make up in the morning; foundation, a little rouge and lipstick. I've got to color my face so that after the operation, I will not appear greenish-white when they roll me down. Hey, I haven't even been wheeled up. I will do it anyway, spare those who will be waiting, from an apparition, fit for sympathy."

I lay everything out. No mascara. That would be obvious. I must just look well, even if the worst happens.

(If I don't know the depth of my well now, I'll never know it.)

"Thoreau? *Walden*? You're the wrong book. Not tonight. Was there a right book? No. There was no book. There was only me. This was selfish time. And I couldn't transcend it. Clear, cold, new time, for I would be different tomorrow. There was no help to be gotten. Only from myself."

I couldn't turn my mind off. My dialogue was a million miles away and I had failed. I was hysterical, with a pain in my left knee and thigh. Where did that come from! My heart began to beat like a clock about to split. "God, help me!" There it was. "The word came, you old atheist. You finally said the word, in context. Which god? Don't limit it. Make it Greek. There are more to choose from.

"Okay. You're in a hospital. Call a nurse."

She gave me a pill called Darvon. An unexplored island off the coast of Africa. "Did Ulysses anchor there? No matter if it works." It didn't work. It was almost dawn. "I must give myself up. I really must. To face the world without breakfast? Go quiet, love. Not 'raging,' Dylan. This isn't death. Now really! Not 'raging.' Just calm, calm into the operating room; that's all I have to do."

I make believe my hospital room is a paraffined existence, and I force myself to cover myself . . . with myself . . . and sleep. I'm exhausted.

My voice, which had been talking for hours was still talking as I slept. "So, I said to the surgeon, the tall man with the ivy growing outside of his building between Fifth and Madison Avenues. So, I said, 'You be your virtuoso self, and I'll be mine. Light the candles. This is a ceremony. We must perform as well as we can. Everyone is watching.'"

At six-thirty, I was up. I made believe it was a hotel room. "Get washed and put your makeup on, dear. You're in rehearsal with a play, and everything that can go wrong will go wrong. Be prepared." I looked great. The nurse came in and made a diagram in red ink on my chest. Indian territory. I knew the warpaint was right. All right. She gave me a shot in the behind. That's serious. That's second to meeting Mr. Morpheus. All the help of twentieth-century medicine I will receive, and give it to me, gently. She did. I waited for reaction. "Get sleepy." Move through revolution time like a sleepwalker? No such luck. I wouldn't give up my consciousness for a jade mountainside.

My husband arrived. He held my hand to the elevator. I was being wheeled like a corpse by two young men I had never met. I introduced myself. They thought my manners were the result of drugs. Not at all. I just wanted to let them know how important they were. Jules said good-bye. And there we were in the elevator, me, and two of them, whom I didn't know and would never see again. They looked embarrassed. I tried to smile.

"What floor are we going to?"

"You're supposed to be asleep," one of them answered.

"I'm not," I said. "Not at all."

They wheeled me onto a bustling floor. It was all wrong. I thought it would be a quiet place, like the little hospital of Papa's, and that it would have the deep silence of a theater before the first word was spoken. This was Times Square before the theater. And who should be walking down the street but the first doctor who told me I wouldn't be able to wear a bikini anymore! Stretchers were being moved back and forth like a battlefield, each figure lying down, more ashen than the next. I couldn't believe it. I was in a traffic jam. Patients were waiting to be operated on like a line in a supermarket.

I was wheeled into an anteroom where four other stretchers were parked. Everyone was out cold except me and another woman, who kept rising up and complaining, in not too normal a way. They all wore little white caps on their heads. God! Am I going to have a white cap too? My anesthesiologist from the night before stood in the door-way. He was holding a white cap, and he came and put it on my head just the way my hairdresser does with his hairnets, jammed it down over my forehead. "No, no," I insisted, and pushed it back to a more rakish angle. "There, that's better." The doctor looked at me as though I'd become unwrapped.

The complaining woman was becoming more obstreperous. Someone came to calm her down. She seemed worried about her jewelry, and her voice rose in unpleasant, vulgar tones. I lifted myself off my stretcher and in a loud voice proclaimed, "There will be no sounds in this room, but the sounds of Truth and Beauty! Quiet! Madam."

I began to laugh at the rule I had just made. It was absolutely insane, maybe I was going under. I saw the eyebrows of the anesthetist raised and remaining there. He was now sure I was nicely "unwrapped." I sank back. Was I reacting to the shot? No, it was to the lack of grace. I had nothing more to say. Mr. Morpheus then wheeled me into "the place." It wasn't an amphitheater. It was a small, neat place with overhead lights, machines, and a garbage can. I know. I looked for it. It was my last look, before my last thought, which was to repeat my name to myself. Pentothol. Who knows what else. They were doing what they knew how to do, well. I gave in to science, and someone else's artistry.

After many an anesthetic moon, the Woman came to a place where a Man, such as she had never seen, stood waiting. He ushered her into a boat. They crossed the River Styx, and with his hand on the rudder, he brought her home. He didn't leave her there. So close they were, not lovers, not even friends, yet he knew who she was, more than any other man. He was saving her—for money. It was science.

Mr. Morpheus woke me and told me. It was a *radical*. "It was a great wonder, the Man's work," he said, but I, the Woman, was full of pain. Six hours had passed. I was in my room with the balcony and trying to laugh when I woke. To three loving people standing over me, I said, "It certainly has been a 'farfalliner morning,'" I had used a Yiddish word for "lost," and they all laughed. It kept them from crying.

"Where's my brooch? I want it round my neck." I remember saying round, and not around. I used the "round" of folk songs. I was singing a lay, not talking.

The nurse said, "No jewelry after surgery." I insisted. The friends prevailed, and someone put my gold chain, with its jet brooch round my neck, and it fell on a large mountain of bandage on my left side. There was laughter in the room. Like a child, I had insisted on my talisman of femininity. I was going to be all right. I felt my husband's face standing in the corner of the room. He knew me so much better. He knew it was not going to be all right that fast. The anger came later. I had been amputated. We both had lost something.

The first day I was sitting up in a chair in my hospital room, a woman I never met walked in, high-spirited, her breasts proud and flaring in her chic dress. She was a member of "Reach to Recovery," an organization started by laywomen out of desperation in a man's world, women who had been disfigured by cancer and who wanted to help others. She walked over to me and said, "Feel me." I was shocked. She saw me pull back.

"Feel me. Go ahead," she said. "Which one is real?" I knew I had to feel her. My nurse was standing by, and they both waited. I felt her.

"Well, which one is real?" she insisted.

"I don't know," I mumbled.

Then she laughed. "This one, dear, this one." And she thumped one of her breasts. "I'm wearing a bra with a prosthesis in it. Just like you're going to. So, there's nothing to worry about. Now, here's our kit. It has a little red ball, and a rope and a booklet with everything you have to know about getting well in the next few weeks. And, if you're a good girl and do your exercises and squeeze the little ball [I can't remember what the rope was all about], your muscles will get back in shape and you'll be as good as new. And [she brought her face close to mine] you make sure you've got your husband in bed with you no more than two weeks after you're home. *That's* a must, or you'll lose him. You've got to be courageous. Get back on the horse."

I thought I would faint.

"You've got to think of him, you know, not only yourself. And if men don't get it at home, they're going out to get it. Keep in touch with us. Come to the office when you're up and about, and we'll give you the names of corsetiers who will fit you and sell you your prosthesis. In the meantime, here's a temporary stuffing, and you can walk out of the hospital with two breasts, in your best dress."

I must have been white as a sheet. She stood looking at me for a moment, not knowing quite what else to say. I was one of the overly neurotic ones, she supposed, and the look on my nurse's face told her she was right.

"Good-bye, Mrs. . . . Get well fast." And she left, wearing her two breasts and chic dress.

"You're a lucky girl," my nurse said, running her hand across my forehead. "Your doctor asked her to come. Not all surgeons do that."

I was in shock. Anesthesia was still in my system. I only knew earthquake, not epicenter. There was a plastic cylindrical bag hanging from my left side, attached to a tube from God knows what hole I didn't have before. My chest was tightly bandaged, and I hadn't yet thought about having lost a breast. The bandage felt like one. I was a slow learner and began to cry for the first time, about everything, from finding the lump, to the day after it was removed, taking everything else with it. Heaven will not bestow on this Jew surcease today. Doom.

"Now, don't be ungrateful," the nurse said, as she maneuvered me back to bed. "That lady is a marvelous lady."

This was a new thing she was doing, the nurse went on explaining—"brave and charitable and innovative"—indoctrinating one of her sisters into the Amazon Club, for women only. It was as new a movement as natural childbirth twenty years ago. I really was ungrateful. Who was I to want my psychology a little less jock! Spoiled rotten, that's who I was, not to have the guts to think about "making love" twenty-four hours after I had been operated on. What was wrong with me!

A few days later, the mound of bandages came off. I look at the black stitches. My left side had become a stranger. The dreamer side. There were no more dreams, only reality. The left side belonged to the doctor and his associate, who came and looked at it each day, smiling, approving. They were pleased with their work, and later I learned it was an exceptionally beautiful operation. The doctor *was* an artist. I felt I had done my homework well and passed the exam. But what of the jewels glowing in the dark of me? They were gone. There were no more secrets. I would have to find new ones. Not yet, though. It was too early. I would have to dig a new mine. The earth was crusty and tough on the top of my brain. My spirit would have to collect itself, raise some loot, buy equipment, survey the scene, find a partner, and start to dig for gold anew. Could I? Were the fortune hunting days over? Could I strike it rich again, with only one breast?

My left side was a battle map. The generals came in each morning, checked the positions of their strategies, left me to do the front-line combat, which would require their analysis the next day, fighting the battle not for me—I'd lost myself—for them, the generals, and above them Fate, which I was not facing at all, it being the first time, face to face. I had never faced the death of anything. I'm a hoarder of memory.

I watched the ooze lessen in the cylindrical bag attached to my left side. I liked it. I got used to the bag. My temperature was normal, I was healthy and fine, and I couldn't remember my name. I woke out of sleep, trembling and frightened, insisting the nurse tell me. She was a lovely, flat-chested woman, especially trained for chest surgery. She had had serious tuberculosis herself and a chest operation to boot. She exuded confidence and calm. Her dreams of voluptuousness had been long since buried. She was my lifeline. She made me eat, walk, talk, and massaged me into quiet. She "laid" her hands on my nervous system and stopped it from screaming. I made believe I liked her.

Slow, slow, after days at home, the pain subsides like an angry river, recalcitrant after flooding everything in sight with muck and disorder, trees uprooted, my house turned over on its side. And, as I stand looking at the fruits of disaster (the stitches moving diagonally where my breast used to be, my favorite breast, the one so quickly stimulated to love) I know there has been a death inside my house (like Mama lying in state in the parlor when she died). And I know other things remain, jumbled, thrown about, wounded, but still there, not dead. I wait for the courage to walk inside and slowly put my "things" to rights, push the broken heart back into its cavity, place my womanhood carefully in its drawer, where it lay for years with my pride and vanity. Lavender and clean sheets. I would have to be more ruthless with it. What must I conjure up to make it strong again? Nothing will ever be the same.

I thought very little about the totality and didn't dare think about whether I would have done it another way or allowed others to do it another way. The idiot phrase, "If

I had it to do all over again," is like another phrase, "In all honesty" (you mean you haven't been honest up till now?). I was too busy adjusting to the life of an emotional amputee. The sensations and meanings of woman-life seated in the breast are incalculable. How do you continue your sex life? Make believe there are two? How does your husband *really* feel, with all his protestations of it's not the outer, but the inner that I love, the whole of you, the history we've shared together. What's a breast between lovers? A lot, particularly when the breasts are full and round and heavy and the loss of one makes you feel light-headed when you walk, because there is an uneven distribution of weight as a constant reminder you are not yourself. The scales are tipped. Aesthetically, it's all wrong, unthinkable. A moustache on a Rembrandt. I had to deal with that. What to do? Wear a bra every waking and sleeping moment? To make believe you're complete?

No matter how much you both try to forget, the natural flow of love making is sandbagged. Your husband has to think first, react afterward. As much as he protested no, I saw the process in action. There was almost a physical sigh as I felt him choose the one breast to kiss and fondle. And try to do it with a forced unconsciousness, for which I thanked him. But it was no good. The abandonment was past. Passion raising could no more be electrically propelled. We would be thrown back to the ancient Archimedian screw. The mystery of breast foreplay was gone, the erect nipples, the magic, flying state of feeding one's love, known only to women, the gift of women to babies and lovers. The remaining breast was a clinical specimen, a survivor to be stimulated, but not to make wonder with.

Right to the seat of pleasure then, which was not my style. I would have to find a new way, be more aggressive, arouse him first, and if I did well enough, his excitement would be able to trigger off the main event. It would have to be a different ball game. Naked, half of me was boy, half woman. What a test, oh Lord, God, Jehovah. There would always be a fence the two-backed beast had to hurdle, before we could gallop across the countryside in delicious abandon. There would be no more that feeling of being perfect when loved. I had to learn a new language and become an immediate translator. Even the dark, that haven for uncomfortable women, couldn't hide the stitches and ridges of ribs, exposed, and my sense of loss. Was that how it was going to be?

Why did I let "them" do it to me? Did I fight for my body as an emancipated woman, artist, wife, and mother, with none of the ordinary conflicts other women complained about? I didn't, because in front of me, I had the tragedy of genetic tendency. There was nothing to gamble with. My mother had had a cancerous kidney removed, and my sister a breast removed. There it was. I thought I would escape the hand-me-down, but I didn't. I had become a statistic. There was nothing to be assertive about in the world of men and science. I *had* to put my body in the trust of that cool, unsmiling, virtuoso doctor. I had to let him lop my breast off, as they have been doing, using the same operation, with slight variation since the end of the nineteenth century. If testicles were removed as often as breasts, would the world of male-dominated science have found the cure by now? I was getting itchy and angry.

A month and a half later, I am working again. A lost kitten walks out of the woods, where I am having a play done. Does it matter? No, it doesn't. She came, one rainy morning, her tail clotted with tears, from the woods. She came, chin up, wagging her angelic face, with its kittycat, star-crossed eyes. "I've come a long way, dear," she said to me. "Cross my tongue with milk, a bit warm, if you don't mind." She asked so little, and I gave it to her. As I did, the pain on my left side left me for a while. I was healing, physically.

꧁

How long will I have? Will it strike again in some other part of my stranger body? I didn't want to acquaint myself with the statistics of survival. I was sure I would be one of the lucky ones. But each day of the first year, as I prepared to stuff my specially pocketed bra with its prosthesis—that was now my breast—rage was all, and fear the unembraceable ghost.

As the day wore on and assumed its shape I would become a functioning "person." But in the morning I was not a "Ms." or a "person." I was a woman in deep trouble, dressing myself in shining, black, wet rubber, flipping in fathoms deep below my ribs.

Perverse? Always. Losing a breast made me think more about being a woman than I ever thought before—when I was physically whole. I wondered if other women were better soldiers, resumed their duties, accepting, brave. I, who had always found refuge in melancholy, began to find the melancholy exquisitely suited to plunge even deeper into the center of this stranger who'd been amputated.

In truth, rage was all. The outside world was a constant abrasive. My private angers were being flamed by public angers. The Vietnam war crackled like a burning cross on which America would crucify itself. Terrorists were plucking airplanes out of the air and kidnapping people as my breast had been plucked and kidnapped. Social order was running riot . . . as my cells had run riot. *And* all around me was Women's Liberation, consciousness raising, bra burnings, angry women hurling epithets at whistling men, women finding the love of "sisters" in spirit and body. A sexual revolution.

Even if I had wanted to (now) I couldn't burn my bra, wear a topless bathing suit, and declare myself free. I was (now) light years away from physical experimentation. The whole world seemed to be occupied with the investigation of breasts and genitalia with the avidity of children playing "doctor" in the cellar. The capitalistic world, that is. And I had just lost one important erogenous zone! I couldn't play. As the economics of myself *and* capitalism appeared to be crumbling, the favorite word of the injured seemed to be "orgasm." How, with whom, how much, when and where. Private pleasure to combat public failure. Shades of Rome and Hitlerian Germany. (As the ship goes down, lie with the nearest lover and fornicate.)

And yet, withal (the fringe craziness) were not women flowering, moving once and for all into the mainstream of equal work and education, expressing themselves as they never had in the entire history of Man? From now on, would it be called the history of "Person"? Was that marvelous or neutering?

Through my own melancholy a voice kept saying something *is* wrong. There *was* a neutering happening. Who were those women running through the streets in fury, dressed in dungarees, their breasts banging in the wind? Why did I think they were flagellating themselves as they screamed "Freedom!" Why did I not feel related? Did I not want to be free and equal too? On the other hand, if women wanted their breasts to hang to their waists, it certainly was their right. I must be a product of bound-up, tight-assed Western society, and couldn't see the longer view for the mammaries. And yet, on still another hand, don't we Westerners have our own concepts of what is beautiful? We do not, after all, pierce our ears in many places to hold large objects. We do not stretch our nostrils, lips and chins to wear meaningful symbols. Those are not our aesthetic decisions. We have our own. Or do we? I went and sat for hours in front of marble statues entitled "Greek Woman," "Greek Girl," "Greek Boy," "Greek Man" at the Metropolitan Museum. The Greek woman stood mature, full-bosomed, with her breasts glorified by ribbons wound about her ribs (empire style). I looked at the delicately contained breasts of the Renaissance, the cupped, high-breasted women of the Age of Reason! All, of course, paragons of balance and beauty, perfection caught in art. I was obviously becoming obsessed.

Was I now to take my cue from homosexual designers of the late twentieth century—bent on bridging the gap between male and female to assert their own place—and let my pectoral muscles do what they will? My preoccupation was frivolous. There was too much for modern woman to do in a man's world.

I sat in front of "Greek Woman" (B.C.) and thought— my rites are thin as an ancient coin. Alas. How come you (man) don't spend a lifetime carving me in marble anymore! Am I not still Diana? Athena? Don't the winds of myth still blow around my mons veneris? Don't I look the same in a body stocking, honey?

I felt ancient and out of step. I could anticipate the weight of my modern sisters' outrage falling on my head: "Heresy! Be quiet! You are in no position to comment. You are filled with self-pity. Tend to yourself and recuperate! We're sure to see our dreams come true—of fashioning a bridge, a symphony, a form not yet conceived of by a man; a vase, a column, a curve, a swirl, a row of scientific thought, so clarified, the world will be able to cook omelets in its meaning. All the things we've never been allowed to do before. So get well and join us. No more on our knees in nunneries. No more tender traps for him to thrust his anguish. No more Griseldas, moist with longing. We're free and equal, love, the captains of our own secretions."

It was so strange. As my sisters talked to me, that's all I wanted was to be a woman in love with her opposite, hormonally. To conceive a king in the light of a midnight sun. The one thing I wasn't going to be able to do anymore . . . as a total woman.

All because of a few cancer cells run riot; and the little wheels of which the cells are built having lost their brakes. The subcellular particles, the molecules, the atoms, the electrons of myself . . . having lost their regulation.

Past Paradigms

I WAS wild for the accumulation of family fact. What else had I inherited, besides the cancer? What other things were handed down, as inevitably, as rain falls on wheat and wheat grows?

"It starts, on one side, at least as far back as I know," said my first cousin, who is a physicist, "with a well-known Chassidic rabbi in Poland." (Laughter.)

Is there a Jewish family looking for aristocracy that doesn't have a famous rabbi somewhere, nestled in a velvet-lined drawer of the past? It seemed as though we were no exception. True or not true, the wish was as good as the fact. Having a famous Chassidic rabbi for an ancestor was the surest way to best the Teutonic emblems of family-tree upmanship. It's hard to feel lowly when you can boast of erudition, philosophy, mysticism, religion, and magic in your genes.

"What are you up to?" my cousin asked. "Do you want a family tree? It's going to be tough. They moved about a hell of a lot. Remember, they were Jews."

"Remember? How could I forget!"

The Jew doesn't need a family tree. It's already on

paper. The Bible. I don't think that's what I'm after. Everyone knows who Abraham was. And that was a bit earlier than the Celts and Gauls, and who could even think of the Mayflower pilgrims in the same context. (There was that eternal snob-victim defensiveness again. That certainly was inherited, wasn't it?)

Just the way an anthropologist lovingly fingers the skull of a prehistoric man, isn't it possible to turn over, again and again, the spirit of one's forebears?

"Why the search?"

"I don't know," I said. "We come from such a distant, removed family. There's so little we know about who they were and what they were up to. Their nests. Maybe I want to find out if it's better or worse to be a Jew from the Ukraine than a pigeon from Samaria."

He looked at me strangely. I hadn't told him about the pigeon watching.

"I'm obsessed with nests," I said. "I'm a Cancer person, born in June."

He laughed.

Why the search? So as not to feel like a genetic accident, a hybrid, scattered in the wind? So as to feel more important than wild wheat in the cosmos or pigeons on a ledge? It really was with Papa that I wanted to talk. He had been so reluctant to share his pictures. And I wanted pictures. The unconscious is such a hoarder of images. They take a lifetime to catalog and decode. Here I was asking for the pictures of others to mix with my own. The accumulation would be a redoubt of memory. I would be armed and rich.

This cousin was the closest tie. He had been brought up by Papa's mother, Grandmother Pearl. My cousin and his mother, my father's sister Edys, and Grandmother were brought to America by Papa. They lived eighteen miles away from us, and we never saw them. Why? I had never thought about it growing up. I was thinking about it now.

Recollection comes in phrases; first, small, one-instrument plaints around a naked little memory; then longer sweeps about a larger cluster of remembrances; semiquavers move into curves, higher, lower, reaching trills that hang midair, defying passivity; then resolution, into solid, unexpected weight; the theme, lying heavy and prophetic in present Time; the theme, prodding the brain doors to fling open and startle the inhabitant inside backward into origins of feeling. Which comes first, the fact or the feeling? The inhabitant insists upon fact. It's safer. Recollection insists upon both. Recollection knows the two, fact and feeling, are forever wrapped, caduceuslike, and, only when entwined, can heal. Around what sort of staff do they wrap themselves? The unconscious. Fact and feeling, wrapped about the unconscious would give me a piton for my left hand. What about the right? In my right hand would be what I would imagine to be the unconscious of the family, no, not from Abraham, I wanted something closer in, like Grandmother, and her father, and Papa. So about the right-hand staff, heredity and environment would wrap themselves, again caduceuslike, the piton for my right hand. Up the rocky cliff then, cousin. I knew I couldn't tell him everything that was on my mind. He was a stranger, yet I looked at him and saw kin and he felt what I saw. And, slowly, the doors opened, and he unfolded things we owned in common. The theme . . . was Jews. It was a sparse, reedy sound, but better than nothing and a little surprising.

Papa had always given us the impression (after a few drinks) that he came from dirt-poor and lived in a hut in the Ukraine. We believed him, because that's the way he felt. He transmitted what it felt to be a Jew in Polonnoye, near Kiev, not what was.

"They lived in a large house, with servants," my cousin said.

"Servants? What kind, Jewish servants?"

"No. Russian peasants. Grandmother ran a business. It had to do with the making of cigarette paper. The franchise was originally owned by her father and handed down to her. Anyway, you know," my cousin added, "you're not a Jew from the Ukraine. You're a Jew from Germany."

"You're kidding! Papa never told us that."

"Our great-grandfather," my cousin went on, savoring the secrets, "emigrated from Emden, Germany, to the Ukraine in 1847, along with a German baron and his family, for whom Grandmother's father worked and shared destinies. They all settled in the Ukraine, bought thousands of acres of land, and were very rich. Not only the baron, but also Grandmother's father. His name was Abel Frankel. He owned serfs, ran his own estates with the help of two sons, and also oversaw the holdings of the baron, who shuttled back and forth from Germany to Russia."

"Who told you all that?" (I was so jealous.)

"Your father's mother."

"My father's mother? You mean, Granny, Grammy, Nanny! Mine and yours."

How formal we were in our family.

My cousin was enjoying himself. We had never sat like this before. And it was all on account of pigeons, but he didn't know that.

"Where in hell is Emden?" I brought an old Webster's to the table and looked it up for both of us.

"It's a seaport in northwestern Hanover, it says."

My eye glanced at the opposite page, as one's eye cannot fail to do when a dictionary is lying open. The heading on the very next page was EMPHYSEMA. That's what Papa died of. I felt a chill and didn't say anything. The Chassidic rabbi was in the room with us.

Emden, the known beginning; emphysema, the end.

My cousin went on. "There were about thirty golden years of affluence, and then Russia clamped down on Jews owning land. So the estates were taken away from Abel, and he became a businessman, as he had been in Emden."

"Family characteristics?" he responded to a question. "There's an intellectual streak in the family, math, science, mysticism, and *mishigas*. Scholarship was very important in families of a certain stature. Let's see, physical characteristics," he went on, "delicate constitutions, nervousness, habit-ridden, tics, anxiety. That's not physical." He laughed. "We're into something else now, not fearful, but anxious, not comfortable outside of family."

"Sounds very Jewish, perfectly normal."

"I, myself," he continued, "don't hesitate to jump off into the deep, but I worry when I do. So I'm always worried, because I'm always jumping off into the deep."

(And, indeed, he had just jumped off into the deep of world energy concern and come up with new numbers and formulas that added up to the use of solar energy for transforming waste of *any kind* into protein, electricity, and pure water. Any thousand acres on earth could be self-sufficient.)

"Am I helping you?" he asked with an amused look.

I felt agitated, excited. He sensed it. What *was* I looking for? I wanted a sense of belonging, beyond my beloved New England. I wanted to dredge up the smell and light of kitchens and bedrooms of strangers yet kin, the feel of other days connected to mine by sperm and ova. I was looking for a rope of kin to wind around my own unconscious, a belt of identity as strong an inheritance as a cancer cell. I wanted the life-giving spiritual cells to be as powerful if they existed.

"Where is it written they don't exist?"

Who said that? I looked at my cousin. Neither of us had said it. It was the rabbi.

"They married Grandmother, the daughter of a prominent family, to a young scholar, full of charm and incompetence. A good match. Riches and learning. She supported him for the rest of his life, and in return, he gave her nine children before he died of tuberculosis. So did two of the children. Your father was the third youngest, healthy, naughty, and bright. And Grandmother brought up all the children by herself and ran the family business. She was quite a gal."

"Papa didn't like her."

My cousin looked hurt. Then he reasoned it out logically, mostly for himself.

"By the time your father was growing up, the Russians were clamping down pretty heavily on the Jews. She was too busy to be a mother and probably left him in the care of siblings and a maid. I know there was a tutor, a young intellectual who was practically supported by teaching all the kids in the family, and later he came to America and became the editor of a left-wing Jewish newspaper in New York."

"Papa, the few times he would talk about the past, said he was beaten."

"Those were probably the older sisters who were nervous Jewish virgins, stuck with youngsters not their own but their mother's."

"He never once intimated the quality of his childhood, except for being beaten."

"What did you think of my father, your uncle?" I asked my cousin.

"I idolized him. He was awesome, very awesome to me. He was a figure to follow, not so much through exchange but by example and watching."

We sat silently for a moment, both thinking, I'm sure, of Papa and wanting him to be with us.

"Well, now—"

"You know," he interrupted me, "your father's house in Polonnoye was the Jewish intelligentsia center of the town."

"I do know Papa was sent away to school, and he ran away twice and came home, much to the chagrin of his mother. That he did tell us, my sister and me. He said he was homesick but hated home and would laugh at the inconsistency."

(This spiritual spelunking was making me very tired. I was gleaning a little something, though. The deprivation Papa spilled over on us was not physical but emotional. He had never resolved his differences with his mother. The role he played as a child never changed. He was the maverick, the unruly one, the recipient of punishment, for which he never forgave anyone. Then he mixed up those feelings with what it meant to be a Jew in an oppressive atmosphere, a young Jewish boy of bourgeois background—fine family, as they say, yet nothing more than a Jew to the whiplashing Russians.)

Papa's mother. I think I saw her no more than five times in her life, and she died a great old age of ninety-two. Her death came as a perfunctory notice when I was away at college. I never gave it a thought. There she had lived, the receptacle of family lore, just eighteen miles away from us in our town north of Boston. We never visited her as a family. There sat Pearl, knowing the Napoleonic time from her father, the American Civil War time of her own girlhood. Pearl, the young girl, whose wedding took place (so my cousin recounted) in a field in the Ukraine, so that the surrounding countryside could attend the ceremony of the daughter of Abel the landowner, with the baron sitting at the head table with Great-grandfather; Pearl, who danced for everyone, and the baron throwing jewels at her feet for her wedding gift. There sat Pearl, now in a tenement in the Jewish ghetto of Boston, removed from all that was familiar, again a Jew in a new land, at the age of seventy-two, whose last workload was to keep house for her daughter and two-year-old-son (my cousin), and to help shape him into an engineer, mathematician, physicist.

"She must have been made of steel."

"Yes, she was," said my cousin. "She was a cool customer but full of humor. She always knew what was going on, to the day she died."

"You loved her?"

"No, I liked her."

"Papa did his duty and brought her to his new land, didn't he?"

"She doted on him. She was very proud of him and forgave his running away. After all, he did keep up the family tradition. He was a man of learning, a doctor, and in a new country."

"Now, what about his running away for good and coming to America?"

"The story goes he disappeared one day with a friend of his. They were both sixteen, rebellious and very radical. They stole five hundred gold piecces from Grandmother and came to Boston, America. The friend didn't do too well. He couldn't adjust, and the minute he got hints of revolution coming in Russia . . . The story goes he went back and organized the youth of Polonnoye to form a Communist party. And he came to a bad end, your father's best friend. He and his brother, along with twenty other young men, were beheaded by members of the White Russian army—in a railroad yard."

"Gorki!"

"My mother and Grandmother witnessed it," my cousin said, "and they said the mother of your father's friend delivered a eulogy at the funeral. She kissed the severed heads of her two sons and told them they didn't die in vain. The Revolution would happen."

"Brecht!"

"Well, the Revolution *did* happen. How come the family didn't stay and reap the rewards of their radicalism and intelligence, Grandmother and all the other brothers and sisters of Papa? After all, wasn't the Revolution going to be the millennium for the Jew?"

"Aha. You're forgetting," my cousin chided me. "Between 1918 and 1921, Russia was a hell. Particularly the Ukraine. It was too unsettled and dangerous. And, of course, the Jew, as usual, was in the middle. One month, Bolshevik forces occupied the town. The next month, invading Germans and Poles; the next month, Americans and Czechs; then the White Russians. *And* everyone was in league with the White Russian army to squelch the Revolution. *And* the White Russians were executing every known radical and intellectual on sight, and if you were a Jew *and* a radical, forget it. They were killed like flies."

"So, what happened?"

"It seems that in 1920 your father's oldest brother, Abraham, who was managing the family's affairs by then, went to Warsaw on a business trip and decided to settle there. It was a more decent and tidy existence. He got out just in time, and then others followed him. A large group of Jews and radicals slipped over the Polish border at night, including Grandmother, my mother, and me. I was a baby."

"Wow!"

"Well, it was either that or be killed, by accident or intent."

"So that was the end of Polonnoye and the memory of land and apple orchards, and cigarette paper and status and—"

"So my mother said. We joined Uncle Abraham in Warsaw, and in 1922 your father sent us money to come to America. Warsaw couldn't have been much better than the Ukraine, for Jews at any rate, newly arrived. Yes, he brought us all over. Abraham remained. He died in a concentration camp in the late thirties."

"And his children? I'm sure there were children."

"Yes, there were. Who knows?"

"And what about Papa's oldest sister—what was her name?"

"Brindel. She fled to the Crimea with her husband."

"Did anyone remain in Polonnoye?"

"Yes. A younger brother, Edward."

"Edward?" (My mind was beginning to boggle with the litany.) "What happened to him?"

"Who knows?"

"And Brindel and her children, another who knows?"

"Grandmother heard that one of Brindel's sons was a general in the Russian army in World War Two."

"Then that branch of the family must have survived well."

"Who knows?"

We both sat in silence for a long time imagining what we didn't know.

"Getting back to the streaks and bents of the family," my cousin broke the silence.

"What difference does it make if half of them ended up in furnaces, becoming bars of soap and lampshades?"

He decided to ignore my cry. We had been skittering around the barest edges of kinship—disaster, rebirth, disaster, rebirth. The Jew, fleeing from Germany to Russia to Poland to America, and God knows where from before Germany. Great-grandfather Abel was a landowner and rich man. But he was still flogged by the baron for mistakes made, because Abel was a Jew. What did Abel think? What did Abel feel? Was Abel in Papa, his grandson? Was he in me?

The quality of the etchings was bad. The ridges were worn, through second- and third-hand telling. It was too late for original impact with the European kin. I was exhausted, imagining tall, blond people from Germany (Papa's whole family were blond and blue-eyed) mixing with shorter, darker people from the Chassidic rabbi branch, people with intensive drive to be middle class, with a lust for scholarship, passionate, cool, like Grandmother, nervous yet intellectually courageous like my physicist cousin (he said Grandmother heard there were others like him in the Crimean branch).

My cousin began to laugh out loud. "You come from a long line of snobs. You talk about nests"—I was amazed he had remembered my saying I was obsessed with nests, it was ages ago—"even when they were finally locked up in the ghettos of Boston, your little Grandmother would harrumph at the kitchen table at the inferior lineage about her. And her brother Avrom, you know, became the first Jewish member of the Boston City Council."

"Now who the hell is he?"

"My dear, Avrom was the young man who got the peasant girl in trouble and fled as far away as he could get. To Boston. Remember?"

"When was that?"

"About 1880."

"You mean he was here when Papa arrived in 1906? Then Papa didn't arrive a waif. He had family here! For Christ's sake!"

"I should say. Avrom's younger brother came too, after the Russians confiscated his father's land. And your father's older sister, Sophie, arrived in 1901. She married beneath her, so the story goes, and when Grandmother (who was still in Russia) heard about the caliber of person she married, candles were lit and Grandmother prayed for a week. Sophie and her husband had a chicken farm. They were the first Russian Jewish family in Lexington, Massachusetts."

"That I do know," I added weakly. Aunt Sophie had always interested me, although I might have seen her once in my life. She had two sons with whom we were allowed to share some sort of kinship. One became a psychiatrist, the other an aeronautical engineer, and Aunt Sophie had a massive breakdown and spent most of my growing-up time in an institution.

"You know," I went on. "Oh, forget it, I'm exhausted. It had to do with someone saying there were sunflowers all around Aunt Sophie's farm, like a gold ring."

"Yes, there were sunflowers."

"I still don't understand. *Why* did Papa separate himself from everyone? There were nests all over the place he could have crawled into."

"They were all helpful to him at first. But, you see, your father was . . ." He was searching for words.

"Go ahead," I interrupted him.

"Your father was a new breed. He turned his back on the old-time religious Jew who strove for middle-class values as the panacea. Even his family was anathema. Your father was the ultimate snob. He was a radical and a very stubborn man."

"I know."

"He never gave an inch," said my cousin resignedly.

"I know. He stubborned and idealized his way through life with a glorious poker up his—" I stopped. My cousin was very much like his uncle, my father, a formal man.

Again, we sat for a long time, saying nothing. It was getting to the end of the afternoon. How Papa would have roared, listening to us trying to put together everything he had purposefully and ruthlessly smashed, the whole kit and caboodle of family pattern, love, and concern, the ways of old Jews!

Our talk trailed off in an almost whispered coda, phrases slithering away from the main theme . . . into the air.

"He wanted it that way, evidently, to find a new way in a new country, without ties."

"Without the Old Testament, without the oppression of old orthodoxy."

"Marx, Lenin, and Freud were the new ones."

"His friend had been beheaded by the White Russians."

"He would pursue radicalism and eschew the nests open to him."

"Yes, with the Friday-night candles, and the women in wigs, and kosher butchers, and kin, turning into business-people, department-store owners, capitalists—"

"—suffocating closeness of tribal ways, and memories of the past with their beak-to-beak Hebraic feeding. What a paradox he was!"

"Well, that was the beginning," my cousin ended. "The rest you know."

"No, I don't know."

"You don't know what?"

"*How*"—my Chassidic ancestor gave me a shove and made me pause for the correct Talmudic time—"*How* can a person be a Jew, throw off Judaism, and remain a perfect Jew in a hostile environment?"

"Who knows?" my cousin said, reaching for his coat.

We were at the door.

"There must be cousins running all around Russia and Poland that we don't know," I said as a parting gesture.

"Yes, if they weren't exterminated; but who knows?"

(There it was again.)

"What made them not lose courage?" I asked, putting my quaking boots on, as he checked his hat in the hall mirror.

My cousin laughed. "Next year, Jerusalem! Who knows—"

"Oh, stop it with the 'who knows!' "

Red-letter Day
for Plucky

MIDAFTERNOON of the eighteenth (December). It was a cold, brilliant, sunshine day—Grandma Moses without the snow. People walked on a phenomenon (New York sun-swept streets) with Achilles' heels that bounced their feet toward Christmas. It was definitely the day to "do," ho-ho, spend money, to be sorry for those who didn't have it, weep and feel lucky.

My head was in a half-swivel away from the typewriter, looking at Plucky and Brownie. Wasting time. I turned back to the keys, again to the dumb alphabet stare. There was a whir and beating of wings. I knew the sound, but it couldn't be the kids; they don't fly! This time I turned full about, and there was Plucky, flapping his wings with such vigor he almost took off! The look on his face was one of such surprise I burst out laughing. I noticed I was laughing a great deal, out loud, in the quiet house, those days of pigeon watching. Plucky kept on flapping, faster and faster, a mad little thing, with the afternoon sun hitting his outspread wings. A mythical brightening shook the air. Everything seemed to be happening on cue. Was it the sun, at that exact moment hitting his back, that made him rise to full exercise? The little wings in extension looked enormous. Oh Plucky, you'll be flying soon! Yes, we're close to flight. An exhilarating, peaceful feeling ran through me. I noted with bemusement I was not observing coolly but with a mother's eye. All through this Olympic display of prowess, Brownie was sitting in a corner of the ledge with a look of "showoff" on his face. Plucky finally settled down in the pot, very self-satisfied indeed, and there they were, one of the innumerable pigeon studies I relished like a secret vice.

To hell with the typewriter. I left my desk for the table next to the window and, chin in hand, sat looking. That quiet of looking. And through the experience of the past month . . . that if I looked long enough, something would happen. If nothing happens, it's called wasting time. If something happens? It's observation. If I understand it? It's perceiving. Perceiving what? That birds fly? I was a little worried about the inordinate amount of time spent in this quiet time of looking. My excitement made no sense. It was childlike, yet I couldn't keep away from the window, as the days approached nearer to the time Plucky would surely take off. I wanted to be around when it happened.

The two little pigeons and their parents had become my chance to connect with an ancient step, "feeling" the nest, the past, the steps of transformation like major chords pealing outward (provided there was to be no aberration). The muscle and nervous system rituals, outward. The strengthening into total usage of all parts till one matter-spirit moment, divined, when everything said "Go" for that little bird, and flight to freedom was not only possible but inevitable (providing there was no aberration). I wanted to see something inevitable, outside human determination. Animals on fours and twos fall and stumble and recover. To fly you have to be perfect. I was "seeing" it for the first time, from inception. I had passed through looking, into observ-

84

ing, past perceiving, into feeling. I was feeling flight! Perceiving with feeling would be insight.

Chin in hand, there was no house, no ledge, no city stone-cold. It was the Garden of Eden, and God was saying again: "Let the waters bring forth abundantly the moving creature that hath life, and fowl that may fly above the earth in the open firmament of Heaven."

Something happened. It was not wasting time. Along comes the male marauder pigeon. Mr. Khrushchev flies through, surveys the scene, sees the kids unattended. He swoops down on Brownie, and proceeds to peck at his head with lightninglike fury. Brownie screams. Plucky hops from the pot and hides in the opposite corner. It's V2 time over London, napalm in a rice paddy. The act was swift and just as incomprehensible. Time suspends. Murder in the nursery. Khrushchev means business. He tries to push Brownie off the ledge. The little brown baby clings to the grillwork like mad. I pray he'll hold. Plucky comes over and tries to peck the fullgrown bird away. It was the first time I saw Plucky peck in anger. He knew how, but it was a vain though glorious gesture. The big bird envelopes them both. Plucky rushes back to his corner. It's Brownie the marauder wants first, little Brownie—to throw him off the ledge! My heart races and there's a taste of blood in my mouth. It was up to me. I was ten feet away.

I rush to the dining room, grab a fistful of what? Of what? Walnuts! Back to the green room, fling open the window and start to pelt the murderer with nuts. The big bird looks over at me with astonishment. I yell, "Get away, damn you!" He turns his back and continues to peck at Brownie, who by now looks like the last scene of *Swan Lake*. I hear myself muttering, "Oh, dear" (how ineffectual). I throw another nut and another. My aim is terrible. I am aware that I'm trying to effect a pitcher's warmup. Laugh at a time like this? How could I! The nuts are hitting the neighbor's window with loud thwacks. I'm terrified the neighbors will rush to the scene, see what I'm doing and call the police.

ANGRY WOMAN THROWS WALNUTS AT NEIGHBOR'S WINDOW. UNDER OBSERVATION AT BELLEVUE.

With one walnut left, I take aim (I think I spit on the nut), and pray I'll pitch it right. A curved ball to the back of the neck. It hits! And "monster" flies away. I sink to my chair, shocked at the brutality of the scene, at my own anger. Plucky comes over to sniff Brownie, who is whimpering, and it makes me cry.

Delicately, Plucky starts to move his beak over what look like painful spots on Brownie's neck. He tries to smooth the feathers down that are standing up like wounds until Brownie stops crying. They both hop into the pot and sit very close and quiet.

By now, the corridor was filled with cold, black shadows. It was after four, pigeon dinnertime. I still sat at the window, stunned. Violence. Always violence, police sirens, accidental death, premeditated death, political death, hunger death. But death from covetousness, in the pigeon world on a middle-class ledge four flights up? Why? Because this ledge had a pot already twigged and cozy? There was another ledge just around the corner, within sight, with another empty flower pot, ready and waiting. Twig your own pot, damn you, if I have anything to say about it. Did I have anything to say about it? I could certainly keep a little brown pigeon alive who was only ten feet away from me. Or could I? Were we related?

Ma and Pa Smith came skittering around the corner. Well, it's about time, for heaven's sake! They sniff at two bullet-walnuts on the nursery floor, touched beaks with both children, and looked over at me in the window. Damned if they didn't know. Pa fed Brownie first. (It was the first time the little one came first, so they must have known.) Then

Ma fed Plucky. Both parents repaired to the parent ledge and hunched up for the night. The kids were in their pot, heads staring out into infinite pigeon space.

It was to be a cold night, perhaps the coldest of the year. Well, I can't worry about that, too. They've got feathers. If they freeze to death? There are three hundred trillion pigeons in the world (an emotional estimate). Knit woolen jackets for pigeons? I don't knit. I was a mass of confusion. It was almost five, and I had been occupied for an hour and a half. A little early for cocktail hour, but I made myself a good, stiff drink and pulled down the shade in the breakfast room. This was ridiculous. I had become a bird-sitter. What would happen tomorrow if I weren't around?

Ma and Pa, from that incident on, were never far away. It took me a few days to perceive that. And Pa, the more worldly of the two parents, had made a definite connection with me and the young ones. He would look over at me many times during those days, checking me out. Then he would fly off. Ma never went with him now. They took their forays down to the river one at a time. No more duets till the kids could fly. I also made a decision. What with the marauder, who was setting his cap for the Smith nursery, and what with the Smiths having to hang about to protect their turf, and what with the cold weather, frosty ground, tightly lidded garbage cans, hot dog vendors few and far between, park-playing cracker-dropping children tucked away in warm schools, it *had* to be an unwritten law that I put food on our bathroom window ledge with commitment, twice a day. Pa Smith and I made some kind of pact with each other. He had what looked like a developing territorial imperative problem, and I would help. Those two kids *had* to fly. So I sensed, he communicated. Who's to say it wasn't so? The aesthetics of perception is up for grabs, the physiology of communication between creatures a mystery. So I said *yes* to Mr. Pigeon-Smith.

I had never fought for territory before, actual land, that is. Sibling territory, yes. "It's mine. It's mine. Don't you touch it!" But guns and horses, hard-riding into distant points of the compass; "I want, I need, I take, I conquer;" hills and mesas and rivers and mountains; to stake out and yell, "This land is mine"—as a natural act it fell strange on a Diaspora Jew. Put me in a ghetto, let me be quiet and teach my son to read, was more to the genetic point and closer to the ancestral river that flowed in the bloodstream. And better than extinction.

I sat over my drink, with the blind pulled down, wondering about all this Jew-thinking. The marauder pigeon had set something off. I had never thrown anything at anyone with intent to wound, never, except a glass of wine at a mediocre poet who tried to rape me under a table of spaghetti. He was unsuccessful, and I never saw him again. When I stormed out of his candlelight, he gave me a gift, *The Man Who Died*, by D. H. Lawrence. Well, indeed, yes. The marauder had opened up a can of peas. They were all over the breakfast-room floor. As I got up to make myself another drink, I slipped and slid until the floor turned into moss. It grew up the walls and turned into New England, and I thought about my own Papa, ghetto-psyched, a Russian Jew, real, honest-to-God, authentic Diaspora. Push the Chagall button. Papa crossed an ocean, young and alone, with the mad look of mud paths and *shtetl*, crooked apple trees, confinement, loneliness in his eyes. Land was where you escaped from and went to, and if "they" left you alone, *that* was freedom. Land was an abstract dream, a place where you could read and think and earn a living. You never fought over it, or for it. Almost never, for a Jew. Real estate, yes. But land, no.

There was no writing that afternoon. There I was, first of my clan, fighting over land, albeit a three-feet-by-eight-inch ledge, and not for myself, but a family named Smith.

Definitely not Jews. But certainly with ancestors who perched on stone outcroppings that looked out over white desert in the underbelly of civilization a few miles from the Garden of Eden, where it was warm and moist.

Ancestors. Sitting at the window, nursing my second drink, it was the quiet time after intense drama. I had the feeling Plucky would fly for the first time, tomorrow. My head was a three-story building. On the first, were images of afternoon sun, hitting Plucky's wings as he rose to exercise, the whirr of black monster feathers, the vulnerable neck of Brownie, his cries of pain, the walnut throwing, my sense of outrage, invasion, the return of the parents, a free-floating anxiety about cold and snow, a sense of rush, a dumb-creature deadliness of purpose, rhythms, preordained. On the second floor was the breakfast room, grown high with moss and memory. And on the third floor were great, empty rooms of deep incomprehensible. Dreams of wood and trees.

Wood. Wood was Papa's house. Wood was the grayish, old-wood floor of the attic, with its special old-wood smell. Wood was the church in the middle of the square that I was not allowed into. It was for the people who believed in God and Jesus. Wood was the bigger houses, half-hidden by trees and set back from the street, the houses of rich, goyish people, whose town it was. Wood was the elms all around. On our street, Central Street, wood was the massive bellies of the elms, in between which Papa parked his car with the little green cross of doctor on it. Wood was our house.

"The wood is peeling."

"The wood needs fixing."

"The wood is rotting."

"The wood looks good this year." Papa loved the wood of our house, but it scared him. Wood requires a man who is good with his hands, like in woodsman, huntsman, boatman, craftsman. Papa was a Jew-talker, and a doctor, and a thinker, and a head shaker, and an arguer, a world planner, and he swam like a Russian, breaststroking away in the Atlantic summers of our childhood. His mind was on other things, and he became angry with wood. If there was money in the bank, he would call in the Pole or the Greek or the Yankee to do the wood thing. Come spring, if winter had been lean, if the factories were idle or closed on strike ("Damn the capitalists"), and his worker patients were out of work and he, paid in chickens, shoes, and meat, then he would approach the wood sideways, with respect, for after all, it was his wood, put on his overalls that hung loose like the carcass of a predator on a peg in the attic, year after year.

"Where are the overalls?"

"In the attic!" And he would tackle the wood of the screens, acres of screens, not as many as the rich, goyish houses, but still quite ample for a Jewish doctor in a small New England town on Central Street, in between the elms. He wrestled with the wood frames of the screens, mumbling, "Jesus Christ," under his breath. Mama removed herself to weed in the garden and keep her temper, as he fought with the screens that meant warm days and the wood slat shades that went up all around the piazza, to cool the house from hot western suns in the afternoon.

Wood was the lovely, heated-up wood smell of the green slat shades, casting a green light on the white piazza with its sky-blue ceiling; shades that made quiet, secret places of wicker chairs and rockers; wood shades that hid the glider from the street; wood shades that enveloped the piazza with a smell of cedar and sun.

Wood was the umbrella tree, fat and old, on the side of the house, of which Papa was so proud. It paid his attention with thanks by growing and spreading gorgeously each year. Even when he pruned it to the quick, it grew back for him. It is still there, falling heavy to the ground, ancient.

He is not. The elms are not. Hurricanes felled them both, rotted their insides, cracked them like brittle bones. Special diseases ate them alive, Papa and the glorious, giant elms. Papa was not the only one who died. Bigger than he gave in.

How scary the elms were. We would stand four abreast, hands clasped, to encircle them. Their lined, thick bark looked like what God's skin was. Did he not make them? Was that not the first goyish poem to be committed to memory in school? At home, it was Walter de la Mare and Hans Christian Andersen and childsize myths from the Greek and Roman and Norse. But was not one prouder to stand in front of the class uttering that magic line, "Only God can make a tree"?

My tree. Papa's tree. Mama's tree. The Yankee teacher's tree. Trees made one feel "belonged." They were the city, school, and country. They were not only holy but national. "Trees" were the honor of Fourth of July parades, viewed from the piazza with its green wood slats pulled up for the occasion. "Trees" were waving to the people who marched under them, who "belonged," who fought and died for the trees and glory (not like Papa), who played bugles and walked into the goyish cemeteries to stand at attention in the late afternoon sun. The wood of elms was, in the final analysis, Yankee, goyish, awesome and unattainable.

The wood of the large weeping willow tree in our back yard was evidently Jewish, for it was ours alone and beautiful. Mama said "beautiful as Anna Pavlova," for its boughs swept over half the lawn, in extensions that would have turned Pavlova green. A swing hung from one of its many armpits like a childhood ribbon of honor. "The babies grew up under it," Mama said. And it also had a sense of humor. It dropped a caterpiller into my sister's mouth when she was very small and gaping at the wonderment of things. Everyone laughed, because it was a doctor's family and they knew it would come out by evening. Everyone, except my sister.

The perfectly marvelous way Plucky flapped his wings, firstborn, normal, sure, staunch little soldier, reminded me of how my older sister wrote. My sister wrote like an angel. She had one of those slanting-to-the-left scripts, each letter a swirl of beauty, each word leaning toward its companion like a perfect dinner guest, intent upon not losing, heavens, the next bon mot. As trees will bend away from the sea, so her letters leaned away from the right, as though there were an awful salty wind there. I dared to emulate this feat, scruffy and squabbly of nature as I was. The result? Gnomes, on their hands and knees, crawled in a state of rout across my smudged pages. Defeat was inevitable with a teacher's "What on earth is this?"

But I practiced, till the slant was mine, not clear as hers, not with the grace and quiet. I succeeded, however, in killing the Palmer method in me for life. By my own hand, you might say, it was the first thing that died in me, that irresponsible way I had of writing before I undertook to copy someone else's lean. It brings to mind the need to be worthy of an unworthy love. If I am not suitable, then I must change into something else. I must be better than what I am. After all, pleasing is halfway to being pleased. (If only Brownie could learn this, then he would flap his wings, please and be pleased, be fed first, grow strong, *and fly*.)

The moss on the breakfast-room walls was winding itself down like an animated cartoon.

The next day, a dazzling morning, white with frost, pulled me out of bed. Without portfolio, I ran to the breakfast room, looked out the window, and Brownie and Plucky had obviously survived the zero-degree night. They were out of their pot, stretching and pecking at the frozen ledge, laced whitish-gray with dung and frost, an appetizer before breakfast. Most "artists" I know, who live in the city, wake up sluggish and angry. It takes a pot of coffee, *The New York Times*, much ruminating and shuffling about and a few aggressive phone calls to agents or friends to get the juices going. I was strangely wide awake, and my nightgown, sea green, seemed to be phosphorescent in the morning light. Ma and Pa were on their ledge, looking over at our bathroom window.

"Where is breakfast?"

"Were you waiting for me?" I got out a box of wheat cereal, flung open the bathroom window, and covered it with wheat flakes. Freezing! Close the window quickly, run to the breakfast room, and watch.

Pa flew over to the bathroom window immediately. Ma flew to the nursery ledge and watched. He ate as much as he needed, flew to Ma, nudged her about the neck. "It's your turn." She flew over for her breakfast, flew back to the family, and fed Brownie. Then, both parents went for a morning constitutional. The sun was already hitting the cold cement corners and perches that only pigeons know.

Leave them alone? Well, well. What evil could happen at seven in the morning? Not much. Nazis enter and attack, predawn. Predawn is dying time, when the body is at its lowest and most vulnerable metabolism, eyes closed and the head heavy with dream. It wasn't predawn. It was breakfast time, and Ma and Pa knew what they were doing. Marauders also need breakfast.

I sat at my table, eating mine and observing. Plucky and Brownie. Plucky had a special zippity-do this morning. He kept hopping in and out of the pot, while Brownie sat watching the show, with his head resting on the rim of the pot. Hmmmm. Tricks at seven. What would happen at three? Plucky wouldn't stay still. He paraded about the ledge, then suddenly looked up at the wrought-iron fence that encircled the ledge.

"Jump up like Ma and Pa? Not really!"

It was a matter of two feet. Plucky began to flap his wings, as he had done yesterday afternoon. Faster and

faster. Then, he stopped, and in a wobbly, split-second, he'd done it! My coffee cup was halfway to my mouth, and Plucky was sitting on the top of the grill work, teetering dangerously back and forth.

"Oh, no, watch it!"

He sat shaking and teetering for a full second, looking around: Hey, Ma, I'm dancin'. Then, he fell-hopped backward to the ledge, righted himself, and hopped into the pot, flapped his wings again, hitting Brownie in the face, and finally settled down, little chest all plumped out. My coffee cup was still midair. I put it down in its saucer, and I was laughing out loud again. What a grand way to start a morning. Only then was I aware that I had turned on the radio. When? Probably at seven. That old city reflex. Flip it on, connect with the outside, hear the tragedy, and wait for the music.

". . . ambush . . . along the Ho Chi Minh Trail . . . Route One . . . body count of thirty enemy dead [with pride, always the enemy] . . . eight casualties American platoon . . ."

I waited. Wasn't the news on December 19 going to mention anything about Plucky Smith having flown solo to the top of the iron grill in a corridor on Eighty-third Street? No? That's strange. It was the feat of an outstanding explorer. I turned the radio off and went about my business. That little box, made in Japan, often annoys me beyond reason. Its litanies of death and destruction. Never resurrection. Why is it always "they die"? Never "they live!" It's enough to make one want to climb a tree, Zoroastrian style, and never come down.

> At five in the afternoon.
> It was exactly five in the afternoon.
> A boy brought the white sheet
> at five in the afternoon.
> A frail of lime ready prepared

at five in the afternoon.
The rest was death, and death alone
at five in the afternoon.

Plucky, it turned out, fortunately, didn't know anything about Garcia Lorca, his poem, and its moment of truth at five in the afternoon. Plucky's moment of truth happened at three in the afternoon. But it lacked nothing in its elements of extreme and fatal drama. It moved with the same complications. Time and the Counterpoints within Time. The pendulum—feat, fact, and emotion—once touched into motion, and there is no turning back. Only resolution. Life or death. Heavy.

Yes, I was watching at three in the afternoon. A magic command brought me to the window. Without it, I might have missed what I had been waiting for.

The winter sun again struck the ledge, as it had yesterday. Ma and Pa were nowhere visible, but they weren't far. Plucky and Brownie were parading about their ledge, marching in and out of pinpoints of sunny cement, children hopscotching in those golden hours of play before the call to supper. Fat hours with the kinetic self. Testing. One, two, three. The mind and spirit and flesh and muscle, alone and free. Plucky and Brownie would meet as they marched, and as they met, they touched beaks and necks.

"Hi, guy. It's the open road, brother!"

From nowhere, the marauder pigeon flew into the corridor, and with a huge whizz and flurry, landed on top of the iron grill. Oh, no. The "kids" stood, stunned. Brownie whimpered, remembering. Khrushchev hopped onto the ledge and started to go for Brownie as he had done yesterday. As the word *walnuts* began sending signals to my feet, Pa Smith appeared, also from nowhere. The kids huddled in opposite corners of the ledge, and the battle was on. Forget the shadow of film. This was real. Pa and Khrushchev start to go at each other, a jab to the left, a jab to the right, a black wing caught between the black grill, wings beating, wings mixing, bits of feather wafting down in the rays of sun. Suddenly! There was another set of wings in action. Small wings! Plucky had flown to the top of the grill, teetering, to join his Pa in pecking the marauder off the turf. The invader flew away to the flower pot on the ledge around the corner; Pa, poised on the grill, still arched for battle. And Plucky! Wowee! was off! In midair, his small wings flapping with a stutter, Plucky was airborne, flying through four feet of space, four flights up off the ground. He was flying to the parent ledge. I thought I was going to faint, for it was the flight of a little drunk. But he landed on the very edge of his parents' bedroom, radar working, tilted backward for a frightening moment of Time, and then, pushed himself deeper onto the ledge, holding on for dear life. He looked over at the nursery in utter amazement. Mission accomplished.

Ma flew down from an upper ledge, where she had been on duty with Pa, and joined Plucky. Much pecking about the neck. Pa flew over and joined them. Initiation rite . . . A.O.K. Receive congratulations. Brownie was in the comfort of his nursery pot, looking over at his family. "Well, that's a fine state of affairs. They're there, and I'm here. How did that happen?"

So we went from pastorale to invasion to combat to victory. Through fear into courage, into euphoria—to flight! And Plucky had sent his little body through four feet of space, four flights off the ground. I was exhausted. Such drama usually takes two to three hours of generally mediocre acting on a modern stage, used to take ten to twelve hours of working it out in an amphitheater under a hot Greek sun. I felt privileged, indeed. I had just witnessed a moment of truth that had a preparation and completion time of one second. Only human time demands the ritualistic, painful elongations that are words, gesture, phrase, dance. And Oedipus—how he suffered—before the blindness became seeing. Darkness into light. Inaction into action. Ignorance to knowledge. Not knowing into knowing. We had often joked, in the family, about how on earth will those little ones "do it." And my son's answer was, "Mom, they have one second to learn!"

I couldn't wait to tell everyone what had happened to one of our little "fowl" of the air. So I picked up Willow, the cat, and hugged her so tight she let out a tiny meow of outrage.

The World Widens

How does a new bird fly? Does he have to work at it, or is he one of the universe's gifted ones, springing full blown when ready? A little bit of both, I learned.

The first day after Plucky made his stellar exploration into space and experienced "the secret of powered flight" (like the Wright Brothers at Kitty Hawk—120 feet in 12 seconds), I expected him to inch his way down and out of the corridor. Instead, he spent the morning *walking* about the nursery ledge, a senior senator expounding in the Presidium on a new law that would change the face of the land. He practiced flapping his wings till I thought they would fall off, as Brownie watched him with annoyance and amazement.

At noon, Plucky was ready to try flight again, and off he went, his little white tail-marking gleaming in the light, to the fire escapes at the end of the neighbors' building. Ma and Pa rushed to join him and brought him his boxed lunch —them. And there was the young hero being fed beak to beak. Conqueror of flight, but still a baby.

Brownie was sitting in the pot, his head resting on its

rim. Where had everyone gone? He was alone—for the first time.

The next day, I was at the window to see how Plucky would implement his craft. I was preparing myself for the change, a sense of loss. Nothing would be like it was, the two little ones together in the pot. New patterns would be forming. But nothing happened. Instead, the whole family spent the morning together. Had Plucky forgotten about his huge leap into adulthood or had he been given orders to stay put and rest his system? It seemed to be the latter— that the parents told the stronger sibling to "lay around." Their being together made Brownie more sure of himself. He was hopping in and out of the pot like mad. Everything was as it always was—babies and parents together in the nursery. As for Plucky, "laying around" seemed to be an intelligent pulling back, straddling both phases of growth— infancy and childhood. Just because I've taken my first steps does not mean I can't have my bottle in Mama's lap, does it? I was reminded of many people I know who never let their babies languish in babyhood but keep wanting to push them into becoming achievers too soon, as though to prove parent intelligence; as though babyhood was a state to be gotten through as quickly as possible. And so, many people never know any more about Time than what was inflicted upon them in infancy. They never know that Time is *now*. It was something one was propelled through—to get to some other Time, where it would be fuller, better, more important.

"Look how quickly the baby walks!" "Look how soon the baby talks!"

About midmorning, Plucky flew to the top of the iron grill, teetered unsteadily. Big shot. At that moment, Willow joined me in my "watching." She pressed her nose to the window. Ma and Pa see Willow. They look at Plucky. They look at Willow. It's a tense moment through glass. There would be no flying out, certainly, while Willow was at the window. I want to push her away, but she reads my mind and gives me a dirty look. Plucky returns to the pot and looks at Willow. The parents cock their heads at the cat and me. Willow is looking at everyone, her whiskers trembling with excitement. It's all delicious. Another still life, alive with Time. Just Time.

Suddenly, a cat's inscrutable schedule called for her to sit in a spot of sun somewhere else, and Willow dispensed with the drama. The minute she left, Plucky flew into the air!

Now that Plucky "flew," I could see I would have to be running from room to room, just as Willow did, window to window, scene of action to scene of action. The "watching" was getting bigger and deeper and going places I hadn't been for years.

Down the elm-lined streets to the kindergarten where I was to be relegated in the morning. Mama had helped import a Montessori teacher to our little town so that a school might be started (mainly for me) and I would have "a worthwhile place to go" before I entered the public school first grade. And whatever Mama planned came to pass. So my mornings were spent in kindergarten much too early in life, in my estimation. How do I know that? I remember great loneliness. I was not ready to leave the first fool in my life, whom I must have loved too much. I suffered from grand ennui at a tender age.

I haven't the faintest notion why, but there was some kind of urgency about my learning to read before I matriculated into the first grade, when I would be barely five.

I already knew my alphabet. I couldn't understand all the fuss. My sister, five years older, had already broken the sound barrier on all levels—music, dance, mathematics, literature. What could I do to equal that! To equal, surpass, cleave out new things—those were the passwords in the family. To climb high and cling to dizzy height. To surprise. To be an artist! At three it was expected.

It was into a wood-wood room—with wooden toys, mathematical beads and string, and weaving on spools, and numbers—I went. One bead, two beads, three beads, back and forth on their leather thongs. We were learning to add and subtract by pushing the large colored beads back and forth. My first sweatshop. Everything was so serious. All I could think of was Mama and home. Only ten minutes away from home, I could have been in India with a tin can tied to my neck, begging, so copious were the tears. Where was Mama? Was she watching the first day I flew? Was she coming to feed me, beak to beak? (How come Ma and Pa Smith "knew" and she didn't?)

As I asked the questions, I tried to figure out whether they were mea culpa or whether they were questions prodding into Past Time to define the quality of Past Time.

Oh, I was a problem that first day of kindergarten. Fool. I rejected taking in learning. I cried till they called Mama, who was terribly embarrassed, to remove me. No one likes an unhappy child, one who cries so loud. If you do it well enough later on, it means you're part alpha, and others will listen and follow. I'm not talking about whining or whimpering. I'm talking about indignant outrage and cries for love—positive, energetic, original response to given situations. It makes actors, writers, poets, composers, architects, statesmen, freedom fighters.

Mama's secondborn was not following the rules. I saw that in Mama's white-faced nervousness when she arrived. Her face gave me nothing to feed on. It was water-repellent.

My anguish made no impact. We walked home, my hand in her cool one, and there was no talk. If we had . . . I wanted to ask her why I had to be kept so busy when all I wanted was to be near her, learning and taking in from her in our own fashion. It was all too soon, all this world activity, and I was losing my own sense of Time because I didn't know hers. Well, there was no coming together, I could see that, to solve our mutual problem—me. Please Mama's face? What could I do to bring her near? Nothing but be myself, tearful, silent, and at the age of three, Chekhovianly depressed. Certainly she could appreciate that, mad Polack that she was.

To this day, I cannot count without a sense of "Is it right?" An overwhelming heaviness with 5's and 4's and 3's, and what they make when added to Mamas and Papas and sisters and cousins. Numbers, added to themselves, subtracted from themselves, making a family. Dizzying mathematics. Subtraction was always a depletion, even unto the later grades in school. How could I deplete myself even more—by showing the slightest interest in subtraction—when my very existence was a subtraction. Or so Mama impressed me with the weight of a second child, another girl, the weariness of it for her. There I was, a startling facsimile of my sister, even though there was a five-year difference. The same eyes, the same face, the same bangs falling over the high brow. How boring for Mama, who wanted change, style, drama. I wish I had known that dark lady. She was disguised and forever closed to me, because I was born with temper, and I had disappointed her. I was not a boy.

Aha. So, Plucky was my sister! Hear, hear. But with Plucky it was pure enjoyment. It's beautiful to watch things being done right when the hate and envy is subtracted and the love allowed. Anger makes you learn on the sly, or in spite of. The utter waste of a forward pass accepted, a mid-air somersault under the circus tent when viewed from under depressed eyes is appalling. Beautiful things must be observed in a state of openness and love, in order to be beautiful. My sister was beautiful, but it was impossible for me to see her because of the nest in which we grew.

Plucky was being trained to do things right. Instinct went directly into action. I'm hungry? They will feed me. I want to be touched? They will touch me. I demand attention? They will attend to me. How simple. Nothing was wasted on the negative. The secrets of bird learning fell into his feathers like rain into well-planted furrows. All was Observe, Learn, Do, Satisfaction. The air encompassed him like an oyster. Plucky breathed the air of the lucky, enough to make one grow, joltless, unscarred, without trauma. His little head sat on the shoulders of a young scion of a very important family. First, positive, up, out, and strong enough to go, one's self. Free. Full. Strong. Fly. Joy.

I sit on my son's bed, thinking about it. It's way past lunch, and I feel I've earned it. Joy is a firm, preoccupied mother. It scrubs you down in a quick bath as though you were her lastborn, a change-of-life child. She plunks you into your crib, gives you a distracted kiss, switches off the light, and leaves you to your own devices in the dark of yourself.

Here I sit, still chewing the fat about the fleetingness of Joy, still surprised, still hopeful, ever longing for its total attention. How about settling for one huge, obese hour, and I'll never mention it again, I say to myself. How about lunch?

Plucky was nowhere to be seen when I finished eating. He was off on his widened world. Where on earth did he go? How did he look with his tender new wings flapping overzealously? He must have been adorable. How far did he go? I'll never know. As the afternoon darkened, he rounded the corner of the corridor at four-thirty, pigeon dinnertime. The whole family was on the nursery ledge waiting for him, and he skidded home with a flash of the little white triangle on his tail, jumped into the pot next to Brownie and dinner was served beak to beak.

※

It was five o'clock, and I was four. It must have been at the end of summer, near Fall, crisp, expectant time. I remember my hand could reach the hem of my dress, I was that old. The lawn was still green. The late sun found its way through the umbrella tree in the front yard up the path to the willow, where I sat in the swing, back and forth. I kicked the gold in the grass. Queens do that. The rough ropes pulled me up to the sky where queens go. Everything comes true when you're four and not weeping about something. Pull and up! Down to the gold! I was almost touching "it." "It" was higher than the gabled roof, closer to the clouds on their way south to Boston.

Mama was leaning out the back-stairs window. Her voice encompassed an octave. "Come up here this minute and get into your tub!" That's funny. It wasn't my tub. It was her tub. The swing moved faster away from the tub, although the sun would still be in it, too. Away from the clock, firm, business hands, away from supper for a four-year-old who dines alone.

"You'll be sorry if I have to come down and get you!"

The neighbors heard it that time. The birds flew away, and the umbrella tree hid the sun. I had to make "number two," she called it, badly. Before, it was a pleasant sensation, holding it back. Now it was urgent. But I'd be damned if I was going to be rushed. This was my Time. The house was too far away, the air too sweet . . . so . . . I did it on the swing!

Crash! The day was over. Crash! The swing returned to grass. Slowly up the stairs with a pantsful went the penitent. How final "bad" is when you're really "bad." I stood in front of Mama and turned my bottom to her. "Bad" slithered down my spine like a spider, even as I wondered how "bad," "bad" is . . . and why.

"March yourself straight into that bathroom, and wash those pants yourself."

Tears fell into the Ivory soap. My hands were too small to scrub. Didn't she know that? Tears fell for the sun through the umbrella tree and for the badness I'd done in the beautiful air.

"Now get into the tub, and when you're clean, you sit on the couch in the parlor till supper's ready."

In the parlor? This must be very serious. The parlor is for guests.

When I was four, I think I liked the parlor, the way the sun caught the cherry woods and locked them in its light and the chairs, decked in grape design and satiny brocades, watching like silly, disapproving spinsters in their Sunday best. And, beyond the bay windows, I could see my giant elms. That wasn't bad at all.

It was later that I grew to hate its every corner, old enough to play a knowing role, old enough to feel the coldness of that room, when I would sit for hours on the couch in the bay window with a book of myths in my lap (required reading) opened to the tale of Loki, God of Mischief.

But at four I was cozy on the couch in my pink bathrobe, savoring the sweet reprieve of sinners, not yet condemned, with the last bit of sun bouncing from the cherry woods to the back of my neck. Sweet-smelling, and alone. I didn't feel "bad" at all. That was my first secret. I paid a price for freedom, and it was worth it. I wasn't "bad." What I'd done was "bad." There was a big difference. She was wrong, but I knew I couldn't tell her. Well, if she had only smiled me back to herself, I would have forgiven her. Just one sign of friendship, and I would have excused her for having screamed, in that exquisite twilight, like a poverty-stricken washerwoman.

The Day Brownie Made It

Bang! BANG! All through the week after Plucky flew, the corridor was alive with drama. Brownie was still just stretching his little brown wings, walking about the ledge, peering over it to look for everybody. That's all. Plucky was flying off, coming back, and the parents were leaving Brownie alone but coming back to give him his meals, reluctantly. One or the other would feed him and fly off immediately. Plucky was on our bathroom ledge, taking his meals there whenever he came home. Then he'd join Brownie, and I could see Brownie sigh with relief. "Just like the good old days, me and him." Particularly when Mr. Khrushchev appeared, which he was doing all through the day, just flying in and flying out of the corridor. A testing of nerves. Brownie whimpered whenever he heard the big bird approaching, and Plucky would flutter his wings angrily. Mr. K. didn't come close to the nursery, not after the big fight with Pa. But he was obviously spending part of his day on spying, swooping over the nursery. Brownie would tuck his body in a corner whenever he heard the strange wings. And if Plucky wasn't with him, I would stand at the window with walnuts in my hand, ready. It wouldn't have surprised me if Mr. K.

knew that. He very often looked over at me as he flew by.

Little Brownie. He looked older and stronger. He would teeter over the ledge, looking down, interested in the passing scene. He would flap his wings furiously, and every minute it seemed he wanted to make it to the parent ledge, just as Plucky did—then he would change his mind and go sit in the pot.

My concern for that little brown pigeon was reaching the abnormal. He was not an achiever! He must have a handicap. Was I imposing a rhythm of growth on him that I detest humans for doing? It seemed that Mr. K. knew there was trouble. He was getting an edge on the Smiths and would just stay about to assume control over the territory by default. He would push the kid off some way or other, and the Smiths, in anguish, would leave. As the week passed, a sense of panic and sadness rose by the hour— an evil tide bearing the red algae plague. The corridor was ceasing to be a place of joy; rather now a home for retarded children. Brownie was pinioned to the pot. Everyone knew it. Ma and Pa were saying: For heaven's sake! You're old enough to start fending for yourself. It's enough with the beak-to-beak feeding for the both of you. Go off, already; do your chores, and find your pleasure.

Toward the end of the week, Ma and Pa spent a whole day at home, doing nothing but feeding Brownie. The reward system was in full gear. He'd flap, and they'd feed. He even flapped his wings, teetering on the tippity edge. OOPS! Not yet. Then he'd go back to the pot and make believe flying was unnecessary. To heck with it. I'm still a baby.

The next day, they left Brownie alone completely! They wouldn't feed him and only fed Plucky on our feeding ledge. Brownie was hungry and furious. He even pecked at a parent who sat on the grillwork of the nursery for a minute. Something had to give, if only to stop the knot in my stomach

from growing bigger and bigger.The whole family flew off
to Riverside Drive, leaving Brownie whimpering and me
wringing my hands. Why did I have to be involved with a
late bloomer? He was dumb, and I was dumber!

And furthermore, Mr. K.! He was as gleeful as a bomber
pilot who had just sighted an enemy village of women and
children only.

I decided to go out, walk on Broadway, and mingle
with the old people and cripples. No, I'd stay. No. I'll go.

There was that familiar whir of wings. Ma and Pa came
back. They were on the ledge *above* the nursery. Plucky was
on the parent ledge. My phone rang. I told someone I
couldn't talk to them, I was too busy. It was two-thirty in
the afternoon. A poltergeist gave me a shove on the shoulder
and said sit down. Brownie was standing on the very last
inch of the nursery ledge! He was flapping and flapping. I
sucked in air and held it. And then . . .

Miraculous order. The lesser became the hero. The
nervous one, fainter in heart, with one big surge mastered his
construction, became Heracles, Jr.—and flew. Little Brownie,
a week later than his sibling, not as Plucky did, normal, careful, testing. Brownie flew in spite of himself. He broke the
circumference of his inherited wounds (that's a hero). He
flew flashy and farther than Plucky. It was Al Jolson at the
Palace. Klieg lights. Lindbergh. Marilyn Monroe marries
Muhammad Ali. The moon is conquered.

Brownie had flown to our bathroom ledge, *across* the
corridor, the big span Plucky didn't attempt until his second
day of flight. Brownie sat screaming with delight and fear
on the feeding ledge. Ma and Pa joined him, and then
Plucky. I watched the family celebration, rejoiced with them,
and wept human tears. I felt smacked in the head by nature
(again). Not a new thought, old girl, but curiously revivified.
I understood what made Jane Goodall walk up a mountain,
sit by herself night after night just to wait for dawn and a

glimpse of a chimp rising to meet it. To find out what his nature would put into his head, there on a branch, attached to a tree, rooted into a continent, floating somewhere on a day in his life. Her voyeurism was totally important to many. Mine only to myself.

Everyone leaves the feeding ledge after the party. Brownie is alone and starts to cry again. Can he get back to the pot? It's such a long way. How typical. The scared one, out of fear, outdoes the fearless one. Then, he has second thoughts about it, and says, "Who, me?" Brownie pulls himself together and flies, not back to the pot, but up to the ledge a floor above! Ma and Pa join him, and they both feed him. It's a great day for brown pigeons.

> I'm becoming an alcoholic. It's three o'clock and I'm making myself a celebration drink. I read *The New York Times.* I think a lot about the derailment of my kind. I'm zeroing in on a microcosm, and the rewards are stunning. A Scotch sour.

There is a new look about Brownie, his feathers smooth; no longer frozen between larval and adult form, no more pupa. He was out. What a day! From languish to hunger to anguish to euphoria. The day did indeed have an off-center-strange-depression-before-action feeling to it. Doubts before the thrust. The possibility of correctness, the probability of instinct being trustworthy. I must remember that. Brownie's day was just like—writing.

Incestus

THE idea of remembering Time was becoming another consciousness as I watched the nesting flower pot. The house in New England was embracing me with all its wall-arms, winking black shutters, benedicting bishop roof. Its space created another dimension, not like "Alice" falling down or up to where she had never been, but back, back into space-experienced; alive as though present, yet not remembered. How curious to recapture where one has been yet not remembered, real time, lost; experienced by no one but me, and not mine.

The sunlight on the pigeon nursery ledge was pricking me with signals from my inner space. Civilizations of my past psyche were sending me coded messages I didn't understand, yet the sounds had a familiar ring. There *was* a place I had been, an air I walked through, clocks that turned in real time, people who encircled me, talked to me, and what they said. What was it they said?

Warm sun on my counterpane. Mama was reading me Robert Louis Stevenson, and I was sick in bed. "You have a counterpane, too," she said, and her fingers walked up my thigh like the little soldiers in the poem. Oh, life is good when you're sick, 'cause Mama sits on your bed, looks you straight in the eye, and reads you poems she loves. To be sick in June is lovely. There are so many days of sun a few at home don't matter. To be tucked into a bed, tight with hospital corners, and a fever, not too high, not too low was solipsistic splendor. Mama *had* to be with me. What is the recipe for a great, hypochondriacal gravy? Just that way. And then Papa walking in to say hello. "How's the little girl?"

"Oh, nothing serious."

Nothing serious? I've got you both in the same room, at the same time, and all for me.

"How's the fever?" Papa would ask.

And Mama would put her lips to my forehead. Her breasts would brush my shoulder, and I wriggled under the counterpane with delight. Papa brought the strong smell of anesthesia into the room from his morning at the hospital. Papa in his summer straw, his cream linen suit for the heat, his asthma coughs, his heavy, frightening, Russian laughter, his worry over patients, his nervousness, his veiled looks of affection, his surprise as I grew—his love for Mama—they were all in the room. Then they would leave, and my hand would find that secret place between my legs, and soon I would sleep, which was good for the fever.

Two days of under the counterpane was all I could stand. So I used to "do it" every so often, not too often. Just when I felt I had to find out who's who and what's what, and whether they loved me in their own way, which they did. They were both trained to be tender with illness. And Papa's nervousness excited me. When I was sick I got the best of him, his worry. How I must have loved him. He and the house were my flower pot. How close we were, never touching, hardly talking. He, not Mama, was my wall of certainty, my rock, my tree, my wailing wall.

Now I was really in "it," remembered Time. Often I've stood on the edge of a grassy plain, free to run, yet back I turned, parched with thirst, to drink the judgment in his face. To him, to whom I said, "You do not exist," I meant, "I cannot live without you."

Most of my waking hours were spent trying to get Papa's attention. I long to embrace the ghost of my childhood. I'm trying to perceive it with the eyes of a wanton. Was it easier for Orestes, beneath his blue and ancient sky filled with gods, listening, ready to supplicate, after sacrifice? Was it easier to love and hate at the edge of the Aegean, or face the white bull, head on, from the warm hills of Crete than in a New England childhood? Was it easier to anguish when the summer winds of myth blew loose the heart from the unconscious and acts of love could draw blood and murder?

Papa loved birds. "Birdies," he would call them. He watched them come, and he watched them go. His heart was light in spring because the birdies were coming. He would stand in the back yard, shyly commenting: "They're coming." And in the fall, a mood would overcome him till the first snow that had its own, white sex.

"Will the car make the icy hill?"

"Jesus, I skidded all the way to the hospital."

How I miss that terrible time, when no words of love were spoken, those days with their ashen hayheaps covered in frost; the countryside gaunt and skeletal, a light, thin, blue air, with the tinkle of tiny needles as Papa opened the front door.

"Mary?" He always called Mama's name, no matter how many times he walked into the house. Her answer was always the sound of a queen clapping.

"I'm back here!" "Supper's ready!"

It was their song, and we listened. There was no touching. How was one to know one was loved, when there was no touching? I never, not once, saw them touch. So, one *knew*, and one didn't *know*. Mystifying.

Yet it was the nest, that winter house, with a smell of apple pie from Mama's kitchen; the smell of ether from Papa's office downstairs; the smell of cedar from the winter closets; the smell of finely polished wood and Noxon-ed brass and copper; the smell of starched school blouses and camphorated serge skirts; the smell of one's own skin, hunched over a desk, studying Virgil and looking for obscenities in vain. Then close the book and ruminate. Listen to the sounds of the house, Mama and Papa, walking up and down the stairs, talking to each other, moving through their hours and days that I'm trying to remember, now that I'm a pigeon watcher, looking for Order.

Which Time do I remember best, in spite of not remembering? I remember the Time denied me. It was theirs.

Do parents know they share their Time? Can they cut themselves in half while it (Time) is happening? Can they say, "All of this is not mine, it's theirs, too, those large, small eyes that watch with such wonder and disbelief."

If parents knew they were being watched with such love, would they give the gift of life differently?

Papa would be surprised to think I remembered his standing in the yard, looking up at the sky, watching for the birdies to fly south (such a tiny moment). We are surely what we eat, and what we breathe, but we are mostly what we watch, as all creatures are. But we higher creatures have something more than instinctive patterns to watch. We watch, and we learn how to feel. What on earth will my son remember that I did when I shared my Time with him? I hope denial won't bring tears to his eyes. I pray he'll remember my touching him, laughing or crying. Who the hell cares, as long as it was real, and shared.

If Papa had taken my hand and said, "Look! The birdies are coming from Canada, and they're flying to Brazil," or, "The winter's coming, darling," then we would have shared a miracle.

But no. He said it way off, in another part of the garden, standing alone, in his grief over the death of summer when we could have shared it together. As it was, I stood in one part of the garden. He stood in another. We both looked up at the birdies flying south, and we shared the wonder of it, separately.

How about that! Past time unremembered and present time merge. Some unremembered time, you fake! Now I zero in on the birdies—alone. Part of me knows it would have been better if I had had a remembrance of having "looked" in concert with someone.

Papa never called me "darling" until years after Mama died. I was safely married, and he had had one too many Manhattans, sitting at the dining room table, reading his beloved Russian authors.

"I was a failure. I never did what I wanted to do. I didn't make it. You'll know what I mean, darling, someday."

There it was. The jack-in-the-box was out for good, unsprung. And where did he get *it* from? Who was he watching in his unremembered Time, when his eyes were big, small ones? Jews in the Ukraine? What was it like?

Poor Papa. He started talking too late. I bet I would have understood, even when I was five.

🍁

The day of the championship fight for the supremacy of the corridor on Eighty-third Street was going to be fought on a clear, cold, Sunday morning. I was sitting ringside reading the Sunday *Times*, drinking coffee. Willow was on the table looking out the window and my husband joined us at my insistence, because I had a feeling Pa Smith and Mr. K. were going to start their Third Punic War.

How did I know? I knew Mr. K had been watching the past weeks' activities just as I had; that Plucky had flown, that Brownie was finally off the nest, that there weren't babies to defend anymore; that the nursery ledge was now conquerable. It was going to be an easy heist. All week, I waited for the ax to fall. And not only me, but many other birds in the neighborhood. That's how I knew the day had come. Other birds were flying in and out of the corridor all morning, some of them taking positions a few floors above the Smith ledges and just sitting quietly. Willow's whiskers were twitching like mad. She didn't know where to look first—there was such wing traffic outside. Either it was going to be a party to celebrate the flight of children or a fight to settle ownership of the corridor. When Mr. and Mrs. K. came sailing in and took their places on the air conditioner around the corner, I sensed not a party but a war.

First round: Mr. K. flew to the sacrosanct nursery ledge, threw down the gauntlet, and sat on the grillwork, daring Pa to make something of it.

Pa and Ma were on their parent ledge looking very nervous. Plucky and Brownie were on our bathroom ledge pecking at some cereal.

Mr. K. called to his mate to join him.

"It's our property now, dear, come on over. He'll never challenge me."

Mrs. K., too, sat on the grillwork of the nursery. It was a revolting sight—Hitler troops marching under the Arc de Triomphe. Pigs.

What would Pa Smith do! He paraded back and forth on their parent ledge to rev up his adrenalin.

Pa attacked!

A large shoo of wings to the right! A shoo of wings to
the left! A jab to the neck! A bite on the wing!

The two birds locked and broke and pecked and flew
at each other.

Mr. K. flew back to the air conditioner. The first round
was Pa Smith's.

(Plucky and Brownie joined Ma on her ledge, and Pa
sat shaking on the grillwork, waiting.)

Back comes Mr. K. Pa attacked. Their wings got caught
in the grillwork. Mr. K. held Pa by the neck. Pa wrestled
free and flew to Ma and the kids. They pecked his neck
feathers down. He flew back for more. Then both combatants
took to the air, and they battled, flying, rushing at each
other in aerial, dogfight fashion.

"Wow!" my husband whispered, as he looked at the bird
spectators and Willow and me with our noses pressed to the
glass.

"There it is," I said. "Nikita Khrushchev and Jimmy
Cagney in a championship match for the supremacy of
Eighty-third Street. You didn't believe me, did you!"

"Okay. I'll place my bet. I bet on Nikita. Smith doesn't
have a chance. He's too light. The other one's going to
murder him."

"You just wait! Smith has something to fight for. The
other one is a pig."

"Darling, ideals have nothing to do with it. Your Smiths
are finished. It's simply a matter of weight and strength."

"All right. You place your bet! Five dollars!"

I was very upset. How could he say such things, when
we'd both been following every inch of the Vietnam War,
looking at the daily horrors that were tearing those gentle,
beautiful people apart. Yet each juggernaut offensive, bought
and backed up by the outrageous weight of America,
couldn't decimate the tiny "enemy," some of them not even
out of puberty. (We argued back and forth. Was there a

spirit in all creatures, not only in man, that made them victor in the face of all odds, because they were on the "right" side? Romantic poppycock.)

"There is a right side!" I yelled.

"Of course, there is, but who's to say what's right?"

"Me!" I screamed.

"What's right can change from moment to historical moment."

"There is an absolute Right," I insisted, "and you damn well know it! They're fighting over the Smiths' ledges. The Smiths made them 'green.' The babies grew up there. It's their home and no Fascist pigs are going to knock them off if I have anything to say about it."

"You don't."

"I know," I said.

The birds were still in the air. It looked as if the battle was going to rage all morning. The thought frightened me. It could be a bloody Sunday massacre. I knew nothing of pigeon "territorial imperative," except what I saw, and that was, everyone had respect for the Smith stake-out. It was inviolate (except for the beefy Khrushchev twosome). I also didn't know whether pigeons kill in combat. That was the worst thought of all. I was not about to run to the encyclopedia. The libraries were closed on Sunday. The Bronx Zoo would think me mad. Anyway, I would miss the outcome, and I really didn't want to learn from study. I wanted to get it straight, through the eyes. If Pa lost, my pigeon watching days would be over. I'd draw the blind and never look out again.

Mr. K.'s strategy was to prolong the war until Pa was all worn out. But we could both see there was a spirit in Pa that the bigger bird didn't have. Pa was fighting for his land, dignity, and right. He had discovered wheat, tilled the soil, invented the sickle—and here was this nomad, riding in from the plains of God knows where, wanting what he hadn't made, a usurper, marauder. That was it! My terror and excitement! I was reliving another "first step." Not of a creature, but of Man.

Pa got Mr. K. where he wanted him, caught finally in the grillwork of the nursery and he held the bird by his neck, held him and held him, till Mr. K. had nothing more to do than wrench himself free and fly out of the corridor, with Mrs. K. fluttering behind him.

There was one more round. Mr. K. came back alone. Pa cornered him on the air conditioner, pecked him, a jab to the right, a jab to the left, a tight one to the chest. Pa's fury was so relentless you could almost hear Mr. K. saying, "I've got to get the hell out of here." And, he did. Flew out as fast as he could.

Both birds had hurt each other. But it turned out this time, they had established a modus vivendi. Rights were clarified, order maintained, without killing.

I decided I was highly prejudiced in favor of lower species. All through the morning, in between watching the battle, I'd been reading the Sunday *Times* about the bombings in Asia.

The next day, Mr. and Mrs. Khrushchev, alias Marauders, quietly flew into the corridor, took possession of the ledge around the corner, preened and pecked each other all morning, and by afternoon, the empty pot was starting to be twigged.

Another family being planned? I didn't give a damn what they did. I would not watch them, and I did not for weeks to come. The greedy ones lost, and peace was assured my dear Smiths. Now the only thing anyone had to worry about was the heart of winter itself.

Away from the Nest

THE caribou will cross this river on its way to summer tundra ground. In the fall, it will go back to the shelter of the green forests.

Snakes are deaf. It's the movement of the snake charmer, weaving back and forth, that makes the snake rise up.

Plucky and Brownie are growing up.

The bee defends itself and dies. Not so the hornet or the wasp.

That bird has flown 10,000 miles to nest on an island—in Alaska!

A young boy was assassinated on a Dublin street last night.

Pigeons are monogamous.

A woman is beaten and raped in her doorway in the middle of the afternoon, everywhere.

Ten thousand Africans will die of hunger next week by twilight of a certain day.

Charming France is selling guns to her friends and enemies. The whore has learned nothing.

The carnivore will kill indiscriminately only when crazed with hunger or fear.

Ice is creeping down from the Arctic, a foot a year.

Angry hordes from the east are riding bareback again, toward the west—on galloping Cadillacs.

The sun will rise at 7:26 tomorrow.

Ma and Pa Smith are mating again.

God help us! They're lining and padding the pot anew, neck pecking and cooing.

Days go by. The order of the building act is excruciating and true. I had missed the nest building for Plucky and Brownie. But now why, in the dead of winter? Zero weather was being forecast. How could they sit on eggs, not moving for hours at a time, and *not* be frozen stiff?

I thought we had everything nicely worked out, with our getting Plucky and Brownie through the early winter rapids. But this? Nature must be mad on that ledge. I couldn't bear responsibility anymore. If the Smiths don't know what they're doing, that's their business. And yet, I looked over at the Khrushchev ledge, and there *they* were, sitting in *their* pot on an egg or eggs. The whole damn corridor was one big gestation center, a giant, swelling womb getting ready to expel tender life, plop, into the frigid air of an unusually cold January.

New York pigeons are crazed, spooked, wrapped too tight. They've lost their marbles. The corridor is a pigeon Broadway. To hell with it. What? Not look at Plucky and Brownie growing up after everything you've done for them? Okay. Look, but look less.

Actually, it was easy to make believe my disinterest was real. Nothing much was happening. Ma and Pa, having lined the pot to their satisfaction, were just sitting, spelling each other with a faith that made me turn away in anguish. It was so simple.

Willow, sensing my inside flailing, came and sat on my lap, tucked her front paws under her the way cats do when they're very sure of themselves, and said, "Listen, I'm a cat, you're a person. Granted, I'm prettier than you are, with my heart-shaped face and white whiskers, but you've got green eyes and not a bad figure, and your brain is larger than mine. But we're both part of the whole thing, and there *is* no answer, so why don't you just *be*—like me. I am. You are. Why don't you just . . . [she was searching for an idea like mad]. There is no Future. Everything just *is*. The Future is nothing but humans trying to define what always was and is. Was always there, and always will be. Unless you do something terrible and destroy it. And even if you destroy it, you can't even do that. *It* will still be there. *You* won't, but *it* will. Why don't you be like me! I'm very pleased, being a cat. The trouble with you is that you're too curious—"

"Oh, shut up. What do you know!"

She got off my lap in a huff.

Ma sits on the eggs all day, from seven to four P.M. Pa sits on the eggs from four to seven A.M.

I assumed, once flight was mastered, Plucky and Brownie would be off on their own and disappear into the pigeon population of the city. Not so, at all. Even though Ma and Pa were busy with the new nest, they were still a tightly knit family.

So if you saw, walking along Broadway, a smallish black pigeon with a white triangle on his tail and a smallish brown pigeon, would you ever dream they were kids acting

like big shots in the big world; that they flew home for
lunch and never dared arrive late for bedtime because they
had a Ma and Pa who would worry? True. If they were a
few minutes late, when twilight deepened, the parents became restive and wouldn't change guard over the new eggs
until all were present and accounted for. Plucky and Brownie
were still the Smith kids. Pigeons . . . observed late childhood and adolescence.

Brownie? He's still a talker and screamer. I always know
when he's around. He's demanding of the parents, and they
try to ignore him. He wants to get into his nest, but it's not
his anymore. He hangs around the grillwork, teetering on
the top, a drugstore cowboy. Plucky? He's away for longer
parts of the day, having sturdy, plucky adventures, no doubt.
He's all put together. Brownie was never all put together.

One day, close to bedtime, Brownie appeared screaming
his head off as though his nervous system had gone wacky.
The light began to fail, and he didn't join his family. He
just stayed on an upper ledge, crying and pecking away at
the cement, a lonely little figure, craning his neck toward
the family, wanting to join them, but not doing so. When
full darkness came, he flew down, edged some space for
himself next to Plucky, cried a few times and went to sleep.
Something had happened. Was he getting enough to eat on
the outside? Could he get to the crumbs of the city fast
enough, before bigger birds pushed him away? Of course,
that must have been it. The next afternoon, I made sure there
was plenty of food on the feeding ledge when he came home
for lunch. Curiously enough, the parents let him feed there
alone, without sharing with Plucky or themselves. It was
his meal, and his alone. That was a first. My instinct was
right. Brownie was hungry. Now I make sure there is double
the food on our bathroom ledge. *Pa knows what I'm doing.*

Several weeks pass. Plucky's tail is getting quite fullgrown and handsome, with its pronounced white triangle. When he flies in, there is a delightful blur of white. Brownie, too, is larger but still wacky, the runt.

The routine is so routine, I scarcely look out except when I'm putting food on the feeding ledge. And late at night, just to remember old days, I check out the pigeon silhouettes on the parent ledge and nursery. All was well, twelve o'clock, the crier said. A few nights Plucky wasn't there, but I never worried about him. I let him go and knew he would make it. Brownie still tugged at me and filled me with guilt—the sediment of parental love.

Confusion. Strange things are happening. I'm feeling loss of control—watching freedom with all its cruelty, all its joie. The bel canto of my pigeon watching is fragmenting like shrapnel. Rhythms are not easily discernible. The play of infancy is over. A new play is starting. The pure lines of looking and understanding are breaking into thousands of sound waves, disappearing into nothing.

The corridor is changing, the scenery is moving, the actors have put on new costumes. I can't leave. I'm stuck in the middle of my curiosity. I'm also remembering another play.

❧

The morning light squeezes itself through the stained-glass window set into the stairwell leading to the front porch, harlequin-ading the carpeted steps. It's eleven o'clock, a slow hour of Time, the top of the curve of the morning for someone who had spent the early part of the day in the attic, with a head lost in the bellies of trunks filled with discard—forgotten pieces of fur, old shoes, diplomas, summer clothes, tinkle and glitter from parties given and plays performed before she was born.

Mama was kitchening, supervising the Finnish cleaning

lady. Papa was completing his rounds at the hospital. Elizabeth, the stranger-sister, was out into the world at school, and she, the smallest head in the family, had the fat of the morning on her hands.

Spring. The air, so clear, it smelled as though ozone pies were baking. Why not down the stairs, dressed in someone's high heels, ten pair of Venetian glass beads around the neck, and the gauze of a Queen Titania costume around your waist. Open the screen door, then the heavy front door, out onto the stage—the porch, with its green slat shades and sky-blue roof. And wait for the audience to go by. What was the script of the actress? At first. "Hi, there!"

A man-audience passes by.

"Hi, there!"

He smiles and answers. "Hi, there!" and walks up the hill. A woman is on the other side of the street. That will require a louder voice to say the speech.

"Hi, there!"

"Hi, there, little girl. How's your mother?"

"Fine, thank you. And you know what? My sister got a spanking last night. She did."

"Really?" The woman stops. "And how's your father?"

"Papa's worried. He yelled a lot about money."

"Really!" The woman is so nice. She stops for more.

"You know," she says, "you look so pretty I'm going to give you a penny. Say hello to your Mama."

The penny falls on the porch, and the woman walks down the hill smiling.

It's working. Everyone is smiling.

There's the nice man who owns the vegetable market in the square.

"Hi, there!"

"Hi, there, yourself," he answers and waves. "And how's the family?"

"Mama's making prune whip for dinner, and she's going

to a meeting this afternoon, but she doesn't like two of the ladies there."

"Why aren't you in school this nice morning?"

"I'm not ready yet. Mama says I'm ready, but school says I'm not. Mama's mad with the principal, 'cause I can read and write and count, and I go to kindergarten, but I'm only four and a half, and you have to be five, and—"

"Why aren't you in kindergarten then? Playing hooky?"

"What's that?"

"You'll know when you're five," he laughs.

"My teacher has a cold—"

"Say hello to your Mama and tell her she's got her own newspaper out on the front porch." He leaves smiling.

A friend of Mama's is walking down the street. Quick, quick.

"Hi, there! Mama's making prune whip, and Elizabeth got a spanking last night. Mama slapped her face."

"My, don't we look like the cat's meow this morning. And how grown-up. Does your Mama know she's got an actress in the family?"

The woman waves, but it's not at the little girl. Someone is standing behind the screen door. Mama, her mouth severe, her eyes smiling. What did it mean? Was it all right to say "hi" to the world, or was it bad to sing out and touch the morning? Was it all right to be seductive? How come Mama wouldn't let you into her bedroom when she was dressing this morning, like all mornings? How come, if you burst in, she would be in her closet? How come she never let you touch her hair when she brushed it, and it was so long and beautiful?

"Don't you ever accept a penny for anything," the severe mouth said, with the eyes still smiling. "You just give it right back, with a nice thank you."

Leaving home, but not for too long, reminds me of a friend who had bought his first motor launch, having arrived at that state in life where he could afford the captain's cap and all that went with it—namely, the boat.

He invited me out for a spin one afternoon and picked me up at the bay front of a house my husband and I had rented for the summer. No sooner had I made the jump from bulwark to bobbing boat than he looked nervous, barely greeted me, pulled out large maps, and began searching for something. I asked him what he was doing as we jiggled up and down in the bay water, just a few feet away from our house.

"I'm finding out where we are."

"Where we are? I know where we are, Alfred. There's my house right there!"

"No, no, the buoys! Which channel I take to get over there," he said, pointing to a saucy mandarin-looking figure darting in and out of the horizon.

"Way over there? Jesus, I'm in the boat two minutes and we're lost."

He looked at me over his glasses with distaste. I had to make amends. I would offer a suggestion. "Why don't you point the boat in the direction you want to go—and just go?"

"We have to find the channel, or I'll run the boat aground," he barked.

"Oh, well, let's find it," I agreed.

"That's what I'm doing, looking at the navigational map of the bay."

"Oh. Do you know how to read it?"

"I'm trying to, if you'll wait a minute." His face looked like crisis time. I didn't want to go to the Chinese mandarin at all.

"Why don't we just loll about here and dunk our feet overboard?"

He looked at me with masculine horror.

"Dunk our feet? Christ, woman, I'm taking you for a boat ride," and he gunned the motor, not without difficulty, and went zooming toward the drunken mandarin.

"Do we know what we're doing?" I asked timidly.

"Of course!" His face was a conflict of resoluteness and displeasure.

I began to laugh hysterically as boats whizzed past us, their owners craning necks to look at us, as if we were driving on the wrong side of the street in London, which we were. I began to hum one of Jimmy Durante's favorites "Did you ever have the feeling that you wanted to go . . . that you wanted to stay," then precipitously into "Row, row, row your boat, gently down the stream," then into "Alfred, are you sure Jewish people should be rushing pell-mell toward a Chinese mandarin," then, into a scream, "ALFRED! take me home!" as a huge fishing schooner Rolls-Royce almost sideswiped us, its skipper looking like a blowfish with a hook in its mouth.

Alfred immediately cut the motor. All was blue-white, dazzling silence. We looked at each other and burst out laughing. The afternoon was lovely.

I said, "At least if we don't know how to go, let's go slowly, you know, like a rowboat." My heart was pounding under my tee shirt. God, my nervous system wasn't worth a nickle a pickle. If I didn't get back to my porch, I would die. I was so ashamed of my fear.

(Wait a minute. What fear? What porch?)

"Alfred, the radio said there was going to be a tidal wave, typhoon, hurricane this afternoon. We'd better get back."

"Aw, honey, come on, let's try and get to the second buoy."

"One buoy is enough," I decided for us, firmly.

The Warren School was very far from home, two streets up the hill, left turn down a long, leafy street, up a short hill. And there it was, the first grade, a ten-minute walk from home. Just about one buoy's worth.

Down the steps from the porch, a little grasshopper on its way somewhere. Halfway up the street, caught suddenly in the mouth of a very large lizard. The leaves on the trees have their mouths open wide. On! Push on! Don't you see I'm not a grasshopper? I'm a very large stag, with rococo antlers, so wide, they're making heavy heat about my head. So heavy, my brain is beating. Now, down the long street. Hurry, the Warren School is close. The antlers grow smaller. The stag becomes a little running grasshopper. Then up the short hill—and the grasshopper is a person of five years, heart beating, cheeks flushed. What a long trip, alone, without Elizabeth, my sister.

"Mornings were hell," she said. "It was my job to teach you how to get to the Warren School. You always made me late for my classes, because we couldn't wrench you out of the house. You lolled over breakfast, had a tantrum about being dressed in scratchy underwear, and only after much hysteria, cajoling, even a spanking, could you be ejected from the house. There was a scene every morning."

"Did we ever talk on the way to school?"

"Talk? Who could talk? My heart was in my mouth because you always made me late for my own classes. Was I relieved when Mama finally felt you could 'do it' by yourself."

Certain relationships never change. The people change, but, curiously, remain faithful to original game plans. My older sister behaves toward me, sometimes, as though she's still dragging me to school. I can see it in her eyes when she's tired with herself, and me.

And who was Elizabeth dragging me to? The first-grade teacher, Miss Nichols, who was probably fifty and looked seventy—my mother away from home. A fifty-year-old Yankee virgin could very well look seventy.

What an exciting time that was. The little Polish boy who sat next to me had bugs on his scalp—and gave them to me. Mama had a fit and almost enrolled me in a private school. Miss Nichols, who ordinarily took orders only from God, was given edicts from Mama, and she followed them with tight, thin lips. Mama ordered that every child take home a sulfur solution, to be followed by green-soap shampoos every week, and my first grade had the cleanest heads in town. Mama was married, after all, to Papa, who by then, was the Commissioner of Health. His word was law. So was hers.

Papa arrived at school one morning to give the first Schick tests to schoolchildren in the town. The immigrant parents had not given their consent. They were terrified their offspring would be hurt by the injection. But Papa insisted and came himself rather than a nurse. He injected the entire town of children, to 'lick diphtheria,' which, of course, he did.

He arrived unannounced. We were asked to stand in line, and there was my Papa, standing at the head of the line, smiling and injecting. My whole body broke out into a flush. "That's my father," I whispered to my classmates, who were so terrified of the needle waiting for them, they refused to acknowledge my importance. But, even so, my pride was excessive. I forgot the uncomfortableness of my scratchy woolen underwear. It became my turn at the head of the line. Papa would show everyone who *he* was, and who *I* was.

"Hello, little girl," he said, and patted my head. That's all. He injected my arm, and I slunk back to my seat.

"He's not your father!" the little Polish boy whispered.

"He is too!"

"He is not!" someone else chimed in. "He didn't know your name."

"He is too!" (My underwear was itching to beat the band.) Did he?

"Now, class, let's thank the doctor. All together now, 'Thank you, Dr. Halpern,'" Miss Nichols ordered.

I poked the little Polish boy in the ribs. "You see, his name *is* Halpern, and so is mine!"

He stuck his tongue out at me. "You're a Jew, then. My mother said Dr. Halpern is a Jew. Ya-ya-ya-ya. Yayayaya, ya-ya."

"*Silence!*" tore out of Miss Nichols like a whip. But I couldn't let the ya-ya's go.

I hissed, "Polack, Polack, Polack with nits in your hair!"

"Stand in the corner, Doris, this instant."

The room was full of snakes. The mortification, total.

The world is full of gangsters, takers, attackers, lying in wait for soft spots. They think if they attack the soft spot, the Whole will fall away. Misconception. But, sometimes, they win. When they win, they spin a world that doesn't belong to them loose from its moorings. Then they take over.

The Whole must stand fast, even though nibbled at the edges by evil. The whole must be convinced it *is* a Whole.

Many a nest has fallen simply through negligence, the Whole never dreaming that its edges were entrances to the parts, never understanding the meaning of circumference— a skin, easily pricked, a doorway to the state of being conquered.

Some clever Mafioso with an all-white tail figured that one out. I didn't think it up. I simply watched him. He carried *Mein Kampf* under his wing, protesting it was just outmoded reference material, but necessary reading for a student of revolution.

"Don't call me a terrorist," he warned. "I'm an instrument for change. Them's what has *must* share with thems what doesn't haves."

Mr. and Mrs. Khrushchev would have nothing to do with him, having settled into their complacency. They honored borders. They were respectable citizens making babies. Their style of aggression had been completely different from WhiteTail's. Mr. and Mrs. K had moved into the corridor, with tanks. It didn't work? Excuse me, they said. But White-Tail was another breed. He was a fringe-crazy terrorist.

> "If ever I wanted to attack an opponent, I would NOT negotiate and prepare for months, but would do as I always did: emerge out of the dark and with the swiftness of lightning throw myself upon my opponent." *(Hitler, at Nuremberg, 1937)*

WhiteTail had a high I.Q., an excess of anger, and one thought in mind: to conquer the entire corridor of the Smiths and Khrushchevs, who were strange bedfellows observing detente.

In the beginning, when I first became aware of White-Tail's plan, I called him the Prince of Evil. He was a handsome, dark bird, with a long white tail. But his appearances into the corridor became so frequent I didn't have time to think "Prince of Evil," and so he became WhiteTail, the sound of which better described his "lightning" movements anyway. If (canny fighter that he was) he was using any image as his model, it must have been that of a medieval Italian prince with great chains of gold about his chest and a large fur hat hiding his handsome, avaricious features, elegant from the top of his head to the claws on his feet. He wasn't hungry. This was an exercise in power, grabbing it, maintaining it—because he might want it later!

Into the bucolic corridor of Eighty-third Street he came, sized up the situation and began to nibble about the edges of the Whole, starting with Brownie, its weak link.

Brownie is a victim, an accident-prone kid. He wears a sign on him saying, "Hit me."

The weather was down to five and ten degrees above zero. Ma and Pa Smith were letting Brownie and Plucky snuggle up to them, even on the nursery ledge, while one of them was, of course, sitting on the new eggs. My bathroom window-feeding ledge was kept crammed full with food. Despite my feelings, I was even worrying about the Khrushchevs, who would never touch a bit of the food on the Smiths' feeding ledge. Quite amused with my turn-around and flowing with the milk of bird kindness, I started to put out food for the Khrushchevs on yet *another* ledge.

Now there were two bird dining rooms in operation. I telegraphed that message to Pa Khrushchev. He watched me warily, and letting a decent twenty-four hours go by, flew over, looked through the window, thanked me, and began to eat like a pig. Now I had two families to feed!

It was no time to feel sheepish about selling arms to a cold war country. It was the right move. The next day, the Khrushchevs had a baby bird in their nest. Not two, but one. Another tiny yellow head. Birth even makes a Gorgon's head smile. The Khrushchevs, alias marauders, whom I detested for the sake of the Smiths, were now a family. How could I not feel sympathy, with the freezing cold and more snow in the offing? Anyway, it made me feel holy, being so fair. I named the baby Bozo. He would undoubtedly grow into a beefy, dopey, clown of a kid, knowing his parents as well as I did. I don't care about Bozo, but I'll feed the family. That's as far as I would go. There would never be another Plucky and Brownie. I had energy enough to worry only about them and the new force in the corridor, the Prince of Evil.

It was before bedtime that WhiteTail struck. Pa had just taken his watch over the eggs. Ma was to be "off," and Plucky was flying about for a last swig of flight before sleep. Brownie was already on the parent ledge, about to settle down for the night. Suddenly, pandemonium. WhiteTail attacked Brownie, got him into a corner of the parent ledge, and was pecking him with the intent of an executioner. Pa Smith could do nothing because he was sitting on the eggs. Plucky was scared stiff. Only Ma could try to get WhiteTail away from Brownie. The cries brought Pa Khrushchev over, and between Ma Smith and Pa Khrushchev, WhiteTail was pried loose from Brownie, whose screams had roused the whole pigeon neighborhood.

Brownie cried half the night. His tail had been injured. Before I went to sleep, I saw Plucky with him, trying to comfort him, pecking his neck, moving as close to him as he could. Ma and Pa were both on the nursery ledge, protecting the eggs. She didn't take her time off that night. I looked over at the Khrushchevs. They were both on their pot, sitting on Bozo. No one was taking any chances. The whole schedule was awry.

That's the end of Brownie, I thought. WhiteTail was hovering about the corridor all the next day. The Smiths and Khrushchevs would chase him away. But he was insolence itself. He would repair to an upper ledge and just sit, surveying the scene. Brownie was back in the pot with Ma, while she sat on the eggs, and *didn't* chase him away. He was home again, recuperating, cozy and not flying. In a few days, he was flying again.

What on earth would be the future of Brownie? Would he make it?

WhiteTail's attack had made everyone alert. Another change took place. Pa and Ma Smith reversed their watches. Pa sat all day and Ma all night. I couldn't figure out why. It led to greater complications and was not the greatest decision in the world.

It was night. For some restless reason, I was bird watching, which I seldom did after dark.

There was Ma, on the eggs, and WhiteTail on the grillwork, just sitting, like a gargoyle that belonged. Plucky and Brownie were over on the parent ledge, sleeping, and *Pa was nowhere to be seen.* Ma's one eye was throwing out fire. She flew a few inches off the eggs, pecked WhiteTail; he flew off laughing and lighted again on the grill. No one had ever dared get that close to the nest and pot and eggs. He certainly wanted "in," that bird.

Wait a minute. Could he be a suitor? Could Pa have gone off for good? I was trying to imagine and adjust to possible pigeon behavior.

During the day, Pa would take his watch and have very little to do with Ma. No more pecking and cooing over the nest and its eggs. It was strictly business for Pa. Ma looked terrible but faithful, and her nights were hell, sitting on the eggs, looking over at Brownie and Plucky and pecking WhiteTail to keep him from jumping into the pot with her.

Something was breaking apart. Where in hell was Pa spending his nights? He would appear in the morning with straw and twigs, because Ma's nighttime activity, fending off WhiteTail, made the lining of the pot fall over the side. Pa was sleeping with someone else. Who? Where?

Was it my fault? Had my food that maintained the family for so long attracted others, and were the Smiths getting tired of fighting for their right to eat on my ledge? Had one of the mates a new lover? Is it White Tail? No. It couldn't be. Ma pecks him away, and she looks exhausted. Is my concern abnormal, misplaced? Do pigeon children never leave? Are the new eggs ready to hatch, and everyone knows it but me?

My desire for the perpetual family is human, perhaps, neurotic, not *ante*diluvian, *in* diluvian. In the Flood is the way I want it. The whole family together in one boat, with the terrors of the world swirling about them, but the family staying Whole. That's the way I want it. Fool.

Why should they stay? To please my sense of order and

continuity? Of course not. Is that what I want so much? The L-shaped farmhouse? Section being added on to section, as the family grows? Children, surrounded by the fat of aunts, uncles, grandparents, all living together. Children learning from the wisdom of their elders: feeling secure, clan-sure, growing among their own; their own stones, trees, paths, fields, harvesting their own, planting their own in turn. Close the blind in the breakfast room, and cry for the moon, love. You live in an apartment with your husband, your son is away at school, and you talk, now and then, to relatives on the telephone, and both your voices are careful not to ask for too much love.

It seems to be ending, and not in goodwill—rather, fighting for place. Plucky and Brownie were coming home, wanting closeness, recognition, no aggression, but life impinged in this new bird WhiteTail, a mythic figure bringing change. He was the outside, nibbling away at the edges. The inside was changing too. Pa had expanded his life. Ma compressed into being only Ma to save the new eggs. Plucky and Brownie knew it was time to leave. The patterns of their days were no longer readable. I had to take my cue from Ma Smith. She was almost letting them go.

Yes, this new bird WhiteTail was the messenger of change. During the day, now, he spent the winter hours with yet another bird, his mate, touching beaks on ledges heretofore reserved only for the Smiths. Pa let them. And they were waiting it out to see how much eating away at the core they had achieved. Plucky and Brownie spent long hours talking to each other. What were they planning? And when they weren't doing that, they were flying through the wide world, gradually unhinging themselves from the corridor.

Pigeon gestures were becoming harder for me to translate. Time was slipping by me, because I was ignorant and couldn't break the code. *One day, Brownie disappeared, and never came back.* A few days later, Plucky stopped sleeping on the parent ledge at night.

He would show up every so often during the day, have lunch, and fly out again.

Then one evening, when I was sure the new eggs were about to hatch (it was time), Plucky came dashing into the corridor, with WhiteTail in hot pursuit. Plucky flew into the nursery for protection. Pa got Plucky into a corner of it and pecked him severely. The son had *never* been pecked by the father before. Something must be going to happen.

Plucky flew to the parent ledge. Nope. You can't stay there either. Pa chased him away. Go away from home, go away. The parental protection was finished.

WhiteTail was watching from a higher ledge. Another kid, down and away.

And Plucky flew off for good. He insisted on belonging much longer than Brownie did, still the stronger and the fittest to the end.

I had to make my peace with the leavetakings. No ownership. They had given me pleasure, and it was done with, the first pigeon children I ever had, one weak, the other strong, off into the world, muscles better because of my bread and, yes, love.

Sometime during the night that Plucky was chased away, a warming trend began, and the Smiths hatched their third child of the winter. There was a new yellow head in the pot. Just one.

Ma and Pa were a family again, sitting in the pot together, neck pecking, talking, feeding the tiny head. *Aria da capo.* Am I not bored with it? Evidently not. A tiny creature breathes. My God, would this loving never end? Here was a replacement for Plucky and Brownie. Who could resist? A lot of sane people, I laughed to myself.

Mama's Church

MY Christian friends and their parents went to church on Sunday. The parents of my Jewish schoolmates went to the synagogue on Saturday, the only one in town; built, I later learned, by my Great-Uncles Harris and Sam; a fact kept from us, I can only imagine, because Mama and Papa, who were so disapproving of "barbaric ritual," didn't think it was information worthy of note. God was a four-letter word, an obscenity, a sign of weakness of spirit, bourgeois pap, "the opiate of the masses."

I was jealous. Everyone else had rules they seemed to relish, unbreakable ones that came from the Outside. They gathered together and observed those rules in concert. It was cozy. They knelt in front of images or wrapped themselves up in strange-looking prayer shawls and rocked on their haunches, dressed in Sabbath-best.

We had to live by the rules that came from inside Mama and Papa's heads. They were atheists. It was extremely lonely. Our Sunday ritual, after roast-beef dinner, was to gather in the "sitting room" and turn on the radio for the Sunday afternoon symphony concert, while Papa read the

Sunday paper and Mama read a book. I was either supposed to study or join them in listening. The afternoon hours stretched out like brown toffee, as though Bruckner and Mahler had invented the clock.

On Friday nights, the house of my special Jewish playmate was bewitched by candlelight and the smell of fresh baked bread made one dizzy with hunger. The phrase *"bench lecht"* had something to do with Fridays. And my friend's mother had a special, sad look for me on Fridays. I wondered why I was never asked to join them. "It's time for the little goy to go home," she would tease me pleasantly, "this is Friday." She very well knew I wasn't a "goy." Her pleasantry had a special barb that I could never understand.

"What's *'bench lecht,'* Mama?"

"It's what Mrs. Singerman does on Friday. They're religious people. They believe in God."

"Do we believe in God?"

"No, we don't, because there is no God."

One glorious Saturday afternoon, my special Catholic friend asked me to join her in a walk to her church. There she was to have a pair of scissors blessed by the priest, because her father wanted to cut an ingrown toenail that had been bothering him. The priest was going to dip the scissors in holy water, she told me. We hung around the screen door in the back of her house, while her parents discussed the advisability of a little Jewish girl entering the church. They decided it might be all right because we were going into the basement of the church, not the church itself. And in delight, because we were such good friends and our friendship transcended the rules, we skipped all the way to the church. My friend was naughty. She said, "Do you want to see 'Him'?"

I whispered back an exalted, "Yes." And she snuck me into the church itself to meet "Jesus." The rendition of "Him" in my friend's church, frequented mostly by the

Irish of the town, was the most beautiful man I had ever seen. His golden locks wound round an exquisite neck, pulsing with sex. His naked body gleamed in the afternoon half-light like a yellow sunset. Oh, how jealous I was. To think that she could see "Him" every Sunday or whenever she wished, even when it had to do with her father's toenails.

Standing in the exalted presence of my friend's "Him," I knew "they" were right about me. More than being a skinny, little Jewish girl with large shadows under my green eyes, I was an alien, an outcast, an ugly behemoth who had strayed into a valley of grazing crystal and pearl-backed gazelles. My place was in the fetid pool of Jews, but they were in the synagogue, and I wasn't even allowed to go there. I was an outcast squared. Double-hexed. I was a Jew whose family didn't believe in God, who, it seemed, was everywhere in one form or another, looking down, except in our house.

I longed for my own church like a spurned lover. On Sundays, the angst was especially bad, as I looked out the bay windows of our house and watched the Irish Catholics going to church, the Yankees going to their church, the Greeks going to their church that had three gold domes on top of it, the Poles going to their church, the other Jews strolling about, not going to church, because they had "gone" on Saturday. I imagined that they all passed our house and looked the other way, their goyish or Orthodox noses high in the air with contempt and disapproval.

But none of them had a sign on his house that said HARRY HALPERN, M.D., as we did. And none of them had a car with a green cross on its license plates, as Papa did. The cross and the sign on the house and Papa's office must have been something very special, because when all those people were not feeling good, they treated Papa with a hush and a deference equal to that of a priest or minister or rabbi.

The green cross on Papa's car allowed him to go anywhere. It was like the cross "Him" was hanging on. And Papa served and loved and healed the way my friend said "Him" did, and does. So maybe Papa was a kind of god, and that's why we didn't have to go to church like ordinary people did. And when I was old enough to walk to the square by myself, I, too, was the recipient of some of that same deference given to Papa. "Oh, you're Dr. Halpern's little girl, aren't you?" But it would go no further. Never a "come home and have a bread-and-butter sandwich with us." They were afraid of Mama and Papa and me and Elizabeth. We were godless. Hell would be the end for such a family. I saw that in their eyes.

But we *did* have a ritual, and it happened every Saturday. It was going into Boston for further studies; Elizabeth, the dance and me, music. *And* the ritual of the Boston Public Library! We dressed up for the trip in the same manner others dressed for church. The set of Mama's mouth was the same as other mothers walking their family down the street to pray. The "going to Boston" was a big and ritual thing. It was eighteen miles away and took an hour, all told, on the Boston and Maine Railroad, and finally a trolley car in Boston that said "Huntington Avenue" on it; and straight, at last, to Copley Square, where presided the queen of buildings—The Main Branch of the Boston Public Library (facing the old Trinity Church). There it was, one of the heartbeats of Boston, center of civilization in America! Our church! And our family had not one but two churches. The other one was where Papa and Mama went on alternate Saturday nights— The Boston Symphony Building, where Papa sat in the same seat for thirty-seven years, and Mama until a few weeks before she died. That was the nighttime church, where music was worshiped with a Boston fervor unsurpassed in America.

But the church that Mama had chosen for me to visit every Saturday was magnificence itself. It was a "palace for

the people." As you walked up the outside steps, you were
greeted by two large bronze statues. One was a figure of
"Art," and the other was "Science," represented by two pa-
cific, flowingly robed women, whose laps caught the snow
in winter, whose faces were peace itself, whose very presence
said: "All is well. The world is a place of dignity, contain-
ment, majesty. Enter, little girl. Even climb up and sit in our
laps when your mama isn't looking." Then you walked up
the outside steps, passing through three huge bronze doors,
and on those awesome doors Mama said were portrayed in
allegorical figures, in low relief (I didn't know what she
meant, but I felt it), Music and Poetry, on the left; Knowledge and Wisdom, center; and Truth and Romance, on the
right door. How could you go wrong! Come in. You were
entering one of the most beautiful buildings in America.
Again, you didn't know it, but you felt it. A national landmark, an Italian Renaissance building of almost perfect proportion, serene, classic, elegant, filled with curves and
columns and great, arched windows (the Gothic arch was
everywhere, man's most beautiful architectural gesture),
light of all dynamics pouring through its apertures and the
glint of gold and bronze and deep reds and marbles of every
hue. In the mosaic ceiling of the Main Entrance Hall were
embedded names that I learned to read almost before I
could make out, "Run, Jane, run"—Adams, Webster, Long-
fellow, Hawthorne, Emerson, Cotton Mather, Bulfinch,
Garrison, Mann, Sumner—jurists, theologians, historians, re-
formers, artists, scientists. The world was full of great people, and anything was possible if one strove to be "learned."
That's what the Library wanted to say to you, Mama said.

Then we would walk up the main staircase, under a
"deep triumphal arch," and everywhere were walls of yellow
Siena marble (yellow!), and floors of ivory-gray marble,
mottled with fossil shells. Halfway up the grand staircase
(fit for a wedding of kings), on marble pedestals at the

turn of the stairs, were two great twin lions of yellow marble, the calmest, greatest lions in the world, each with great paws leaning over the front of their pedestals, paws that would never hit out, because they were the Boston Public Library lions. As you made your way up the second half of the staircase, there they were—the murals by Puvis de Chavannes, wreathed about the second-floor walls, looking down upon the entire Main Stair Hall. A gargantuan, artistic statement called *The Muses.*

Splayed across the walls of the second-floor Gallery were the nine white-robed Muses of Greek mythology, hovering midair about Apollo (Genius of Enlightenment) in a setting of olive and laurel groves, the work of the French nineteenth-century muralist. All was muted, green grass, flowering bushes, trees, ocean, sky, air, light, serenity. All was soft blues and greens, and Mama would stop and rest, leaning back on the yellow marble walls. And she would sigh, half from the climb of the stairs and half from the lyricism dominating the space, idyllic, romantic, yet classic; real, yet unreal. The-hailing-of-The-Muses-of-the-Harbinger-of-Light-whammy-of-the-glorious-walls. Sensual, but without sex.

Maybe others had their Ten Commandments. We had our Nine Muses, Mama and I on Saturdays in the Boston Public Library.

There could be no question, looking at the pre-Impressionistic Romanticism (out of classical elements) of Chavannes' art, that the soul of man was beautiful and the world, though dark at times, always cradled the possibility of light, joy, happiness, fruition, truth, beauty, and peace. *Only* because the mind of man, at its greatest, was all those things. Man, not God, Mama would remind me. She was never one to shirk responsibility. Atheists know they have to go it alone.

Spinoffs from the great mural were smaller ones, imbedded in arches of the yellow marble side walls of the staircase. I tell you, a walk up that staircase and you were surrounded by concepts of the glory that was Greece, enough to make your head reel. Some of those Chavannes images stay with me to this day. What was it that he was trying to do? Depict Absolutes. Breathe life into nouns to live by.

There was History! the Muse of History, in a red toga, standing above the partly buried ruins of a Doric temple, conjuring it to yield up its secrets. Beside her is the genius of Learning, with book and torch.

There was Physics! Two female figures, symbolizing Good and Bad News respectively, float in the air with their hands upon the wires of the telegraph, magical carrier of happy and sorrowful tidings!

There was Philosophy! Plato is talking with one of his disciples, in a beautiful Athenian landscape, with a noble Ionic colonnade at the left and in the background, above (the ubiquitous) grove, the Acropolis, with the gleaming Parthenon. Other students of Philosophy are grouped about the colonnade.

There's Pastoral Poetry! Virgil, in an idyllic landscape, visiting his beehives, while two shepherds of his Eclogues idle at a distance.

There's Epic Poetry! Blind Homer is holding his head (thinking) sitting by the roadside, greeted with gifts of laurel by two female figures (in those wonderful Grecian robes). And the ladies typify his great poems, the martial Iliad, with helmet and spear, the gentler Odyssey, with an oar to suggest her wanderings. My God, what a plethora of images for a small hero.

You think that's all? There's Astronomy! Typified by two Chaldean shepherds, earliest observers of the heavens, and they look into a deep blue sky dotted with stars.

But the acme of childhood impression for me was the

mural Dramatic Poetry! There was Aeschylus, seated on a cliff overlooking the sea, with his hero, Prometheus, in the background, chained to a great rock, where the Oceanids circle round him (again in white, diaphanous robes), to comfort him from the pain caused by the vulture that tears at his vitals (his liver, Mama explained to me). And all because Prometheus took pity on Man and stole fire from heaven and gave it to him, and it made Zeus angry.

"It has a happy ending. Prometheus was eventually saved by Hercules," Mama said.

"Where's the liver, Mama?"

"Ask Papa, and he'll tell you exactly."

I never did. And I don't know where the liver is to this day. Well, vaguely, but not exactly. What I do know is that it kicks up with too much booze. Papa offered *that* when I was old enough to have two gins before dinner. But what I do know is that goodness is boring, very often punished, and evil, often rewarded handsomely, constantly fascinating.

Mama had a copy of this mural in our stairway at home. I saw Prometheus every day, hanging on his rock (like Christ), as I went down the stairs to the front door. Aeschylus reading, in the foreground, sea nymphs in undulating positions, with long, blond hair waving in the wind, hovering over the naked figure of Prometheus chained to his rock, rising out of the sea, and that damn vulture overhead, ready to gnaw another bite out of the liver! Gnaw! Another bite, the minute I turned my back.

What fright, beauty, what wonderment, what curves, swooping and dipping, what whites and yellows and greens and blues, what seas and skies. What weirdness, and with what humor I think back on those first impressions stamped on my little mind, just by a walk up the grand staircase of the Boston Public Library.

Mama made sure I would become a "romantic." Her job was well done. It must have been. Whenever my mind takes refuge, it snuggles into the myths of gods and men of ancient Greece. Why else would I write, years later, after a cancer operation, in a little blue notebook, picked because the sky (freedom) was blue.

". . . will I ever flower again—if, in fact, I ever have? How will I know, if I never have? Now, maimed, will it be easier to perceive? I need to stand close to a temple, somewhere in Greece, high on a promontory, where a few columns stand against the wind and blue sky, proud memory of a house broken . . ." Yes, Mama did her job well. She, with the help of the ridiculous and beautiful Chavannes murals in the Boston Public Library, infected me with the need to search for all the unattainables—Truth, Beauty, Wisdom, Balance, Perfection. Her love for those nouns has pinioned me to her memory.

Directly across the street from the Library, on Huntington Avenue, was the now torn-down S. S. Pierce Building, housing the famous food emporium, and up the street a few doors was the Faelton School, founded by two German brothers, purveyors of in-depth, disciplined music training.

The minute my sister and I conquered the three R's, we were enrolled in the "Preparatory Course" at the Faelton School (preparatory to becoming genius). The Faelton School didn't fool around. I was seven when I started my music studies, and even then, I knew in no uncertain terms that I was working toward "the diploma." Every Saturday for eight years, I was trudged to Boston via the Boston and Maine Railroad. To this day, the smell of smoke in a train tunnel gives me a cow kick in the chest and reminds me of music lessons not ready, memorization of passages from Mozart, Beethoven, Bach, not quite sunk into the unconscious; of looking at my reflection in the dusty window of the ancient train, searching for clues of who I was, with the silly hat I had on my head, a Mama-must when we went to "the city"; reminds me of a sticky brew of great loneliness yet the possibility of adventure away from the nest; of searching the new trees, the new houses along the way, wondering what the people inside said to each other and how they said it; of envying the fleeting figures of children, "wasting time" about the edges of the rivers and ponds along the railroad tracks on an early Saturday morning.

My kingdom for a horse! To ride through indolent hours down by the railroad tracks. What did I do wrong! Instead, I had a goony hat on my head, and Czerny and Clementi (in the early days) writhing in my lap at the injustices I would do them, and a silent Mama beside me, probably reading Thomas Mann, whom I detested, because Mama talked about him and how *he* felt more than how *I* felt. How did she know so much about him? He never came to visit. Maybe at night, when I was asleep.

Mama had special powers. She could just look at you and know what you were thinking. That meant that you were always naked. You had to do your heavy thinking far away from her eyes, far away, under a tree, up the street, or in the winter clothes closet, with the door closed. Even so, she had a magic eye that penetrated wood, metal, bone, muscle, straight into my brain. It was the most amazing thing.

And so she would say (on the train) without taking her eyes from her book, "Why don't you spend this time to get ready, instead of looking at the children?"

Now how did she know there were children down by the railroad tracks?

At first, Mama accompanied me to Boston to break me in, the early years of music lessons. Then, I was "taken" by a slightly older cousin, Dorothy Copeland, who also had matriculated at the school, because her mama, along with mine, insisted she be in a state of musical grace, like my sister and myself. My sister was five years ahead of me in her cultural chores, and so, our paths never crossed. We never did anything together. Elizabeth went into Boston on Fridays for her dancing lessons. That was her concentration. Mine was to be music. That was Mama's master plan. If there had been a third child, he or she would, undoubtedly, have been on the train to Boston to pursue the art of painting. An older male cousin, she fashioned into an architect. Another even older male cousin, she maneuvered into hospital management, and he became the head of a large hospital. Another cousin was encouraged to go into dentistry, and after a lifetime of service, at the age of seventy, he became the first Jewish president of the North East (New England) Dental Society. She would have loved that. She loved firsts. My cousin Dorothy and my sister Elizabeth were sort of perfect. I was not. Dorothy abhorred having to take me to Boston. I wouldn't keep my gloves on, and I kept losing my music. The trip to Boston made me so nervous I would acquire a case of hiccoughs by the time we reached the North Station in Boston, an ugly stone shell of a building that made my hiccoughs sound so loud Dorothy would make believe we were not together, with me running to catch up to her, laughing and crying and hiccoughing. Dorothy was the kind of person Mama approved of. She was an achiever, a good girl, a magna cum laude at Radcliffe, worked for a graduate degree and became one of the first female vice-presidents in a large New York bank. Thank God, Dorothy had a sense of humor that grew as she did. It wasn't born yet in the days of my hiccoughing.

Mama was the Athena of Peabody; Goddess of Truth, Beauty, Wisdom, and Reason; guidance counselor, protector of the less Wise. She was, definitely, the reigning Goddess of Cultural Achievement and had sprung directly from the head of Zeus (the one who punished Prometheus). But Zeus was Papa, so I could never figure that one out.

Mama touched everyone with her olive branch. She

made sure the poor of the town had food and medical care. She guided the reading habits of every child within her circle. She barnstormed for compulsory study of the ARTS for all progeny within hearing. In the early thirties, I understand, she issued a bull forbidding the purchase of silk, because Japan insisted on overrunning gentle China with murdering hordes of soldiers. All adolescents within earshot of her gave up silk stockings and wore lisle or cotton, not really knowing why but feeling good that they did, that they, in a little town in Massachusetts, were part of something bigger, something important. But these young people, I was told later by one of them, started to read newspapers, ask questions, challenge the status quo, become curious, go to lectures and concerts, and gradually move away from the fate of small-town-mindedness. All because of her. "Yes," this person said, "all because of your mother, our growing up became something different, and we turned into people we never expected to be. Your mother must have been a very lonely, frustrated woman. There was no one else in town her equal, much less able to understand her."

Mama snubbed the wives of factory owners, with whom a doctor's family would ordinarily associate and earn his living from, because the husbands were refusing to unionize their shops. No one in town was ever at her dinner table. She imported her guests from Boston and New York. How resentful the town must have been of her aloofness.

Every summer, there was some starving poet, writer, or artist living in the attic, rubbing up against her apple pie and roast beef like a grateful cat and joining in the conversations at night that fed her culture-hungry soul. Mama ran a hinterlands salon. And she must have given as much as she received, inspirationally. To be "inspired," *that* was her sine qua non-est of all desires. And to have those around her in the same state was her sweetest wish for them. It was the dream of a non-artist and drove her mad. She demanded beauty and became a killer if disappointed. More often than not, the victim must have been herself. Those artists, whom I've met in later years, still remember, describe the quality of light around her and her things. They evoke the house as a haven in the midst of madness. How strange. I don't remember her carrying an olive branch, but rather a club. One of her lifelong friends confided in me, when I was old enough to understand, that, "A walk in the woods with your mother was like reading a poem."

One of the few sobs in my life almost escaped me when I heard that eulogy. It was the sadness at having missed being Mama's friend, not her child.

Life with Mama and me was war from the moment I appeared on the scene. We never understood each other or tried to. She had to, forcibly, drag me into her world of absolutes, and she died too soon for me to be able to "have it out" with her. For years after, I was frozen in guilt, because I didn't like her, and there was so much unsaid between us. But all of that came later.

The Time we did spend together, unsprung from the house, its rules and commitment to "duty," was the Time she took me to Boston on those Saturdays to the music lessons; then, a brief lunch, a visit to the library, where we sat looking up at the Chavannes murals or read quietly in the children's section or visited the rare-books room, where she would read and I would sit looking at her neat head with its crown of braids, wondering who *she* was.

I don't remember feeling comfortable with any clothes in which Mama dressed me. Standard features of the outfit "to go to Boston in" were always hat and gloves and patent-leather shoes. The hats were made of velour, brimmed, with grosgrain ribbons hanging down the back. The gloves were always white and a constant anxiety factor. They dared me to return home with them the same color with which we left. They wanted to touch railings when I didn't. They managed to throw themselves under train seats and play hide-and-seek with me behind public toilet bowls. My dresses and coats were those Elizabeth had outgrown or something bought especially for me that had to be taken care of exquisitely. Elizabeth's were always too tight. My own were always too big, so as to last for several seasons and then be handed down to someone else's child.

Public toilets figured heavily in our going-to-Boston scene. Mama had had a cancerous kidney removed before I was born, and relieving herself was always an urgent thing. Of course, I wasn't privy to such facts. Physical things were never discussed. One never peed or defecated. One only "felt." And poor Mama, I was always looking for her under the doors of public toilets, despairing that I'd lost her or she, me. Oh, that Victorian radical. What a friend I could have been to her, if she had only let me, even at seven. There's no greater friend than a child who's been given facts about loved ones at his digestible level.

Mama always looked like a million bucks. She wore severely tailored suits, sensible but expensive shoes, and hidden under her almost mannish suit was an astoundingly feminine blouse of lace or chiffon or georgette. She wore sweeping large-brimmed chapeaus (not hats), the subject of many a money fight between Papa and her. And for all the life of her, she could have passed for a DAR Boston Brahmin, while under her clothes was beating the heart of a flaming, card-carrying Communist. True. She spread the gospel of Lenin and Marx in style.

If I had been a good music student in the morning at the Faelton School, walking the gauntlet of a solfeggio class, a sight-reading class (with twelve students working on twelve pianos in the same room, it was kind of exciting, reluctant student that I was); a private lesson and a performing class in the recital hall; *then* we would lunch, amble through S. S. Pierce, where Mama replenished her larder with orders of baked beans, brown bread, and glassed fruits; thence a walk down Huntington Avenue to Boylston Street and the entrance to the Public Garden, where we would sit on a bench and feed the pigeons(!) with crumbs Mama would save from our lunch bread.

Boats, in the shape of swans, float about in the man-made pond in the Public Garden of Boston. As the final prize for a worthwhile morning we boarded the "swan" to sail around the pond and watch what seemed hundreds of ducks that followed us like an honor guard, through a carpet of water lilies.

It was awesome Time. The boats, filled with children, looked as though they had sailed directly from the set of a Wagnerian opera right onto the Garden's pond.

Mama was the queen, and I was the princess. My straight black hair turned flaxen like Rapunzel's and Mama wore breastplates and carried a spear! We were an impervious two, floating through deep, sonorous chords that made a stairway to Olympus, where, strangely enough, Rhine maidens hung around like butterflies in a Grecian sky. Was it any wonder? Mama was myth-ridden. She tried to make of us candles that would burn with unending memory of the beauty of things past. As a child, my head was a grab-bag of art nouveau renditions of Greek, German, Norse, Gaelic scenes of ancient heroic bravery and love and death. (It still is.)

There were a couple of things wrong while Mama and I cruised about on the swans. One was that we never spoke. The other was that my friends at home were, at that very moment, sitting in the darkened moviehouse in Peabody Square, watching a new cowboy movie, which I would never see until I went to college. American movies were verboten. That was another of Mama's edicts. They were for the lumpen who had to be retrained, reeducated, and made pure one day, in the not too distant future, when socialism would launder the lives of the entire populace of her beloved America.

Until then, I couldn't go to the movies in Peabody Square.

"Don't you think you're fortunate to have seen Peter Pan at the Boston Opera House, with Eva Le Gallienne?"

"Nope."

"Aren't you a lucky little girl to have heard Rachmaninoff play at the Boston Symphony?"

"Nope."

Nope, nope, nope. I sat in the swan boat next to Mama, forcing myself to watch the movement of the water till I made myself dizzy, knowing that things were happening somewhere else. I would never know what they were, but I wanted them more than anything else in the world. Ordinary things, taking place with no time limit, no overseer. A moviehouse full of kids screaming over Dracula! Oh, to be one of them for one blessed afternoon. I would have murdered Rachmaninoff for the pleasure and gladly carried his huge body from the Boston Symphony Hall to the front door of the Peabody Strand moviehouse and laid it there as a burnt offering to the manager . . . if he asked me.

I search into those Saturdays like a miner with a dimming headlight. I'm looking for something precious. Ah, yes, on one of those Saturdays, there is a memory of Mama laughing. A rare Time. As we were sitting on a bench in the Garden, feeding the pigeons, one of them perched himself on my velour hat and wouldn't leave until Mama fed him his own crumbs. She was laughing like a girl. To have a pigeon sitting on one's hat was ignominy, but if it made Mama laugh it was worth it. But was she laughing with me or at me? Without the fog of childhood misconception, it seems that she was laughing *with* me. When it happened, it seemed that she was laughing *at* me.

"How unusual you look—a hat with a live pigeon on it,"

said Mama, who loved hats, finally shooing the bird away. "Oh, dear, he's done something bad on your head," and she sat next to me and giggled.

Why wasn't she angry? I began to cry. Mama was a stranger.

I'm walking in deep mud. I don't remember Mama! Only through broken glass of a bombed-out house do I catch shadows of a woman pacing back and forth in chiffon. She loved chiffon. When her favorite niece was married, Mama created a gown for herself of dusky mauve and made her entrance to the wedding trailing chiffon and the smoke of late autumn burning leaves, her hair piled high on her head, blue eyes blazing, a veritable Minerva on a binge with the humans. Right behind her was Elizabeth in ivory moiré, and behind Elizabeth was I, in apricot moiré, with pale tea roses on my shoulders. Mama and her girls had arrived! Now the wedding of her rich brother's daughter could begin. That's the way it was when Mama was alive, even though she was the wife of a poor country doctor. Even so . . . even so . . . she was the queen.

🍁

What if there's a pipe rupture in a nuclear reprocessing plant? What about all that nuclear waste piling up, and "they" are running out of storage space? How many people will die if "they" make a mistake? How contradictory, how insane, put side by side with my sitting in a bathing pool of memory, playing with pebbles, making arcs of remembrances around me. Outward Time does not match inside Time.

The Outside convulses beyond history's wildest memories of plague and dances of death. Never before has there been such anarchy, such . . .

That's what *The New York Times* said this
morning. And furthermore, it went on, we are
back to early cries, not in the voices of healthy
animals screaming to survive but now, animals, weak in spirit, hurt, beyond redemption,
emasculated by the fruits of having become,
ha, civilized. We are back to original thrusts,
and they are not attractive; hunger, natural
cataclysm, lust for territory. Man's knowledge
has never been greater, more magnificent.
Man's spirit, more mystifying, unpredictable,
terrifyingly powerful in its search for . . .
goddamn it, WHAT?

"You have a choice, baby. You don't *have* to read *The
Times* at breakfast."

"What can I do, sitting in this offal?"

"Take a deep breath, try to be a lake at noon, when
leaves rest and birds quiet themselves as the clock hits midday."

"You must be kidding."

"No, at noon, take a deep breath, and place your hands
on twelve."

"Then what will happen?"

"There'll be a breath of silence—"

"For what?"

"You'll find out when you do it. I promise you, it will
be like lifting your hands, filled with spring water, to your
lips."

"That's not going to stop the destruction, conquering,
fakery, besting, stealing, fuckery, Macaroni shit outside, if
I lift my hands, filled with spring water to my lips. Come
on!"

"My dear, don't fight me, or we'll just talk and wait for
Death like lovers."

(My unconscious is quite a card.)

"Feel better?" he asked.

"None of your business!"

We look at each other. I make tea. We drink it together in silence. Suddenly, he disappears, diving down to almost bottom, jock that he is, always the athlete, impervious to strain, showing off what he knows best how to do—diving. He's the most independent thing I know, my unconscious. Who wouldn't be, born into money, educated in New England, dictatorial, well read (I remember nothing), sponging off me for half a lifetime, feeding off my nervous system. What form! Chic! Memory? Infallible. Tennis of the soul? Masterful. And ready for a game any time of day or night. Never sleeps. I remember dreaming of Papa, driving a car whose body was made of lizard's skin, custom-built in Detroit, had the whole factory in an uproar. Expensive? Astronomical! That's my unconscious. I wonder how I afford him. He laces my day with intrigue. He supervises me in the garden when I'm pruning roses (after convincing me I have a garden!). He knows everything. When I curl the petal of a flower around my tongue, he watches me carefully and adjudicates what I feel. My unconscious is a "he" this morning. Well, how about that!

"I wish you'd leave. I have to write."

"Not without me, love," he says, perching on the top of a lampshade, then diving right into the electric bulb, just to worry me about getting burned. Swimming around the General Electric filaments, I could hear him saying, "Talk to me, talk to me, baby, even if it's sad, talk to me, and don't worry so much about the outside, it's gonna be there long after you're gone. Get yourself straight, an' the outside's gonna look much better."

He was beginning to sound like Willow with her philosophical pronunciamentos. How come everyone was full of wisdom but me?

Ariel, Blithe Spirit

SING to me, sing to me, even if it's sad, sing to me? The Smiths have a new baby. Today, seeing the new, silly head sticking out from under Ma's breast, I put out food for the parents.

So, here we go. A new progeny—to eat and grow and fly away. For what? To be a pigeon. What else!

I am faithful to the second family. Winter progresses, unusually mild. Then suddenly, snow, winds, freezing. I must admit, my interest is not the same as when Plucky and Brownie were growing. But my eyes continue to go to the nursery ledge three or four times a day. The feeding and the watches and the care goes on by Pa and Ma. The cold weather continues. I hope Plucky and Brownie will return on a surprise visit to the old "nabe," but it doesn't happen.

Whether it's my injection or not, there seems to be weariness about the nursery ledge. First, there is only one, not two babies. Secondly, the parents seem to be exhausted from the freezing weather and the ritual of regurgitating their hard-found food into the little one. Pa is very sympatico to my ministrations. Ma holds back. I scarcely have the window open and Pa is there, unafraid. Many times, he gives me a high sign that he's hungry by cocking his head in my direction. I don't think they're getting enough food, because the baby cries, and Pa pecks it to stay underneath him.

We're into February now. I watch Pa Smith, irritable father, scrunched down over his young, looking miserable, with the snow covering his back. My heavens, it's 10:30 A.M. I had forgotten breakfast for him. I put food out. Pa was there pronto, leaving the little one. Where was Ma to spell him? She was perching a few ledges away. Ma joined Pa and didn't go to sit over the baby while he ate. I didn't like that, but maybe I shouldn't worry. Pa flew back to the nest to feed the little one, and I put out even more food for Ma, who waited for me to do it. Then, she finished, returned to the nest, and I put out even more food for Pa, so he would have some for himself. He knew exactly what I was thinking. After feeding the baby, he came back for his own breakfast. And Ma was giving the baby what she had just eaten. Now she would be hungry herself, so I put out even more food. Busy! We were an emergency Red Cross Unit in action. I had a funny, nervous feeling about it all. It just wasn't like the days of Plucky and Brownie. I was feeding the baby directly through the parents. There was no disguise. They were no more pigeons flying through the air, doing what they needed to do and using my feeding ledge as a pleasant afterthought. They were in trouble. It must be the hazards of the weather making them so dependent. I'm really stuck *if* this weather continues. I'd be tied to feeding a baby pigeon. Pa is aware of my *every movement*, and he must sense my radio going most of the day. He must feel my concern.

But it turned out a better morning than anyone had thought. Everyone was fed. The little one was quiet, and Ma and Pa are in the pot *together*, pecking, talking, *calma*, *calma*. Pa is telling Ma that she can go over to the feeding

ledge again, that's how good he feels. Dvorak's "Silent
Woods," for cello, piano and orchestra, is playing itself out on
the radio. An adagio accompaniment to the fast-falling snow.
There is a smell of Vermont sugar maples in my study, rising
high and hiding the sun—thick fern wave in a summer heat-
shade. I hear the crackle of my feet as I walk calf-deep in
ground growth. Willow loves Mozart. Why not pigeons,
Dvorak?

Then Ravi Shankar plays a concerto for sitar and orchestra. Ma and Pa close their eyes and both sleep in the pot
over the baby. The morning pulses on.

I must name the baby. Let's see—only child—born in
cold—a nonsensical thing at best, particularly when one's
nursery is a pot catching falling snow. Ariel, Blithe Spirit.
That's it. Ariel, or Arielle, if female. Anyone who has the guts
to be born in a pot set out in the dead of winter deserves
to be called Ariel!

I don't believe it. I've hooked myself right into a third
pigeon baby.

And what a sweetie. So much smaller than Plucky and
Brownie. But we'd make it grow. We were all working very
hard.

> Ariel, Blithe Spirit. I must come to you, close-
> up. Shall I shoot you through gauze, a la Die-
> trich or Carole Lombard in a white, shim-
> mering light, transforming cheek and body to
> edited romantic? It would be kinder that way.
> What knives it has when it wants to . . . the
> recollecting psyche. It spares me nothing.
> Let's go for broke.

Yesterday, February fourth, it poured cold, almost snow.
My family looked desperate. Pa demanded I feed him. Ma
looked sick. When Pa flew off the pot to eat, she sat in the
pot, but didn't cover Ariel with her body. She sat next to it.

Ariel cried. That was unprecedented behavior. Then she flew off, and the baby cried again. That was unheard of. What was happening? What was I *not* tuned into?

Pigeon babies are silent when the parent takes off. They make a big fuss when they return, and tuck themselves under the protecting bodies, blissfully. Something was very wrong. Both parents were leaving Ariel exposed to the weather.

I was getting collect messages about survival and selection, and I refused to accept the call. The cold rain came down harder and harder. Ma came back, sat again in the pot, but not covering Ariel. She was so scrunched up she didn't even puff out her feathers to keep herself warm. Pa came back and joined her and *did* hide Ariel. Thank God, someone was using his head.

The next day, cold and clear. How old was Ariel? About a week and a half. Something continued to be wrong. My husband said he had fed Pa early. I'd slept late. I looked out. It was more than premonition of tragedy. I couldn't believe it. Pa was sitting in the pot, but there seemed to be no squirming little one beneath him. At noon, Ma let Pa go off to feed. They were maintaining some kind of schedule. Then she, too, was sitting on what I imagined to be no Ariel. It must be there. My "watching" can't crumble like this.

Pavane for a Dead Infante, or Liebestod, or Mahler, take your pick. Intensive care unit. Ariel's slipping away. They know. I know. Ariel knows. Pa shifts his body, and I see its tiny yellow face shrinking into itself, as though the shrinking were not fast enough—the Time too long before sleep.

Ariel is dead. Pa sits, covering the body. On the Khrushchev ledge, where I glanced just to rest my eyes for a second, Bozo was growing like mad. They seemed to be managing the weather perfectly, and doing their pigeon thing to perfection.

Bozo chirps, and Pa Smith thinks it's Ariel, and pecks him helplessly, for there is no answer.

Cold and clear and bright as the day is, it is a day of mourning. The worst day in the corridor. My heart is dressed in black and throws itself over the little body of Ariel, crying out its name. The microcosmic mourning is as bad as other ones.

All day long, I sit and watch. I'm going mad. The instinct to protect the young is still going on in Pa. I become stubborn. I will sit as long as he does. I will live out the decision with him. But he's restive, looking about constantly, almost saying, "Where are you, you little devil?"

I let myself go completely and cry.

> There's a scene in a Eugene O'Neill play, *Marco Millions*, in which the Great Khan sits looking at the body of the princess, Kukachin, his grandchild, who died of a broken heart because of her love for a fool, a senseless death. And he chides her playfully, saying, "I think you are hiding your eyes, Kukachin. You are a little girl again. You are playing hide and seek. You are pretending. . . . You have made your face cold, you have set your lips in a smile, so remote—you are pretending, even, that you are dead!"

All right. I'm going to pieces over a five-inch-long pigeon, substitute for all the loves and deaths I own. I call the zoo, full of self-pity and recriminations.

"Parents will reject the dead bird," the woman says.

I tell her, "Poor Ariel, yesterday, his little head, peering into the rain, and its mother beside it, not on it, the little body getting the full rain and wind. Why?"

She says, "A parent never leaves the baby bird unless the other parent is there to take over."

"What went wrong?" I ask.

"I really don't know," she answers. "Maybe the parents sensed there was something very wrong with the bird and decided it shouldn't live."

"But there didn't seem to be, except the weather's been so bad."

Her silence tells me she thinks I am out of my mind.

"What happened to the father bird?" I ask.

The zoo woman didn't think my feeding had anything to do with the tragedy. "However, he did make a relationship with you, evidently."

"The mother would never leave the nest when I put food out, only Pa. I thought him bright and her dumb," I add weakly.

"Yes, something happened to the father. There's no question about that. But don't worry. They'll reject the dead bird and throw it out themselves."

"Thank you," I say, shaking my head no.

The Smiths *didn't* throw it out themselves. They sat on the dead Ariel all the next day. Pa was terribly agitated. He would sit, then fly off, then come back. Then Ma took her turn. They were terribly confused. It permeated the day. I indulged myself in a miasma of feeling. They were not doing what the zoo lady said they would. Not my Smith family. I blamed myself again for wooing Pa away with my food. Yet, it helped, didn't it? It made Brownie and Plucky grow. Why can't I accept Nature's decision about Ariel? More of the death scene from *Marco Millions* floats through my eyes and gives me instant cataracts:

> "Our Princess was young as Spring, she was as beautiful as a bird or flower.
> Cruel, when Spring is smitten by Winter, when birds are struck dead in full song, when the budding blossom is blighted!"

I will have to pull the blind down in the breakfast room and close out the sadness, for my mind is jumping, transferring the sadness into anger against everyone and everything outside. What if there's a pipe rupture in a nuclear reprocessing plant? What about all that nuclear waste piling up? How many people will die if "they" make a mistake? Is Man truly only a mirror of nature at its pinnacle of cruelty? Little Ariel is nothing and everything. European, Asian, African children of war and hunger are nothing and everything. I rail against death as though Ariel were my first pet and I was five, and *knew* nothing. The nursery ledge with its pot and the snow congealed over the body of Ariel, looked like a macabre Georgia O'Keeffe painting—crystal, cracking, cold loneliness. I'm a wreck. The nursery is *fini*. I am pleased with my sorrow and my anger. I pull down the shade. I feel very much alive.

"This Is the Place"

PEABODY, city, Massachusetts, in Essex County, on the Boston and Maine Railroad; two miles west of Salem, and eighteen miles northeast of Boston.

On the wall of the small library in Peabody is a portrait of Queen Victoria. It is an exquisite miniature, imbedded in gold filigree, red velvet, and jewels, and was commissioned to be painted just for George Peabody, philanthropist, by the Queen Herself, to thank him for helping the poor of London.

What did that portrait mean when we were taken to the library at an early age to watch the librarian open the huge wooden doors that hid the gift? Slowly, slowly, he would swing them open, and behold! the small figure of Madame Queen, tiny, elegant, in full regalia, symbol of power (who even had an Age named after her). How come a poor boy born in Peabody in 1795, who never went to school beyond the age of eleven, could rise to such heights and goodness and love? America was truly a beautiful land to be born in and George Peabody, banker, one of its famous sons; and he belonged to us, and his name, the name of our

town, would forever line the inside of our skulls as surely
as our own.

To this day, I'm sure, if the awful moment came and
I were being given a sanity test, after a dreadful brain injury
or in the grip of senility—to the question, "Where do you
live?" I would answer, 'Peabody," having lived most of my
adult life in New York City. Strange.

There was something very serious about the air of Peabody. Perhaps it was the example of Old George himself,
the industry and benign reasonability of his eighteenth-century rise. Add to that a sub stratum of Yankee pride. Mix both
with the hopes, generations later, of twentieth-century immigrants arriving in what was to become "one of the great
leather-processing districts of the world, with over thirty
tanneries."

There was about Peabody something else—the wildness
and passions of the early settlers. Peabody is known by that
name only since 1868, when the town fathers decided to
honor their favorite son. Before that, it was called South
Danvers. What a beauty spot it was then, with its large mill-
pond in the center of town, its springs and brooks and pasture land, gargantuan elms, gentle lanes and gardens. But
even before that and until 1756 it was known as Salem
Village, the center of witchcraft excitement.

The whalers and sailors and seventeenth-century tycoons
and empire builders lived in Salem. Peabody was where the
farmers of Salem lived. Everywhere were reminders of those
days of strictness and passion. We breathed it growing up.
The names of the early settlers were still around on street
signs, and it was hard to associate some of the modern nobil-
ity in town (bearing the same names) with the burning individualism of their ancestors who ran to Concord and
Lexington like crazy hippies, leaving their farms and families
to show the British what for. Still, the Fourth of July, when
I was growing up, was a very great celebration. Indepen-

dence was a word never taken lightly in Massachusetts. On the Fourth of July, you went up to Gallows Hill and saw the bonfire being lit to honor the word. After that, someone would always whisper, "This is where they killed the witches," and your eyes became filled with pictures of the poor ladies with their bonnets on, caught in that vice of Calvinism-madness, swinging in the wind just where the bonfire of barrels was going to topple in flame. And the band would play, and people would scream, and there were Yankee ghosts everywhere, not only women ghosts, but men ghosts, like John Proctor, who wouldn't admit his wife was a witch no matter what. Everywhere were remnants of those spooky days (are not all days spooky swinging as they do from reason to madness and back again?).

I love the suppressed passion in the real New England, its very orderliness belying the Furies underneath. The way the houses sit on the land, the care and love—to build in order to catch the setting sun in the parlors; the trees set about the houses to shade the times of day humans might want the cool; the stone walls proudly defining hard-won land, the paths and hidden gardens for privacy, the cleanliness of architectural lines; the simple strokes of Grecian revival in the wooden clapboard; the elegance of the more ambitious and vain red-brick Georgian homes; and the humor of a startling cupola, a window seat popping out of nowhere; bull's-eye glass set into one pane of a many-paned window. Form, content, thrift, grace. You see it everywhere in the architecture of New England. When I'm away from it, my eyes hunger for the images like a waif.

And just a mile or so away was Salem itself, after Boston the Puritan center of the North Shore, with its grander brick houses and chestnut trees. Deeper into town there were the houses with widows' walks for the wives of sailors to stand watch; the winding, tiny streets; the harbor where the ships came in filled to the gills with bounty from the East. In the tiny museums, the vases and silks and glories of China that found their way into the parlors of the well-to-do, blended into Yankee-English decor without a moment's hesitation. And the masks from the wild African coasts, and the scrimshaw on whalebone carved by sailors too long at sea, and the Oriental rugs and damasks. There, too, was the House of Seven Gables, with not only its own ghosts but now the ghost of Hawthorne, with its secret stairway and stories of Indians and the slaves running away to freedom via the underground railroad, and the gardens bending away from the Atlantic winds.

As my son would be taken to ride a ferris wheel on a bright afternoon, we were taken to the House of Seven Gables to be frightened and excited by its darkness and stories and longevity, to touch the pots ghosts ate from and tread the stairs they walked. Our hands would smooth the spreads that covered beds from which, still, came sighs and dreams of people long dead. Mama would make me count the gables and it taught me to count till seven. Mama would take me through the house as though she had lived in it as a little girl. She would stand at the window of an upstairs bedroom facing the harbor and look out over the water for many minutes. And I would stand, holding onto a bedpost, inhaling the damp, dusty smell of past Time, and wait for Mama to finish her silent conversation with someone.

The moist, pungent smell of the ocean and its great, barnacled rocks sloping into the Atlantic was all around us.

There was a funny separateness, snobbishness even, about the people born and bred along the North Shore of Massachusetts. You never went south, Heaven forbid, for a summer's jaunt to Provincetown or Martha's Vineyard or Nantucket. Oh, no. The rocky coast of the north was the only coast. Perhaps "down to Maine" to breathe the wild pines, or to New Hampshire, or "up to New York" for a touch of gaudy madness, but never to the southern shore.

If you wanted to bathe on sandy beaches away from the punishing Puritan pebbles and rocks of Marblehead, then you went north to Gloucester, Rockport, or Ipswich, where the last offered a bonus of tiny, delicious clams for lunch, either bought or dug for.

It wasn't till a few years ago, living in New York but still observing the strictures of my Massachusetts North Shore, that I set foot on Nantucket for the first time. I stood there in its cobblestoned, beautiful Main Street and laughed. It was Salem all over again, just floating in the Atlantic. The shingles, gray, trimmed white; the clapboard, white, trimmed black. Gray, white, black. (Salem's rules were not as strict.) In Nantucket you ask for permission to paint a color on a landmark street and the answer is no. Architectural neatness everywhere, except the heart that's filled with womens' thoughts on widows' walks. While waiting, did she plant peonies in those hidden gardens? Yes, they're there, behind the fence. And the roses, are they twisting, three years higher on the trellises I made before I left? Oh, Yankee ma'am, can ya hear me stompin' on the cobblestones? I'm in my sailor's pants, stained with sea and waiting. Light a candle fast behind my white-curtained window. Can't ya hear me comin' closer on the cobblestones? That's my chimney there, my door, my window-wife! Hell! The devil take the sea! Let her fog roll in. I'll not get lost in her tonight. I'm on my way toward home, my other "her." My hand is on the knob! Good evenin', ma'am. Let us not subdue . . . the overdue.

There it was again, the suppressed passion of New England, hiding behind its elegant search for order—a seesaw that's had me on its precarious tilt ever since I can remember.

When it wasn't the smell of the northeast wind from the Atlantic, it was the smell of leather that permeated Peabody. And leather was what brought Great-Uncle Harris to

Peabody at the turn of the century. This was Mama's side of the family. They were good, solid burghers, coming from a comfortable brick and tile-making family in Poland. The family name was Polivnick, makers of tile, and the story of aristocracy (again) goes: When Great-Grandfather Polivnick walked into the synagogue, everyone stood up!

"Why?" I asked.

"Why? Because they were an influential business family, that's why."

I laughed. "That wasn't good enough for Papa's mother. She complained that he'd married beneath him. There were no scholars or artists in the family. Just to be successful in business wasn't enough."

"Ho, ho," answered a seventy-year-old cousin on Mama's side.

Again, for the Polivnicks in Poland, as well as for Papa's family from the Ukraine, continuity and solidity for Jews was a fleeting thing. Depending on the whim of the Christian air around them, Jew-hunting (pogroms) would kill the dreams of acceptance. The rich became poor, and the poor fled. Great-Grandfather's three sons fled Poland. Harris and Sam emigrated to London. Jacob, the eldest, didn't join them. He chose to go to New York and eventually Boston. Jacob was Mama's father.

The Peabody story, however, started in London. Great-Uncle Harris apprenticed himself to a leather manufacturer in London, learned all there was to know about the art of processing leather, acquired a slightly English twist to his Polish-Jewish accent and arrived in Peabody with a letter of introduction to a factory owner. He was a skilled worker and was immediately hired as foreman of the factory in the new land. It was heyday time for the immigrant who had even the smallest special gift and expertise. It was hard for Harris, but things went well. Soon, he sent for his younger brother, Great-Uncle Sam, who in the meantime had had the benefit of education at Lord Rothschild's Free School in London and so arrived in America quite Anglicized. Unlike other immigrants pouring in, he spoke a clear English, which helped in a Yankee town, Irish-run in part and reeling from the thud of the Eastern European influx of cheap labor for its swelling factories.

Harris and Sam were snappy, dapper, proud, quick, humorous men. Harris was the gentler, perhaps the more soft-spoken. Sam was more roguish, perhaps the smarter. But it was Harris who became the tycoon of the family in Peabody. Soon he owned his own factory and became one of the first Jews in town to be "in leather." Sam went into the building business, as the family had been in Poland. The early days were halcyon, there was no doubt about that. The two of them made a good team, and they were close.

"Harris's success was because he was lucky," a cousin offered. But was that all?

"Of course not," another cousin countered. "It was because he was an able, gentle, honest man and no threat to the Irish and Yankee. He wasn't like the other foreigners. They could understand him."

They understood him so well he became the first Jew in town to be a director of a Yankee bank. By then he was commuting to Boston, where he had an office. On his return to Peabody each evening, he would be met by his liveried chauffeur.

One evening, the train was late, and his car was not waiting. So he walked home in the company of a fellow businessman, a Yankee, who offered him this confiding thought: "You know, Harris, you're not like the 'others.' You're different. You're a—white Jew."

Great-Uncle Harris didn't say a word. It didn't matter. By then, he was rich and still gentle, by leather-success insemination part Brahmin in the hinterland scheme of things. Both he and his Yankee friend knew that. Anyway, you scratch a goy and you'll find anti-Semitism an inch beneath the skin. Every Jew knows *that*, Great-Uncle Harris thought as he walked toward home, "the best new house in town."

They were an industrious lot, the Polivnick clan, rising to upper middle-class status, again, in a new land. Was not his younger brother Sam living in a large 125-year-old Yankee house, with a brood of children growing up, playing the games of the Gentile—tennis, golf, and skiing, and God knows what—long before it was ordinary for young Jews to be in country clubs and on mountain slopes?

"What kind of daughter are you bringing up your Dorothy to be?" said Harris's wife to Sam's wife one day. "In the summer she plays with small sticks, and in the winter she plays with big sticks!"

Had not his older sister, Sarah, arrived with her husband, Harry Leo Mincovitz, a large, imposing man wearing greatcoats trimmed with sable and lined with lynx and carrying a cane with a silver handle, who had made a small fortune running an underground railroad that extricated Jews from Poland and Russia to freedom in other lands? *Had not* Sarah arrived with a personal maid and trunks of belongings? *Had not* his older brother Jacob started a cement-block factory in New York—Jacob, the handsome, intelligent ("when Jacob spoke everyone listened") jolly tippler whose son Isidore would one day become a very rich Brooklyn builder of apartment houses? *Did not he,* Harris, and they all have first cousins who chose to emigrate to Argentina instead of America, becoming owners of a large textile mill, summer house, winter house, and gaucho-worked ranch? *Did not* he and his brother Sam help build the first synagogue in Peabody? *Was not* his wife, Sarah Malke, the president of the Ladies Auxiliary?

If the goy wanted to think of him as a "white Jew," let him. He, Harris, was successful on both sides. He was getting comfortable with goyish money, and was a leader among the Jews, at the same time. He had the best of all possible worlds.

Was it any wonder that one of Mama's favorite books was *Buddenbrooks*, Thomas Mann's family chronicle of the German bourgeoisie? She had conflicting feelings, for she loved her family yet had nothing but disdain for their success under capitalism. Their bourgeois status was a constant embarrassment.

Harris's wife, Sarah Malke, was a big spender. She lived in a house of many rooms and felt she and her husband deserved all they had dreamed about, after the hard days of the beginning, when Harris was a foreman in someone else's factory and she untiringly kept a boardinghouse for newer immigrants. A totally untutored woman but strangely blessed with good taste, her home was a beauty spot, her clothes fine, and her husband's Packard, chauffeur-driven, had lap robes and violets in its glass vase. Mama would wince when the Packard passed her on the street. All the same, she loved her uncles and they her, even though their favorite niece refused to play the bourgeois game of assimilation.

Between Mama and her family they had the entire Jewish Question all tied up and neatly solved. The family would assimilate by becoming "all-right-nicks." Mama would assimilate by attempting to change what existed by radicalizing what existed, even to eradicate what existed. Mama had a younger brother, Zachariah, who felt the same way. He also was a burning independent. But her older brother, Isidore, was to become the very rich builder in Brooklyn, New York. Her brother's wealth was another source of irritation to Mama, but, oh, how she adored him and he, her. Mama's way would exact a not insignificant toll, for she loved beautiful things.

The Yiddishkeit (Jewish way) of my Polivnick family, still observing the medieval religion and Orthodoxy that was the ancients', is as sweet to me as the nineteenth-century intellectual, rebellious Yiddishkeit of Mama and Papa and their modern friends. Both will forever line the inside of my brain as has the countryside of New England. The older I am the more tearful I become, hearing Hebrew on the one hand and Yiddish on the other, the two mother tongues of my ancestors. From their cadences, insisting, wailing, extolling, celebrant, I learned never to take no for an answer. I learned to be too touchy, too sensitive, too listening, too doom-shaped, too independent, isolated, introverted, too euphoric. Withal, I learned to survive, rail, go quiet, rail again, survive.

In the spring, Passover (the celebration of Jewish deliverance from slavery in Egypt) was one of the high points of the year, even for my own nonbelieving family. Uncle Harris gave the first-night seder (family feast) and Uncle Sam the second-night seder. At Uncle Harris's, all was crystal and formal and full of dishes with tiny rosebuds on them. The second night at Sam's was jolly and free because Sam was that way, and so was his wife, Jennie, a casual woman with four rambunctious children close in age to Elizabeth and me. I was the youngest for many years. Mama would relax, and we were allowed to drink wine and eat candy. All together, there would be more than twenty people at table.

For those two nights of celebration, Mama and Papa would throw off their atheism and become like the rest of the family—observants. A lot of Jews together in a room for the serious observance of Joy was loud and resonant and their prayers mesmerizing in their certainty. Even Papa sang the prayers of his childhood in a strident voice, marveling each year that he remembered them. Mama would explain to me the symbolic food that was laid out and partaken of, and one year I knew them by myself, finally and forever; the bitter herbs for the bitterness of slavery; *charoses* (a mixture

172

of nuts, apples, and wine) for the mortar the Jews used to build for the Pharaohs; *karpas* (celery, parsley, etc.) for the terrible toil of the Jews in Egypt; saltwater for the tears; a roasted shankbone and a roasted egg, reminders of ancient Passover sacrifices in the Temple; the empty goblet in the center of the table for the Prophet Elijah, in case he decided to drop in; the unleavened bread (matzo) to remind us of the haste in which the Jews fled to the desert with bread not fully baked. It was a magic table at which you rocked and let yourself go with the abandonment of a clan belonging. You nibbled, chin-high to the table, on tradition, like a glutton. Even the bitter herbs were sweet and exciting. The matzo balls, lolling in yellow waves of chicken soup, were mountains of sensuality; the roast chicken, laminations of protean kinship; the *tzsmis* (carrot pudding) confounding as a court jester's gambol ("Oh, the *tzsmis* is even better than last year. What's in it?") And the wine! The wine was holy, ruby sweetness of life itself. Even Mama, stranger within their midst, would bend and whisper what all things meant and shared the Time with me:

"They [the elders, her uncles] will drink four times. The first drink God is saying, 'I shall bring them forth'; the second drink, 'I shall deliver them forth'; the third, 'I shall redeem them'; the fourth, 'I shall take them to me as a nation.' "

It was so heady, Mama's saying the word *God* so seriously, the uncles' "God," the Almighty. It seemed that even she consented to be a member of that delicious society of worshipers.

Then she would go on with a different face, the one I knew when she was at home with her friends:

"Seders mean . . . [she would pause, take a deep breath] are . . . a symbol of humanity's first festival—"

"First?"

"Yes, first festival . . . of freedom. It reminds us that we can all rise—"

(Now the whole table would be listening.)

"—to a level where it is understood that all men are created equal, and no one has the right to make slaves of anyone else."

She approved! It was all right to be happy and feel "belonging" in the bosom of worshiping kin, even though we were not "believers." Yes, it would seem so on the first and second nights of a holiday *we* had, and my friend, with her "Him," didn't have. It almost made up for the lack of Christmas, and Easter, when "Him" got off the cross he was on, in her church, and "rose" high into the sky. If "He" *did* do that, he would most certainly have to bump into our "Almighty," who was the God of Everything, and "Him" was only the son of Everything, and there could only be *one* God of Everything, so what was all the fuss about? Why was everyone in Peabody separate and funny, unfriendly, the "others," the Polish Gaiski(s), the Irish Cavanaugh(s), the Greek Papacostas(s).

Why did my cousin Dorothy whisper to me: "Every time a Jew sees a cross he has to spit nine times, so when you walk by the Greek church with the three gold domes, you have to spit twenty-seven times, 'cause there's a cross on each dome. And three times nine is twenty-seven."

"Twenty-seven times in a row?"

"That's the trick, and if you're a good Jew, you'd better!"

I tried it in the back yard and only got to seven. I wasn't even a good Jew for one cross, so I'd better not walk on the street where the Greek church was. It was hard enough being a good "me," without trying to be a good Jew-me, too. What my cousin Dorothy neglected to tell me was that she and her friends couldn't do it either, and avoided that street like the plague.

(If one *could* spit even nine times, certainly it would be a reminder of the parched mouths of the Jews in the desert, fleeing Egypt, in the dawn of a very important morning and for forty years thereafter.)

Passover at the Great-Uncles' was a lovely Time of "Family, Kin, Clan, Tribe, Nation." It was all so bright and shining. I always felt like Cinderella, leaving it to return to the Spartan house Mama ran, her subdued cooking without the benefit of gloriously vulgar chicken fat, her delicate desserts, whips and mousses, a far cry from the head-on kosher culinary statements of the Great-Aunts, opulent and overweaning. I loved the richness, sexiness of their Hebraic ways. I loved those ritual nights of belonging, an all too rare emotion.

Secondary Theme
of Pigeon Fugue

Bozo's Dilemma

THE Smiths were finally acknowledging the death of Ariel. It was starting to snow again. White chords of resolution were falling through the air of our corridor. Pa Smith sat *behind* the nursery pot, Ma, away on the parent ledge. It looked lonely and unnatural without a child.

I'm in mourning. I'm not looking out. I'm not interested. I'm being faithful to the memory of Ariel, and I'm sick to death of pigeons.

My husband tells me there's adventure in the Khrushchev family pot.

"The little one—what do you call him, Bozo?—was testing his wings this morning with great hue and cry, flapping about, exercising."

I don't care. I will not look out, but I'm surreptitiously developing pictures of the Khrushchev ledge in my head, setting them aside to dry. Something about that family reminds me of the Polivnicks. Something about stolid, well-fed burghers. . . .

By 3 P.M., my curiosity gets the better of me. If I *should* turn my attention to the Khrushchevs, it would be like getting back on the horse after being thrown off.

My resolve not to "watch" the enemy family is dissolving as fast as the snow hitting my steaming window. Time had certainly passed. Bozo is big enough to be left alone. The parents are nowhere to be seen. (I get my notebook, out of habit.) Damned if the little tyke doesn't pick that moment to jump out of his pot for the first time. He marches drunkenly about his ledge. I feel my mouth smiling. The neighbor's window is open a smidgeon behind him. Bozo notices that too. The smidgeon space is just big enough for a small, fat pigeon. He sidles *inside* to their windowsill and disappears. Oh, no. I can't see him anymore. He must have fallen to the floor. Silence.

Ma Khrushchev returns, looks for her offspring where she had left him, in the pot, and in a state of shock, flies about madly. Bozo, sensing her presence, sets up a howl, a veritable pigeon uproar. She talks to him, but doesn't know where he is. He's inside, and she's outside. I begin to laugh, and remember that I'm in mourning.

Inside, outside; alien, familiar; belonging, not belonging. The symbiotic fire machine is rolling again. I'm at the wheel, the ears of my Dalmatian are flapping in the wind, and we're hell-bent to save! Now what? Are the neighbors home, or is Bozo wandering about their living room like a drunken sailor? I hear him calling his parents. This is ridiculous. The neighbors are obviously not at home. Ma Khrushchev sits herself in Bozo's pot, waiting for him to return to where he's supposed to be. She doesn't know Bozo is warm and dry, marching around on an Oriental rug—with another snowstorm in progress. That's a plus of sorts, Ma.

I look over at the Smith ledge. Ma and Pa Smith are hunched up behind the catafalque that holds Ariel. I feed them, they eat, and go back to continue their death vigil, or wake, or whatever it is they're not doing that the zoo lady said they would (throw the dead overboard).

The neighbors, definitely, are not at home. They've had no idea what's going on in the pots on their ledges, or haven't indicated as much. We have to think about how to get that silly baby back to its nest. Would the neighbors know where he belonged? When are they returning home? What if they left for an extended vacation? Their lights were often off for days on end. What should I do? I can't jump across the ten-foot corridor! I could go to the neighboring house, ring every doorbell on the fourth floor till I find the right apartment that faces us. But, if the people aren't home, what good would that do? Would the police break down the door for me if I called them for help? No, they wouldn't do that. They'd put me away, that's what they'd do.

"All right," my husband offered with a big tongue in his cheek. "I'll call a scaffolding company, and they'll build you a platform to walk across. You'll climb inside and save the little bugger. [Pause.] It'll take a couple of days to build, though."

"Oh, you're a big help. For Christ's sake, this is a crisis. The kid's lost."

"You'll just have to wait till those people get home. When they do, they'll find tiny pigeon shit all over their rugs. They'll figure it out, don't worry. It'll all work out."

"Oh, my God!"

"Now what?"

"I just remembered something. I think they've got a dog."

"Well, we'll just have to hope the dog has a sense of humor, won't we."

Bozo's Pa returned, sized up the situation, but there was nothing to be done, so, he too, sat, close to his mate in their pot. The snow was coming down harder. It gathered on their backs, and they waited, creatures of Time, listening, waiting. A chirp came, now and then, from inside the apartment. Bozo must be having the time of his life. He hasn't done all that walking since he was born. Another pigeon soap opera, living itself out dumbly.

The inability of the Khrushchevs to take an action in their own behalf upsets me.

Bozo's walk has made me feel dumb in the face of Fate. The Khrushchevs' very stillness told me to mind my own species. They weren't made with hands to open windows, feet to climb with. They had to wait. Of course I, of another species, could act, carry concern to the end of its line. They had to wait. *C'est la* bird *vie.* I would wait too, let it play itself out. No, I can't do anything, or I'll end up on the evening news as the end piece, a human-kook-interest story: "Woman breaks into neighbor's house to retrieve lost pigeon."

My eyes panned the entire corridor, now white and chilling. It looked like a disaster area. There were the two formerly busy pots. One had a dead baby in it (Ariel) and the other was a vacant crib with its silly occupant gone for a premature walk. Who says that isn't news!

We had our cocktail hour, our dinner, and the neighbors' house was dark all evening. How dare they be away from home so long! What were the bums doing! There were no more chirps from the inside.

At midnight I looked out. The neighbors' lights were on, and silhouetted against their window was little Bozo back in his pot, with a parent on either side of him. I let out a "Ha" of delight. My husband joined me, and we stood there roaring, imagining what the neighbors had encountered when they returned home: the dog asleep in a corner and Bozo in the middle of their living room floor, feathers and pigeon droppings everywhere. How on earth did Bozo thwart the jaws!

Tomorrow, I'll open my window, call across the corridor,

introduce myself, and share life on their ledges with them. No, I don't think I will. They saw us standing there laughing and pulled their blinds down. They wouldn't understand. It turned out I was right, but that was much later.

The next morning, the ledge holding the Smith pot was swept clean. The Smith nursery was no more. The neighbors had taken care of Ariel's burial. Ma and Pa Smith's vigil was over. They sat on their parent ledge, not knowing what to do.

"Dot, dot, dash . . . the Smith family had their pots taken away from them." Dot, dot, dash . . . it went through the pigeon population. By noon, all the birds in the neighborhood were flying by to observe the loss of Smith territory. But by late afternoon the Smiths were sitting on the nude ledge, Pa Smith chasing everyone away with a "even though the pots are gone, the turf is still ours."

I felt akin to the birds and alien to the neighbors. For weeks after, they kept their blinds down and I'm sure were blaming me for the life and death on their ledges. I was an aider and abettor of dirty pigeons, a pigeon feeder. They left the Khrushchev ledge intact. Evidently they were going to let Bozo grow up, so I couldn't be too put out with them for the razing of the Smith land that I'd fought for and helped "green."

Little did they suspect that it was going to take a very long time for Bozo to grow up.

🍁

We were almost at the end of February, and the coldest weather yet had moved in from western Canada. It was zero for days on end. Bozo was having a rough time. He seemed traumatized. The day he squeezed into the neighbors' apartment and spent many unusual hours inside must have done something to deter him.

"If that's what happens when I become investigative, then I'll just sit in my pot till kingdom come."

And just sit in his pot was exactly what he was doing. He was almost as large as his parents. Nothing was happening. It was becoming strange. I began comparing Plucky and Brownie's maturation with his, how they got the idea or were directed into the idea of flying. Brownie was a little hero in comparison, as afraid as he was. With all his hardship, he did get the idea of taking off. As of this moment, Bozo looks as if he'll be the pigeon who wouldn't fly.

I put out food like mad for Bozo's parents. It would be heartless not to. They have a real problem in their nest, Bozo not being able to fly off and find food on his own, and needing more and more of it. The lady at the zoo said pigeons starve themselves in order to give food to their young. But Bozo's not so young anymore. A bird who is big enough to fly and doesn't is a dilemma. Bozo's parents have done everything to try and show him. They feed him quickly and fly off. They come back and feed him slowly. Nothing. He doesn't exercise his wings in anticipation of feeding. He just settles down in his pot with a full stomach, a huge child, unable to take off.

I know several teen-agers like that, but they usually get some "help." What do you do with a pigeon who needs "help"? I didn't dare call the zoo again. First I ask her for nutritional advice, then medical expertise. Now I want a psychoanalytic referral.

I remember a story from my childhood about a little English boy, Limby Lumpy, who was so spoiled, so overfed —whose parents gave him anything he wanted—that he became more demanding and naughty till one Sunday, when they were having a leg of mutton for dinner, he demanded to ride the sheep on the dining room table! His ill-advised parents, giving in to his every whim, picked him up to place him in an astride position over the leg of mutton as the servants watched in horror. He wriggled and fussed and fell into the gravy. That did it! His Sunday clothes were soaked with hot juices. Father said, "Enough is enough." He was put to bed without supper, hungry. Bozo reminds me of that little boy. Trauma plus parental guilt plus overindulgence makes for disturbance.

If I talked to the zoo lady about all of that, she'd fall off her chair.

Dare I assume a similarity in human and bird behavior, given like circumstances? Well, I saw it. More than that, I perceived it.

Dare I wonder if his parents will abandon this creature? I find myself wanting to disengage, as we do when we see something unnatural taking place in front of our eyes. It's difficult to identify with accident. We must turn our backs . . . or laugh. Or . . .

I had this crazy feeling that if I kept on looking at Bozo, there might be a magic healing. I must *will* him to fly. I allowed myself to move into foreign, metaphysical space. If I watch over him, someone will watch over me when the Time comes. A strange peace took me over, just the way it had in the hospital room when, on the advice of my fanatical friend, I counted and talked to my own cells. But being new at the game of transcendence, I didn't throw calm emanations across the corridor to Bozo. I opened the window and yelled, "Fly, damn you! I've got other things to do than watch you and your dumb, traumatized pigeon head!" That ended the séance. I'd never pass the witch's exams. I'm not a healer. I had an uneasy feeling someone was observing me and laughing.

Water was building up, pressing against my pigeon-watching cornea, threatening to break through the viscous dams. Not one drop at a time, but a bursting, longing angst for normalcy, now, then, way back then. I take a deep breath and aerate the angst. Oxygen quenches unease as

182

water does fire. Bozo, fly, damn you. Down goes the window on my impotence.

❧

There was something about Bozo that brought to mind a little girl who wasn't very good "at figures," and so acquired a tutor in order to be perfect.

Mrs. Gilman, my tutor, was Mama's best friend in Peabody. She was a Yankee from Marblehead, a descendant of Roger Conant, a spinster till forty, when she married a man fourteen years younger than herself. Her husband, Sam, was one of my best friends and my champion, even though I wasn't very good "at figures."

When Mrs. Gilman was somewhere in her midforties, she and Sam had a child, whom they called "Little Alice." Mrs. Gilman was "Big Alice." Little Alice was a porcelain-skinned, delicate girl with long, blond hair, a perfect resurrection of Lewis Carroll's love, always dressed in pinafores and Mary Janes. We become very good friends. As I was a constant visitor in the schoolroom run by Big Alice, Little Alice was also constantly "at home," since she didn't go to regular school. Her mother disapproved of the quality of public education, and Alice was taught by her mother until she was twelve. Thereupon, she was sent to a Catholic seminary, where her skin got whiter and her bones looked as though they really would break. Once she went to that terrible place with nuns and priests and had to wear a uniform, she became a stranger. She had become Alice in Prison. In the early tender days of almost-freedom, she truly was Alice in Wonderland, and her presence—in the heaviness of my dumb-trying-to-be-smarter days in her mother's schoolroom— lightened the agony of numbers.

Sam, Mr. Gilman, didn't work very much. He was afflicted by a very punitive arthritis, stayed home, tended the gardens, and fathered Alice, while her mother taught and tutored everyone, from little girls who couldn't subtract to college students having trouble with calculus and Greek. Mrs. Gilman was a tall, imposing lady who wore her glasses on a ribbon, spoke impeccable King's English with a strange, little-girl voice, and would, on occasion, during the day, emit a high, shrill shriek that would break the air and disappear like a shout of pain or a "hurray." I didn't know then that the shrieks were nervous spasms and a manifestation of hysteria. It just seemed to me that Mrs. Gilman had hiccoughs more often than most people. There were many things that I found disconcerting. Big Alice was an atrocious housekeeper and made no pretense about it. A Greek and Latin scholar busy uplifting young minds didn't have time for the nonsense of keeping house. There was a wacky feeling of disorder, except in the schoolroom at the back of the house. Her attempts at cooking were equally atrocious and, worst of all—there was crude plumbing. The Gilmans had an indoor outhouse, whose seat was too big for me, so I always had to be held over the hole, which act invaded my privacy immensely. I can't remember exactly how the waste was flushed into the ground. I think there was some kind of attachment to a well, making a whoosh that shook the foundations. I connected these discomforts with my difficulty in figuring 15 take away 12. They were commensurate problems and complemented each other.

Big Alice and Mama were thick as thieves. They were the two women suffragettes in town, emancipated women who found each other and formed a life friendship on the basis of being outsiders, "above" the others. They went to concerts, read books together, exchanged avant-garde magazines, spent hours in the museums of Boston, and partook of the "finer things," the unpopular causes. They also shared the heartache of Doris, who was rebellious and not very good "at figures." So Big Alice took me on, to help make me a perfect person, teach me work habits and how to become a tamer, more trainable animal.

"You see, it's not because Doris is dumb. Oh, no, Mary, it's simply that she's intractable. She doesn't apply herself. She dreams," said Mrs. Gilman.

I wondered what all the fuss was about. And so did Sam. When my lessons were over in the schoolroom, he would extricate me and along with Alice, who would read quietly, the three of us sat under their big tree on an emerald green lawn. Unlike his wife, who exacted Time, he gave me quiet, indolent, noncrucial Time.

"Now let's make believe Doris is an Indian princess, because she looks like one, doesn't she?" he would say to Alice. Long hours of quiet would go by while we sat, stringing miles and miles of beads, enough "to cover the entire chest of the chieftain's daughter" with necklaces. Slowly, my frown and wondering about dumbness would disappear. Slowly, I would become myself, having to do no one proud, having to reflect nothing but my own Being. Sometimes Alice and I would leave Sam playing with the Gilman Boston terriers under the tree, in between snoozes. We'd go into a dark part of the house upstairs, where Sam had built her a two-storied, five-foot-high dollhouse. The two of us would shut out all imposition and demand and play in the heavy green light of shades drawn against the Outside.

("It was a wonderful childhood in many ways," Little Alice said with some amusement and irony many years later, "even if we were under pressure to excel, to make those itchy people proud of us. And with my being so delicate and your being so dumb and your sister, Elizabeth, being so smart and the two of us never able to keep up with her. . . . Still, it was a wonderfully idyllic childhood, don't you think?")

Maybe she was right. After all, how many little girls had a five-foot-high dollhouse to dream with, their very own classroom, a teacher and mother who made funny, startling sounds, and a Sam Gilman who whiled away pleasant hours with them on an emerald green lawn?

🍁

WhiteTail is back. The Prince of Evil never succeeded in taking over the Smith ledge. This ledge will be a snap to conquer with a pigeon, big enough to fly, who does nothing but sit in a pot all day long and parents seldom about.

Bozo has progressed to walking about his ledge. I spend my afternoon throwing walnuts at WhiteTail, who's getting outrageously arrogant. He hops right into Bozo's pot, while the monster baby presses his nose into a corner and cries. "If I turn my back, I won't know he's there," Bozo reasons.

I don't care what the neighbors think anymore. I throw walnuts with abandon. The parents return, chase away the gangster with dispatch. He runs like a rat. This character WhiteTail mystifies me. He's spent the whole winter wanting someone else's place.

Today, my dear Plucky came home! I'd recognized him anywhere. He looks small and scruffy, half the size of Bozo. Getting out into the world for him must be a "tough dollar."

My eyes are crossing with busyness. It's an extremely cold afternoon. The sunlight on the ledges is mercury-silver on white frost. I put out food for Plucky. He tries to eat, but Mr. Khrushchev suddenly appears and chases him away. Plucky sits huddled on the abandoned ledge of his babyhood. If his own parents had been there, they, too, would have chased him away. When you leave, Buddy, you leave.

The next morning, he flew off and never came back.

I continue to put out food for the Smiths *and* the Khrushchevs, my Russia and China. They need separate feeding ledges. Forces, immovable, they will not share. God, what a busy winter.

The next five days were nothing but war, WhiteTail on

one side, Pa Khrushchev and I on the other. The language barrier made it difficult to set up an effective strategy room, but we did the best we could.

The villain keeps hopping into Bozo's pot and pecking him. I throw walnuts. Pa arrives and pecks the enemy away. Bozo spends his time crying and tucking his body into a corner of the ledge. The bang of my walnuts is scaring Bozo out of his wits, but it was either that, or kaboom. The parents are staying away most of the day and coming home only at night. I'm in charge. They feed the "baby" and fly right out.

If Bozo doesn't fly by the end of the week, I'll have to call the ASPCA. He just can't sit there getting bigger and bigger, prey, victim, a burden to his distraught parents and me.

By the end of the week, Bozo was becoming more alert, trying, trying. His father is performing every trick he knows to get the bird to follow him. Flap, flap, teeter, teeter. No soap. Follow me, try. No? Damn. That went on all afternoon of the sixth day. In the evening of that day, the parents didn't spend the night in the corridor. Bozo was all alone.

We were sure he would be abandoned the next day.

The seventh day, I left the house for a few hours, came back, looked out the window. Mayhem, the overthrow of the universe. No Bozo anywhere. And his father was fighting WhiteTail. They were having a vicious mix.

As in the past, when something big was happening, a pigeon crowd gathered observing oddity, accident. Pa Khrushchev chases WhiteTail off his ledge and out of the corridor. I make an old obscene Italian sign as the villain scoots, and at that very moment, my female neighbor chooses to look out her window. By now, she'd never testify to my sanity, so what the hell.

A moment later, my husband arrives home expecting a gourmet dinner, but instead finds the cook hanging out a window, hair streaming in the cold wind and eyes wild. He joins me, and leaning farther out than I can, says, "There *is* a bird down there, on a narrow strip of cement without snow on it."

"Does it look like Bozo?"

"Yes, it looks like Bozo."

"Hurry, please, get down there and see if he's all right."

The sweet man, indulgent with my bird madness, took himself off, armed with bread, down the elevator, into the basement, out into the side alley to see if Bozo was alive or dead. I lean way out the window to watch, and yell, "Is it?"

"Yes," he yells up. "It's Bozo all right." The bird begins to sidle away from him. "He seems to be able to walk."

"Then he can't be seriously hurt," I answer.

My husband moves closer to the bird.

"Try to get him into a protected area," I yell down again. (What in hell were we going to do with him?)

Bozo, scared, each time my husband got close, *flew* a few feet in the air to get away. My husband walked to him again. Bozo *flew* a few more feet.

"He's flying but not very well," he screams up to me.

My husband bends and tries to pick Bozo up. The bird *took off*, a few feet in the air again, but this time continued to fly out of the corridor, just high enough to avoid a back fence—and away. Jules had made him fly!

Bozo never came back.

His parents kept hanging around, but no return of the prodigal. Something was very wrong. He was still being fed by the regurgitation method. Did he *not* come home because he couldn't fly four flights up, back to the nest? Were his parents able to find him? The little clown either decided to grow up all at once, or he came to a bad end.

The next day, the neighbors cleared the Bozo ledge of pot and excrement that must have driven them crazy. The nest was gone. Mr. and Mrs. Khrushchev still hung around, looking, noticing the change, but it was the end of an era. The Time of Plucky, Brownie, Ariel, Bozo, *et al.*, was over.

Not the Smiths, though! Heracles and Sarah were back on their denuded ledge in spite of all. Ma had her head nestled against Pa's body. They were clucking and cooing, housekeeping again, in a furnitureless apartment. Indomitable monoganimity.

If they mate again, I'll move!

Dear March, Come in!
How glad I am!

I'm glad it's over, February. Bozo was "caught" in a dumbness that made me feel I was writhing on a bed with a gargantuan Scoutmaster twelve feet tall peeking in the window—a presence observing, superegoish, knowing the outcome, not offering a word, just knowing.

Energy, It (God), is too swift, laconic, has "No comment." "It" says nothing. How dreadful to "see" and say nothing. How awful to be a twelve-foot, obese Scoutmaster in that dreadful hat; to look through everyone's window, climb down everyone's chimney, receive everyone's prayers —and say NOTHING.

I must not mince words. I am as frightened of my cancer as I was that Bozo wouldn't fly. The claustrophobia of being caught. That was it. Events over which I had no control. Having a dreadful disease is walking into the mysterious climes of Fate. My joyful journal of the birds is really a notebook about Death. I'm still, three years after the operation, traumatized. I react to stimulus like a starfish on a busy beach. Shadows cause me to turn sharply. The most innocuous event creates impact, and my senses implode to the center of myself. I would curl up rather than risk the weight of one unsuspecting foot. The fear of the tread alone makes me try to disappear into myself. The impotence of my position, waiting. Another part of me wants to explode, lacy, fanlike, around all I love.

My surgeon said: "You are now as healthy as any woman walking the street." (What an unfortunate use of the colloquial—turn a trick, now?) He continued: "You're in the same percentage group as any other normal person— who might acquire cancer cells."

I doubted it. Part of me wanted to make love to the world (while I could). The other part was a starfish after a storm on a low-tide beach. My hair was limp. My skin, shocked. The nipple on my right breast, numb. My lean stomach was collecting fat. I was in hormonal embarrassment. Lingerie ads in the Sunday *Times* grieved me and then filled me with anger. I wanted to shout, "No nude pictures of women in this house!" I felt caught in Mama's memory. Was I not, too, now dressing "in a closet" as she did?

I was walking proof of the Lamarckian theory of inherited, acquired characteristics. I was enslaved to a genetic and psychical program over which I had no control. The stifling brought on respiratory distress, asthmatic episodes of loss, gasping, not for air, but light. I was in love with nothing and no one. I wondered how long there was movement in the cells of a corpse. When did it stop for good? I swore no moon would find my nakedness. I stopped writing of any kind, music or words. I wondered if Bozo died in a strange alley.

I was glad February was over. It was a very depressing month.

> How out of breath you are!
> Dear March, how are you?

Gimleting

PAPA was the first Jewish doctor in town. The sentence makes me sad. It was the beginning of fifty years of "service." A news picture of his receiving a plaque at the end of his life for that service makes me even sadder. He stood for the photographer, in the company of hospital officials and another crony of his, an Armenian doctor, also being honored and booted out. They had been pals most of their lives, both considered out of the ordinary, and bonded in a kind of friendship because of their unusualness. But Dr. Manoogian, poet, philosopher in a small town, had it easier. He was Christian. Papa was a radical *and* a Jew. They seldom saw one another at the end of their days. There was nothing more to fight about, to band together about. They were out to pasture. Dr. Manoogian was a gentler man. The poetry writing that lifted him cuts above the town "others" Papa called "dotty" in their old age.

"He's a nice man, but he's a fool."

There they stood, two old men, posing for the news photographer, a hundred years of living and medical expertise between them. Papa had his shy, slightly embarrassed smile that he used as a shield when out in the world

190

of Gentiles. Behind the smile was cynicism. Behind the cynicism was tears. Behind all three was a vulnerability that could break me in two even now, years later. Papa's acculturation into the land of New England goyim was a hard fight, which he judged he had lost. Perhaps it all would have been different if Mama had not died so soon. If he had had his ally beside him, perhaps the denouement would have been easier.

"I was a failure."

"No, no, don't say that. I refuse to let you say that," I insisted.

Some old, professional men retire gracefully. They feel they've earned the grace. They putter about their hobbies and gardens and friends. A new love, made of dependency on an old mate, shores up the crumbling building. Papa had no hobbies. His life had been politics and medicine. The battle was over. Mama's strong influence was no longer there. The hospital didn't want a seventy-two-year-old doctor in the operating room. They kicked him out of his club with a testimonial. He woke early and had no place to go. His habit was to breakfast at the hospital at 6:30 A.M. He began to sleep late and stay up till dawn, drinking Manhattans and reading Russian novels and, still, medicine. He had outlived most of his enemies. The people who gave him the plaque were strangers. Society didn't need him anymore. Most of it was in the cemetery, going north, out of town. A new generation had taken over. The feisty history of their burgeoning city in the early days of the twentieth century meant very little. They were part of the now, modern Peabody that had become a "bedroom community" of Boston. Distance was different. Throughways ringed the place, shopping centers, the old church in the square torn down to make way for a huge gas station and car wash. The Boston and Maine Railroad didn't make passenger stops anymore. There was a do-nut emporium in place of the station. A pizza parlor infiltrated right into the street where Papa's house sat. No one knew him when he made an afternoon appearance in town for a Coke or coffee (a beloved ritual). I learned sadness from a master. He went out raging, roaring mad.

I'm finding it hard to put one word in front of another. Each letter is made of lead. I'm trying to burrow into a love affair with life that crashed into smithereens long before it was supposed to, a love affair that brought me here, built the sub-basement of the house that is "me." I'm trying to breathe the air, walk down streets, sit in rooms I'd never been, rooms before my Time——Time inherited. I'm trying to remember people who wanted only great things to happen, who tried, died, and in their view, never gave themselves their due or evaluated their contributions kindly. Irritable, anxious, excitable, innovative, creative people.

Withal, the early days were full of sun and promise. The *withal* meaning—in spite of being a Jew in a Yankee town, Jew and Gentile were young alike, together in the growth of the town, sharing destinous things, alike. There were great leaps to be made in the early years of the twentieth century, not the least being the leaving of the nineteenth. And the most: preparing oneself for Lenin, Marx, Freud, Henry Ford, electricity, coal to oil, Stravinsky, Picasso, Einstein; the emancipation of the Diaspora Jew, the Jew as citizen, the Jew as voter, the Jew taking a giant step from medieval tribalism and *shtetl* life into the modern Gentile world for the first time. Papa and Mama, young intellectuals from Russia and Poland, were "doing it" in Massachusetts.

What a typical town Peabody was: a large Greek-columned, clapboard South Congregational Church in the square; two-story red-brick and white-stone buildings with signs—"Counselor-at-Law," "Five and Ten," "Dry Goods"; trees nuzzling the sky; a fifty-foot Civil War Soldiers and Sailors Monument dominating the crossroads of the square, with lettering to remind the citizens of all the right things:

"The town to her sons who died in the great rebellion, that the Union might be preserved, and liberty secured for all. *E pluribus unum.*"

Diagonally across from the monument was George Curtis's drugstore. He was *the* apothecary, and Papa and George made special friends. They circled each other like equal alphas, although both knew Papa would never truly be an equal alpha in the eyes of a Yankee. But in the silent battle Curtis was on Papa's side, and a fine ally, president of the savings bank, trustee of the hospital. He seemed willing to forgive Papa for his Jewishness and respected him for his doctoring and intellect and "love of finer things." The "love of finer things" separated the bigots from the almost acceptors.

In the early days, George Curtis filled Papa's prescriptions with care and respect. Later it was with love. Curtis was an early widower. After Mama died, the two would get drunk together every few months in the privacy of Curtis's home around the corner on Elm Street. It was just a short walk down a dark, elm-lined street at midnight for Papa. No one ever knew. He would arrive home with a "Jesus Christ! I almost fell down the back stairs!"

Every day at three in the afternoon, they drank lemon phosphates together. As the afternoon sun fell on the large glass bottles in the window of Curtis Drugs, the shoestore owner arrived, the mayor, one or two counselors-at-law, the judge, the fire chief or the police chief. The leaders met, casually, at Curtis's soda fountain, talked politics, the growing town, this one and that one; fellow Gentile doctors joined them. Papa's wit, acumen and exotic (to them) controlled Jewish intelligence won them over, temporarily, at three in the afternoon. They were loath to admit, but he had cleaved out his place at the fountain, accent and all. Peabody was home. Freud could not have found a better, more fertile ground in which to grow a masochist hero. "They" had to be

won over anew every day. Inherent in being the Jew in an
alien society were the elements of heroism—the one who felt
more, thought more, complained more, wanted change and
redemption, absolution—more. The right-to-be-more. Professional goyim listened, in spite of themselves. They knew
Papa was dangerous, but no fool.

What brought Papa to Peabody?

"Come, Yidel," Papa's fellow medical students would
say. "We'll buy you dinner if you help us study." They liked
him, suspected he was hungry. It was their way of helping
the Yidel and helping themselves. Those who went on to
specialize, after internship, became the fine doctors of the
East. That's what Papa wanted to do. Specialize. In those
days, that decision was an unusual one, and it was quite
a coup to get into graduate school if you were called "Yidel."
Papa must have been a brilliant young intern. He was offered
a scholarship to further his studies at Harvard. His dreams
of being "important and valuable" were coming true. It
looked as though the dreadful and funny days of college and
medical school were behind him—the days he and a fellow
student decided to open a laundry for the ghetto Jews of
the West End of Boston. They collected laundry from the
housewives, talking them into a service they had never had
in their lives, rented a storefront, filled it with bags of dirty
laundry; then they looked at each other, not knowing the
first thing about how to run a laundry business . . . and ran,
leaving the storefront and the bags. The women who came
to collect their clothes had to spend weeks finding what
belonged to them and swore if those two young men ever
showed their faces in the West End, they'd kill them. Then
Papa and his friend decided, well, we'd better stick to our
studies, but we need one good meal a week. So they pored
over the wedding announcements in the Jewish newspapers
and would show up at the celebrations of strangers, sit down

for a sumptuous meal, making believe they were distant cousins of the groom. Sometimes it was difficult to kiss the bride, but it was worth it for the chicken. They ate and ran.

At the end of his internship, something very important happened. Papa met a strangely attractive dark, blue-eyed young woman named Mary. She was a nurse. They fell in love. He was blond and wild. She was dark and quietly wild. Modesty? Sensitivity? Intellect? And from a fine Jewish Polish family? Hair, when loose, that fell to her waist? Blue eyes in which a man could drown? A sensuous mouth capable of driving a man mad with its edicts, illusions? Papa wanted it all! Someone had already committed suicide over the love of her, a young fellow revolutionary who had followed her to America to marry her. He blew his brains out in a blueberry patch behind her house in Arlington Heights, Massachusetts, where she lived with her father, Jacob, who'd first settled in New York, the stone contractor, elder brother of Harris and Sam; her mother, Laya; and her brother Zachariah. Mary wouldn't marry the unfortunate revolutionary. She was in love with Harry (Papa).

What kinky days!

They had so much in common. They devoured books and ideas, clove to each other, not from lust, oh no. Vaginas and penises were descendant. The mind was ascendant for those young revolutionary puritans. Hand in hand, they wandered through the streets of Boston on their days off, in the early nineteen hundreds, and they *knew* the streets were there for them, radicals, burning to acculturate in the free air of America. They sucked in what New England civility could offer like catfish. Culture-hungry emigrees, anything was possible in libertarian New England. Even marriage. But first Mary would finish her nursing studies and Harry would go to graduate school.

"Oh, Harry," she reasoned, wheedled. "Let's move to Peabody. Forget graduate school. There's a medical practice there waiting for someone. Let's make it *us*. My Uncles Harris and Sam have seen to it. We'll have our own house, a garden, and you'll be the first Jewish doctor."

If I had been around when the decision was made to move to Peabody, I would have said, "No!" Papa's temperament was ill-suited for a general practitioner. He was a clinician, an investigator. He was a shy and angry man, overqualified for small-town living.

"I was a city person. Why did I do it?"

It was a mistake. He gave in to Mama. She married a flawed, neurotic man, capable of great love, a brew very often drunk by a woman not in touch with her strength.

Papa *did* become a fine doctor, withal.

At Home

So, they married, moved to Peabody, and Papa became the first Jewish doctor there. They lived in a sprawling house on Main Street, and Papa bought his first Model T Ford, and Mary's uncles introduced them to the small Jewish community and had him voted in as their Lodge doctor. Soon, the Russians and Poles discovered him, because he could talk to them in their own language. Soon, too, the Greeks and Turks discovered someone who would take the time to learn their language, enough to treat them and make them well. Papa became a very busy doctor. He said good morning to the Irish and Yankees, but he didn't treat them. He was the immigrant doctor.

Mama and Papa planted a garden. Papa built himself a dove cote and raised birds, and they ate their own sweet corn and vegetables in the summer and picked their own flowers. Mama surrounded herself with antiques, learned how to cook, made a few Yankee friends because she talked well, looked so interesting, and couldn't be pigeonholed in the Jewish immigrant category. She confounded "them," the goyim. Not only that, she was "a reader" and believed in "women's suffrage" and all kinds of strange and new things.

And she was a nurse and helped her husband in his office. Everything was up and up and up and yet . . .

Papa wasn't doing what he was "supposed to do." The uncles looked on aghast. Their nephew-in-law was rejecting the few Jewish factory owners and favoring the workers. *Unionism* and *strike* were new words. He put his blessing on the new words. He refused to cross picket lines. Papa accepted the offering of chickens and milk instead of a fee with the dignity of an Aesculapius receiving a sacrifice for his healing. The upper class of the town were horrified. Who was this young doctor who burned with a stench and wouldn't play the game? Mama joined him. The uncles had to look the other way, but they were embarrassed. The lines were clear, and they would have to live with it. They had imported two radicals into town.

The factory owners who could have made Papa rich were the aliens. The workers were the Americans. Would Papa's time have been better spent at Harvard, becoming a specialist in Boston? I don't think they ever gave it a thought in those early days. They both loved the smell of a fight. There was a war to be won—decent wages, decent hours, safety in the factories. If the "uppers" of the town had wanted to print a calling card for Papa, it would have said "Dr. Halpern, Socialist, renegade, betrayer." A professional man shouldn't behave the way he did. He was pariah —double—a Jew and a reformer.

What innocent days those were, just ordinary fights for rights, days before the collapse of capitalism, to be rebuilt by Roosevelt; days before Hitler; days before American aggression; days before napalm and genocide; days before world hunger; days before atom bombs; days before Russia, the grand experiment, turned into dross and the Jew was being hunted again as prey; days before a Communist China; days before Nixon, and the homicide of the American Constitution; days before the threat to drive the Jewish state of Israel into the sea.

In those innocent days my sister was born and brought to the house on Main Street. I know nothing about those days. I wasn't there, except to *know* that she was the first, and was and has always been beautiful, and still is. By the time I was born, six years later, they had already fashioned her into a dancer (with tutu). I was to be The Boy. I wasn't, am not, will never be, even though, sometimes, my unconscious is a "he."

One day, according to my sister, unplanned, I arrived. A strange aunt came in the early morning hours to announce that Mama (my sister's mother) was in the hospital, and that she, my sister, had a sister, who was born in the middle of a night in June (imagine my sister's consternation). It was Midsummer Eve, the night Puck mixed things up, offered his love juice around, and everyone fell in love with unlikely partners. Midsummer Eve, when mistletoe is its most potent, festivals their wildest and happiest; night fires burned to scare away the witches and all frightening forces. Midsummer Day, summer solstice, the longest day of the year, the first day of my life.

Puck was at work in the house on Main Street, there's no doubt about it. That night, Papa fell in love with me, who was to have been his son, and Mama, more in love with her firstborn than she ever was and quite offhanded with me. Only Puck knows why.

Before the Fall, we were all in a new house on Central Street, a bigger, whiter, finer house. There they brought me, and I was put, placed, encapsulated, the new member. That house is my skin. It is I, and I am it, even though years span the time of arrival and the time of now, even though all are dead and the house itself owned by others. The trees are mine, the small half-acre is mine, the roof, the shadows on the roof from the shading elms (which are no more), the grass, as it winds round to the back, the cracks in the cement walk, the bushes, the trellises, the garage with its Halloween party sounds, the sun, when it hits each part at any hour of the day, it is, was, will always be mine. I drew a fence of ownership around it with my urine and feces, as surely as any wolf in the forest makes his invisible fence of ownership. Perhaps the span of space between us is less infinite than I imagined.

It is where I learned about love and hate; predator and prey; first wondered if there could ever be a heavenly balance; and where I never did what I was supposed to do. I learned from a master.

⁂

My heart slips off its wheel remembering. I remember nothing, so I gimlet and spelunk for clues. Why? Is it because the I is wearing thin in its middle-aged clothes and longs to be blown up and up and up? If only it could, presto, wear a suit of light, white and young again! If only. Ha, if ever, I would laugh myself sick with the magic of it. Capturing Time, I *am* laughing. I'm wearing a suit of light again. My body is whole, as it was, my mind not yet a black box of numbers and equations, adding up to formulas it will take another lifetime to understand.

The afternoon sun is playing on Mama's sleigh bed, its burled wood on fire with movement. She is at her dressing table, fixing her cuticles, polishing her nails with a chamois cloth, carefully, then whitening them underneath, with a long stick, one by one. The room is very quiet. I'm standing behind her, just watching. She's wearing a dressing gown of chiffon, pulsing with blends of green, purple, and blues. Suddenly, I'm overcome with love and throw my arms around her. She catches me and holds me, it seems like hours. Her hair is falling all around us. I stroke it, and she strokes mine, so silly, short, and straight. I count her heartbeats, and then she kisses me on my forehead, laughs, and continues to do her nails. I run out into the sun, screaming with delight. *None of it is true,* except for the dressing gown, and her doing her nails. (How little "at home" I was in that room.)

I carried that gown around with me for years, like a nu-nu, until it became shredded, brittle as unfulfilled wishes. Not until I lived alone in my first apartment did I throw it away. Then loneliness was so excruciating I needed nothing to remind me of denial.

What Mama did say to me was, "I don't like being watched."

"Well, you know," an old friend with whom I grew up said, chuckling, "we were the products of emancipated woman, you'll excuse the expression. The early ones who blazed the trail, straight-backed suffragettes, albeit ultra-feminine, even flirts. But if you called them on it, they'd run like mad. Their heads were too full of words, new ones, and ideas. They couldn't relate to scruffy, palpitating little persons. *The* child, yes, *the* masses, *the* bosses, *the* movement. Being women, they felt it their responsibility to have children. 'Children' was the grand gesture to Motherhood with a capital M. Anything more was belittling the independence of liberated women—becoming a cow. Offspring was The Child, the abstract concept of The Child.

" 'Why,' I once said to Reva [she called her mother Reva], 'I am *not* some abstract idea in your head. I am me!' She didn't know what I was talking about," my friend added ruefully. "And, you know, those women were prudes. Repressed. I would almost say sexually dead. I never saw my parents touch each other!"

"Really? Neither did I. Isn't that interesting."

"Not once," she added firmly.

"But they were such sensual, passionate people about music, dance, politics," I said.

"Not at home where it counted! To give you an idea

of the avoidance . . . when I couldn't have been more than fifteen, I was saying goodnight to a boy. I finally closed the front door behind me. Reva was waiting up, with a stern face and pursed lips, and she said, 'Did I hear the sounds of osculation in the hall?' I said, 'Yes, Reva, you did. We were necking!' She walked into her bedroom and closed the door. I was an animal."

My friend Evelyn's face flushed in anger, and we both laughed. It was all such a long time ago, and we were both now mothers, as old as the women we were reminiscing about. Gimleting into the spirits of dead people is painful. The fine powder of their exhumed souls flies about in the air and catches you in the throat. Tiny filaments of it drop into your teacup, and you sit watching the specks of Past Time float about and slowly drop to the bottom, quiet sediment again.

I decided to ask a big question. "Then where did you learn love?"

Without a moment's hesitation, she answered, "My father!"

"Isn't that interesting," I said again. (It seemed to be the only thing I felt like saying.)

"Yes, isn't it," she answered. "The women were the cool ones, the men the hot ones. Well, hot in comparison. But at least they tried."

I began to remember my friend's father, Papa's dearest friend, another doctor, like Papa, and his name was Harry, too. But he was called by his Russian name, Greisha. A dear, soft man, who looked you straight in the eye and took your face in his hands and kissed it by way of greeting. A good man, married to a strong, pretentious woman, Reva, Mama's best friend in Boston.

I looked across our dining room table at my friend Evelyn and felt I loved her very much. She was my past and my present. I felt surprised to think I was surprised that I said to myself, "I love her." I was never taught to say "I love you." I never heard it. I had to teach it to myself and have used it like a deaf-mute trying to sing.

Evelyn looked at me. "Now your mother, to me, was the epitome of mother."

"You can't be serious."

"Oh yes. When I used to visit you on weekends, I thought I was in heaven. You had a mother who was a mother, not only a political creature. Your mother, Mary, cooked and sewed and made desserts, always my favorite when I came, apricot whip. Do you realize how important that was to me? Do you remember her sewing machine that sat in one of the windows of her bedroom, and the big sleigh bed? I sat for hours on it, watching her sew and talking with her about everything."

"Talking?"

"About everything. That's why I loved her. Reva and I never exchanged two words. She was too busy and really disinterested. But Mary? She had all the Time in the world for me."

"You're talking about someone I don't know. Isn't that interesting. I'm going to say something not very nice," I said. "You know what I think? Those two very special women had a competition going between them that was stupendous. They vied with each other at political meetings. They vied with each other over which revolutionary leader was their friend, which artist would be entertained for dinner. Being nice to a child of the other was another game, the game of being the perfect mother. But in their own nests? Nobody was home. On this business of loving, I flew myself and learned it, here and there, on the outside. I don't know about Reva. I accept what you say. But I always thought *she* was the perfect mother. She always said, 'How are you?', as though she really wanted an answer. I never gave it to her because I didn't know how. That was my failing. I couldn't practice it at home. Nobody ever asked me, 'How are you?' Never. And you know, Evelyn, I think you're wrong about no sexuality. Why, it was one of the most exciting and original notions to me when I visited you on weekends—to wake up and find the door to your parents' room slightly open, both of them nude, their bodies entwined about each other, as they slept. It made me think maybe that's real, and where I come from not real at all! Reva was more overtly feminine than Mary. She dyed her hair (like a courtesan, Mama used to say). She believed in high heels and gentle artifice. Mary was the true Puritan. No makeup, no perfume, no card playing, no cheap movies. Come to think of it, their friendship was unfathomable, those two intelligentsia ladies. I assume the radicalism tied them in blood. Virgin bastard queens, both of them. Mary's regime was the tougher to live under when everything else in America was going crazy with change. Remember when Mary first gave in to lipstick, her Tangee sticks of translucent pink? Wow. Shocking. Maybe Reva's very offhandedness, her piquant bezazz, in the long run made you healthier than I."

My friend raised her eyebrows in silence, not knowing what I meant. We saw each other only once a year or so. She never made mention of the "operation." Out of kindness, I thought. I wanted to scream, "Don't you see, I'm not the same anymore? Don't you wonder why I'm spelunking?" How could she know? She lived a thousand miles away, in Wisconsin. And I didn't mention anything about pigeons. It would have taken too long.

Maybe someday, on a beach somewhere, with long hours of nothing, we'd gimlet and spelunk again. I saw from the strain on her face that it was something she didn't do easily, and when we said good-bye, she leaned against the wall of our outer hall and said, falteringly, "I'm amazed at how much I've forgotten, purposefully. I couldn't answer

any of your questions: what was Reva really like? What
was Mary like? How did they behave in the quality of their
days? How did they move through their Space? What were
they like with their husbands? How did they show love? I
could only talk in generalities. And as for Reva [she sighed]
why do you want to know, anyway? I closed those doors
long ago. I'm embarrassed at how completely. But as you
said, it was our Time too, wasn't it?"

I felt I had made her sad and emptied and wanted to
yell after her as she walked out, "Don't feel bad! I'm the
strange one, trying to net Time, as though it were a thousand butterflies, pinning them, setting them on my desk,
gazing at the patterns of their wings, imagining, hour upon
hour, how they looked when they flew."

🍁

Papa's table manners were atrocious. Eating as a peasant
seemed to be his last line of defense. He refused to behave
like the American goyim at the dinner table. He held his
knife and fork in the European way, never letting go of
the knife in his right hand, shoving the peas and carrots
in orderly groupings in a way a sheep dog driving his herd
home might envy. He would lean into his plate, eating till
it was clean, using his bread to mop up the gravy, making
great sounds of chewing and swallowing, ignoring everyone until his stomach was full. When it was, he left the
table. His eating presence dominated the table. No sooner
had he finished one course, the next would be placed before
him, whether anyone else was ready or not. To feed Papa
seemed to be the reason we all sat down to table. There
never were comments of protest or criticism. Mama just sat
there, eating quietly, in the American manner, resting her
knife on the rim of her plate, changing her fork from left

to right hand, pausing between mouthfuls. I sat opposite
her and learned. I never dared look at Papa. It seemed
indecent to watch his passion at dinner table, an orgiastic
ritual in the presence of others. It was depressing, and one
felt shut out.

His intimate, relaxed, self-absorbed eating habits were
Papa's arrogant way of hanging on to the *shtetl* ways, Jewish
ways, feeling comfortable with one's own. "Niceness" was
not necessary in the privacy of home, haven away from the
demands of "niceness"-gentility of the goyish outside. Food
was placed in front of you to be eaten. You ate! Then, if
there was time, you engaged, you talked, you looked around
to see who was there. The manners of the Gentile dinner
table were anathema, only for disguise. Anyway, there
wasn't time. There was too much to worry about. The disdain *and* fear he held for new Gentile foods was almost an
obsession. Artichokes, creamed or whipped anythings—except Mama's delicate desserts, her chocolate mousses and
apricot concoctions, light as angel's breath—he ate without
a word of praise.

Food was the one area where he refused to give in. He
was a meat-and-potatoes boy to the end. It was lucky for
us all that Mama was such a good cook and managed to
make the *shtetl* fare with the light hand of the New World.
Her roast beef and stews were magnificent.

It was all very strange, Papa's schisms. Hating acknowledged refinements in food, he insisted on the most elegant
clothes, always English cut, made to order in the finest of
wools and worsteds, herringbones and twills, ordered from
the most Gentile store in Boston. His fedoras were of Italian
felt and his overcoats only Burberry. In that department, he
outdid the Gentile in his game of gentility and was aware
of fine haberdashery long before many of them could afford
it, the parvenu Irish and Greek and Polish doctors. They

were still sporting white socks and black shoes, while Papa looked like an English country gentleman.

As public a life as he led, Papa was never comfortable in the public places of the outside world, which demanded neutrality for the sake of manners. Papa was an unruly man. He had great difficulty in being neutral, noncommittal. He knew his behavior was offensive to the Gentile code. Papa hated codes. They hid true feelings. The codes made it possible for you *not* to know what the other fellow was thinking. Papa had to learn to be quiet, and it was painful as crucifixion. He had to look into the glacial eyes of the goyim and *not* wonder what was there. Their hate was fathoms deep.

He had to go about being the best damn doctor around, the doctor other doctors called in when they were ill or consulted with privately when they needed advice about their patients. When Papa didn't know something, he called in specialists from Boston, friends who had gone on to specialization, as he had wanted. He admired expertise. At first, this habit he had of calling in the expert worried his patients. Their doctor didn't know enough. Then they saw the wisdom and relied on him like children.

"Doctor, I can eat a few carrots?" (It drove him mad.)

"What our doctor doesn't know, he would find out who knew. That's a good doctor. After all, one man can't know everything."

Papa was a practitioner of Socratic humility. (The wise man is one who knows that he does not know.) Gradually, this earned him respect. But it took a long time for him to see that he had become a virtuoso diagnostician.

"I walk into a sickroom, and by the smell I know the illness," he would say offhandedly. "My God, after forty years of practice, if a doctor can't do that, he can't do anything."

He never admitted he was unusual.

If he was worried about a difficult case, he always had the "lab workup" done by Harvard technicians, not his own hospital people.

"What was wrong with the Peabody facilities? Couldn't they give him what he wanted?"

No, not always, in the early days.

Treading on toes was his vulgar Jewish way. He was such a mass of contradictions, for himself, and the goyim watchers. He retained his *shtetl*-ness and accent his lifetime, and yet had fancier ways, was more of the modern world and avant-garde than "they" ever dreamed of being. His itchiness was always putting them down. His intellectual Jewishness, with its inherited attitudes toward justice made him want to spread those feelings and share them with everyone, Jew and goy alike, and if they didn't want to share, he'd ram it down their throats. His Jewishness forced him to.

The religious Jew in town resented his nerve to be an atheist. The goy was suspicious of his love and probing. So he became depressed, angry, and his striving for justice even wilder.

Attempted civility outside; depression inside.

Sometimes it didn't work and exploded. If he watched an unnecessary operation being performed at the hospital, he would storm out of the operating room, yelling to the surgeon, "You're cutting her open for a fee! She's a terminal case with a few weeks to live. Let her die in peace, for God's sake!" By afternoon, it would be all over town, and took months to heal, the gashes *he* had made in the epidermis of civility.

In the early days, a Polish doctor against whom Papa had made some professional accusation cornered him in the square, in front of Curtis Drugs, called Papa "a son of a bitch Jew," and Papa "walloped" him.

"Jesus, I gave him a left hook, and he fell to the sidewalk. I could have killed him, I was so mad."

It was all over town by evening and took months to cool, but they became friends, with George Curtis the peacemaker, and remained so for a lifetime. They both knew it was important for ethnics to remain bonded, in the face of the Irish and the Yankee. Oh, those were complicated days. Papa was never again called a Jew to his face.

Withal, Papa *did* make adjustments to "goyish." His innate shyness made it easier. His manner of dress was so elegant. His was a charming, quiet way of greeting people, with a courtly "How-di-do," a touch of his hand to the brim of his expensive felt, a slight bow of his head. It was attractive and removed at the same time. There was a superior intelligence in his eye, and the smile of a nobleman on his lips. Removed, remote, concerned, foreign, with a history of outbursts and passion, he scared the hell out of the locals. For the minute he opened his mouth, the Jewishness came pouring out.

How the world has changed. Today he would be considered an eccentric, deliciously European man. Then he was a pariah. The first.

Sub rosa, I often wondered if this man was a good lover; whether all the schisms came together in one lovely, giving person when he made love to his adored Mary.

🍂

Breakfasts were easier. He was more relaxed. A day of parry, thrust, engagement, healing, worry, hospital politics was not behind him; after-supper patients not ahead of him, downstairs in the waiting room, their bells of arrival ringing through the evening supper.

At breakfast, he was a man of almost ordinary tension.

The morning Boston paper was laid out next to his coffee cup. He ate his bacon and eggs slowly, with mannerly relish, and I, whose duty as girl child was to watch every aspect, with an X-ray eye, of an adored and feared male, will never forget the smell of the marvelous coffee Mama made, which he sipped, not gulped, drops falling on the newsprint, crinkly circles of light beige, leaving seals of guarantee that a Man had passed on the news of the day. No one dared touch the paper before he had dropped coffee on it, read it, end to end and left it, exhausted, editorial page face-out. When we all left the table, Mama folded it back into proper order and read it quietly in toto, I imagine, because either at dinner, which was midday, or at supper the analysis of the day's news began across the table between the two of them. Judging from the tone of their voices, I was sure the end of the world was at hand. Every day, I was certain it would happen: doom, threat, gloom, the terrible uphill fight of the radical to see every-man-light at the end of the capitalistic tunnel—revolution; their voices filled with urgency, apprehension, determination, terrible anger:

"Bastard!"

"Negroes . . . chain gangs."

"Depression . . . banks . . . bla, bla."

"Roosevelt . . . Hitler . . . Hitler . . . ach . . . ing . . . tung."

"Mussolini . . . C-i-a-o-o-o-o."

"Manchuria! Run; running; overrun . . . rape . . . murder . . . land."

"Poor China . . . lovely, poor China . . . millions."

"Something's rotten in . . ."

("Everywhere . . ."?)

"No . . . Russia . . . purges . . . trials . . . insky . . . . . . Stalin, Lenin, Trotsky."

"Traitors?"

"No!"

"I say yes!"

"Socialism, Communism . . . ism . . . istic . . . istical."

"Bosses, workers . . . masses . . . masses . . . masses."

"Refugees . . . children . . . soldiers . . . fighters . . . freedom . . . slavery."

Left . . . right . . . left . . . right. I was sure our back door would fling open and the soldiers of "oppression" would march through Mama's clean house, defiling it with their European-Asian boots. It was enough to give one indigestion or not want to eat at all. I chose the latter. It made for less gas. Papa could, but we were not allowed to burp at the table.

Whether I chose to eat or not to made no difference. What was put on my plate had to be dealt with. Those were the rules, whether countries on the outside were being taken, falling, rising or not; whether it was *all* coming closer to our house or not. So I very often sat chewing on cold chunks of food or hiding it under the table, long after the sounds of battle had dissolved into ordinary life sounds, wondering how everyone could go off and do ordinary things when the end of the world was in sight.

The raising of voices in political discussion, still, makes my heart jump until I laugh inside, remembering that the end did *not* come; change, yes, but not the end; that history has always been the same—Sisyphus rolling his stone up the mountain, Sisyphus stopping to rest, Sisyphus tied to his stone, the dumbness of Sisyphus, the courage of Sisyphus, the crashing down, rolling up, fright, despair—hope, that one day, dumb cluck, he'll roll it to the top and it will stay there, a monument to worked-out guilt, shame and greed, and *all* will be free, rational, fair, peaceful, and beautiful.

Learning Love

I: Holy Communion

"**I** COULD tell you things that would open your eyes," said my Uncle Zachariah, age eighty-eight.

"Tell me, tell me," I coax.

"Oh, no, you're not old enough. You wouldn't understand."

"Don't be silly."

"No."

"Tell me now."

"No, when you're in your eighties, too, I'll tell you."

"I'm grown-up, remember?"

(He laughs.)

"But you're not in your eighties and when you will be I won't be here. So I'll never be able to tell you things that would open your eyes."

(That's my Uncle Zachariah.)

"All right," I say, thinking I'm throwing him a curve. "What do you think of Freud?"

Without a moment's hesitation he answers, "He wrote too much. He could have said it all in one book."

"What do you think about what he wrote, albeit volu-
minously?"

"If you were born a little horse, you'll die a big horse."

"You mean, you feel environment has very little to do
with it?"

"You heard me. If you're born a little horse, you won't
die a giraffe!'

"Are you saying it's all predestined in the genes?"

"There's very little you can do about it."

(It occurs to me that maybe he is a true revolutionist.
If the "way" itself were not right from the beginning, no
amount of attempted change would be affective, unless the
"way" itself were changed.)

"About being Jewish. How do you feel?"

"Never bothered me for a minute. I was neither Jew
nor Gentile. No one ever called me a damn Jew."

As I'm thinking about this exchange with my
Uncle "Zack," our male cat, Killer Kelly, is
curled up in my lap, his stomach, pulsing
with purr, against mine. He must know I'm
thinking about love, avuncularly.

"What is an artist, Uncle Zack?"

"Oh, I'll have to write that to you in a letter. It'll take
some thinking."

"This is a silly question, but who is one of your favorite
artists?"

"It's not silly. In your eighties, you should know who
you like. I'll have to think about that. [Pause] But there is
a painting called *Chess Players*, by Thomas Eakins, an
American, in the Metropolitan Museum in New York, that
is as good as Rembrandt. So, who knows!"

"And Picasso? What did you think of Picasso?"

"Do think!" he corrected me.

"I'm sorry, yes, do think." He resented the unintended
burial of my verb.

"He's the best drawer of the twentieth century. But I love Degas."

"A romantic, eh?" I tease him.

(No answer.)

> ". . . peaceful gains, the swept hearth, his best wine for a friend at the table, his wife singing to the children."

Mama's younger brother is Zachariah. He outlived them all. He was, and is, married to what I remember as an angel, Pooney. When I was small, they were childless, living in Boston, where he worked as a bricklayer and she as a nurse.

Puritanical Papa, the unruly Jew, had to admit there was one even more unruly than himself—Zachariah.

Zack arrived in New York as a young boy. His father, Grandfather Jacob, settled in Brooklyn and continued to do what he did in Poland, manufacture artificial brick (cement blocks). I'm told it was a new concept in building here at the turn of the century. The oldest son, Isidore, remained with their father and learned how to lay brick. Zack, the youngest, was sent off to college in Valparaiso, Indiana. He lasted there a few months, disgusted with the idiocy of formal education, returned home, and joined his brother—bricklaying.

Whereas Isidore rose from laying brick to become a rich builder of apartment houses and a landowner, Zack remained a brick layer in his spare Time, refusing to play the bourgeois game. Playing chess, the horses, studying art, writing poetry, making up jokes, conundrums, riddles, reading philosophy, and what some members of the family called "bumming around" was how he spent his good Time.

When Zack first set eyes on the ghettos of the Lower East Side of New York City, he was so horrified he immediately decided to become an architect, "to tear it down and design a heaven for immigrants." He never did. Much later, when he saw the ghetto of the West End of Boston, he immediately decided he wouldn't rebuild it but that what they needed was an art gallery "to shake them up." He opened The Gallery for the Common Man, to which many came, but where no one bought. So he gave the pictures away.

He was brilliant, exciting, original, and naughty and still is to this day at the age of eighty-eight. I think Papa secretly envied him his freedom. Zack was neither Jew nor Gentile. He, in his not caring for social acceptance, bourgeois things, power, status, home, garden, car, travel, clothes had achieved nirvana—universality. The price it cost was in his laugh, his restlessness. Uncle Zachariah found a dime in the streets of Boston. To prove his honesty and purity, he put an ad in the Boston *Globe* to find its owner. He was disgusted that no one had the guts to answer.

Way back then, when Mama didn't know what to do with me, she sent me to visit Zack and Pooney. And it was heaven to visit them. Hers were the peaceful gains (from nursing). Hers was the swept hearth. Zack supplied the "best wine for a friend," and the only thing missing was "a wife singing to the children." But I supplied that when I came. They loved me and said so, over and over again, and Pooney sang to me by the hour.

Mama was at her wit's end. I refused to eat meat. Dinnertime was murder. We both played our roles to perfection. I refused, she forced. The rules of the game were anger and control. My object of the game was not to eat meat. Flesh was verboten.

When I was small, the phrase "starving Armenians" was in vogue. I looked like one—straight black hair, a tiny, long face, mostly eyes, and a thin, long body, always overtall for my age. The subject must have been lengthily discussed out of my presence. I was taken to see a Harvard pediatrician, who put me on a diet for the malnourished. Mama was horrified. It cast aspersions on her mothering ability to have a child who looked like a "starving Armenian," not to mention the psychic overtones of a child who refused to eat.

When things got too bad between us and Mama needed a rest, she would ship me off to spend a weekend with Uncle Zack and Aunt Pooney. I was treated with all the dignity of a visiting diplomat and ate like a pig, everything except meat.

But then, food was not the intense drama it was at home. Other things were more important—helping Pooney cook, or learning the names of chessmen, or being read to by the hour, or sitting in laps and cuddling. Rubbing noses was pretty big with them both.

"Where is my Eskimo girl?" Pooney would call, as I watched Zack pour schnapps into a tiny glass thimble, drink it, and smack his lips; or better still, put my tongue on the rim of the thimble to taste the fire that made him smile when he poured it down his throat.

My aunt combed my hair by the hour, clucking over its baby black-silk straightness. She would stroke my forehead and run her fingers about the contours of my face. When we were all tired of Inside, we would take a walk Outside, through a large park, an aunt holding my left hand, an uncle my right. I would blissfully watch the shine on my patent-leather shoes jump up and down with joy at each step.

They spoke my name with the weight accorded a dignitary's. It made me walk straight, filled my lungs with air, and I got very hungry, forgetting the game of "No." By the time I was five, I had become the owner of a tic. My head turned to the right saying, "No!"—especially at mealtime. When I visited Zack and Pooney, it disappeared.

On one of those fascinating weekends, Uncle Zack sat me on his lap close to dinnertime and said he was going to read me an unusually interesting story while we waited for

Aunt Pooney to prepare the dinner. He proceeded to read me a story with very grown-up words, which I tried hard to understand. I knew he wanted me to, or he wouldn't be reading it. As he read, more than the usual pungent odors of cooking were assailing us.

"Is something burning?" we sniffed.

"No, no, go on with your story. Everything's fine," Pooney replied.

When he finished reading, I was terribly impressed. The story was "A Dissertation upon Roast Pig," by Charles Lamb.

"Dinner's ready," Pooney called the second he had finished the last word. They obviously had rehearsed the scene very well.

"Tell me the story again," I said, as he led me to the table in a tiny mock parade.

"Now," Uncle Zack said, smacking his lips, "you know what Aunt Pooney has done for us? She's serving us burnt, baby lamb chops for dinner. Lamb in honor of the writer's name, Charles Lamb, and burnt lamb in honor of his story about the 'natives' whose straw hut burned down. But as you heard, the pigs they owned also got burned in the fire. The natives began to smell something that made them so hungry they started to eat the burnt meat of the pig. It tasted so fine, they almost forgot their house had been destroyed. The next time they felt like eating burnt pig, they figured the only way they could taste that wonderful meat would be if they burned down their hut again. The pigs, again, would get burned by accident! They didn't know the word *cooking* yet and they didn't have a stove like Aunt Pooney's. She's burned our lamb chops without having to burn the house down. Isn't she smart?"

The irony and fun was not wasted on me. I ate every morsel of my baby lamb chop, burnt crisp and juicy pink inside, and when they sent me home, I had become a meat eater—only if Mama followed my instructions, according to Charles Lamb, master chef.

II: *Absolution*

One hot spring afternoon, I arrived at the Gilman house to play with Little Alice upstairs in the cool, green-shaded room where the dollhouse waited for us. But I delayed Alice's repeated invitations of "Let's go upstairs." Other things were on my mind, and I went out to the back lawn where I knew I would find Sam, her father, sitting under the big tree, playing with the dogs. I sat next to him in such silence, I forced him to ask, "What's wrong?"

"Do you have a Bible?" I asked.

"Why, yes, of course we do."

"Could I look at it?"

"Of course you can," and he went inside, brought back a huge family Bible, and placed it on my much too small lap. He resumed his place beside me and began to oil a gardening tool as though it were quite ordinary for little Doris to ask to see a Bible and as though I were perfectly capable of reading it. The huge book teetered on my lap as I resolutely turned the ancestral tissue-paper pages, edged in gold, making believe I understood every word of it. I turned slowly, trying to catch sight of familiar words, hoping they would pop up and help me find what I was looking for. I didn't let a page go by, carefully fingering each one. There it was, sitting between my legs on the emerald green lawn of the Gilmans, the book "they" all talked about and carried to church on Sunday, the book with all the "thou shalt nots," the book we didn't have in our house, despite the fact we had more books than anyone else, except the library.

"Are you looking for something in particular?" Sam asked gently.

(No answer.)

I continued to turn the pages and minutes went by. I turned faster and faster, and Sam saw my despair.

"What are you looking for? Maybe I can help you."

I shook my head and stared at the pages, helpless and mute. I wouldn't answer him. He lifted the huge book from between my knees onto his own lap.

"It's a very big, heavy book for a little girl to handle. If you tell me what you're looking for, I could help you, I'm sure."

(Silence.)

With my head lowered, in a tiny voice, I whispered to my friend Sam, "I want to see which page has my name on it. I want to see where it says in the Bible that 'Doris Halpern is a Christ Killer.' Two Polish boys in my class said if I didn't believe them, I could find that sentence in the Bible."

(Silence.)

"Oh, I see," Sam said, immediately realizing the seriousness of the search and the depths of my anguish. He began to turn the pages slowly, one by one, from the very beginning. He beckoned me to move nearer, to lean against his knee. Carefully, and as surely as the minutes of the afternoon passed, Sam gave me unhinged Time as he exposed the pages for my eyes to see, running his hand across each one saying, slowly and quietly, as the smell of wet, green, spring grass tied us together, "It's not on this page, or this page, or this page, or this page. No, there's no 'Doris Halpern' on this page, or this page."

By the time we had reached the middle of the book, Alice sensed something of monumental importance was going on. She joined us on the other side of her father's lap, and the three of us took turns turning the fragile, tissuelike pages, sibilant as dead leaves to the touch. When we reached the last page, Sam closed the Holy Bible and sat for a moment in silence.

"Well now, you see for yourself, nowhere in this book is it written 'Doris Halpern is a Christ Killer.' Those boys have told a lie."

I looked up at Sam and I believed him. He patted my black bangs and his touch told me he knew he had delivered me of a terrible weight, at least for one afternoon.

"Alice?" he said. "How about you and this Indian princess going upstairs? I didn't build the dollhouse to sit up there all by itself."

The news of my having been absolved from the killer role must have reached Mama, because she mentioned it a few days later.

"I understand you and Sam read the Bible the other day."

"Yes, every page of it," I answered proudly. "It's a beautiful book, isn't it?" I knew my sentence was a taunt, and I was right. She didn't answer me. That was the difference between her and Sam.

III: Benediction

A friend brought me some tulips the other day. Five of them, the first of Spring. Full, yellow-with-red-trim tulips, bursting with energy and even sporting buds, promising bloom. I put them in a crystal vase in the white, wainscoted dining room so that no other color would interfere with their bravado. A few hours later, I walked through the room. One of them had died, its long stem, its head was lying limp on the mission table on which the vase was placed. "Why you?" I cried. "Why did you die and not they?" My reaction astounded me. "You're going to make it, if I have anything to say about it. This is no time for death," I scolded the limp yellow thing. My talking to it continued to astound me, as I lifted it up and tried to place it among its peers, trying to convince it that everything was fine. But it just fell over again. I prodded its petals, but they gave no resistance and rested on my fingers in resignation. "We'll see about that, young lady. What you need is an operation, and I'm going to do it!" By now, the sound of my voice talking to a tulip in shock seemed like such insanity, I decided to go for broke. I operated over the kitchen sink. "It's going to hurt for a minute, but it will do the trick," and I snipped off part of the young, strong stem that looked so healthy yet had given in to nonbeing. I put the stricken tulip back in the vase. It fell over. I lifted it up and leaned it against the white wall, using the wall as a splint. The tulip fell over again. I felt nausea rising. I lifted it once more and, with all the tulip-empathy I could muster, found the right angle in which it could lean against the white wall and not collapse. I thought I heard a sigh, as it miraculously stayed where I had insisted. The tulip looked as though it was using everything in its presence to please me and remain propped. I sat in a chair and stared at the strange sight of four bursting tulips and one within their midst expiring, splinted, operated on. "It's up to you now. I've done all I can," I threw over my shoulder as I left the room. "That is, I think I have. But *know* one thing—I would like you to live, if you want to!"

A few hours later, I peeked into the dining room and couldn't find the invalid. It had lifted itself from the wall, four inches in space, and was standing, tentative, weak, but alive. To think I might have just plucked it out of its vase and thrown it away, as I have so many times in the past, with seemingly dead things.

🍁

"Home Nook" was the name of Uncle Bob's house in New Hampshire. It sat at the top of a steep, dirt-roaded hill, overlooking Lake Winnipesaukee. When we were small, the twenty-five-mile lake lay as pristine as when the Indians had left it, surrounded by pine forests, dark, damp green, ringing blue water.

Mama and Papa were always happy when we went to visit Uncle Bob. He was one of their most special friends till death did them all part. Death was very far away in those early years when Mama would gather us together on a Saturday morning, saying: "We're going to New Hampshire this morning! Papa's taking the weekend off because Uncle Bob needs some medicine."

That meant Mama's mood would be marvelous. She got Papa to carry the wooden icebox from the attic and stuffed it with food for us and for Uncle Bob and Aunt June, bringing them things she knew they couldn't afford but needed, like fresh vegetables, fruit, chickens, and meat. In my childhood, Uncle Bob was a minister without a church and, so, dirt poor.

But before that, his life had been one tempestuous year after the other. He always seemed to be present where strikes or meetings of violence occurred. Prior to his arrival in Peabody, he was pastor of a church in upstate New York. He had to "leave town," however, when he became unbecomingly involved, for a minister, in a local strike, was arrested, denounced, and forced to find another church. And so Peabody, burgeoning leather factory town, inherited a most amazing man for its time.

Robert A. Bakeman became pastor of the Second Congregational Church in Peabody—until he decided to run for mayor and won. His election, minister to mayor, brought all the Boston papers to Peabody. His political success was a fluke and newsworthy and was obviously the result of the immigrant vote in a conservative town. There were new winds blowing, and they blew him right into public office in 1925. He was "known as championing the rights of the underdog and as a friend of the laboring man."

"He's a radical," they whispered in Peabody.

Papa and Bakeman discovered each other at a town meeting. The young Jewish doctor stood up, made an impassioned speech about "rights," and the two became thick as thieves. It was a friendship made in heaven. Uncle Bob, when he became mayor, appointed Papa the head of the Health Department, and a Greek lawyer, James Liacos, as City Solicitor. Uncle Bob ruled four years that the town still remembers. To this day, an honest act politically is called, in certain quarters of Massachusetts that remember, "a Bakemanism."

During the reign of Uncle Bob, the famous Sacco and Vanzetti case was raging, not only in the Commonwealth of Massachusetts but in the entire world. It was the Rosenberg case of *their* time.

During the height of the McCarthy era of suspected Communist witch-hunting, Papa would say, "Oh, this is mild in comparison with *our* days of the Palmer Raids, when government agents would appear in the middle of the night, haul immigrants who were suspected of being radicals out of their beds, and in the morning they would find themselves on boats headed back 'where they came from.'" It was in that repressive atmosphere of the early twenties that Sacco and Vanzetti, two radical Italian immigrants were framed for a payroll robbery and murder in Braintree, Massachusetts. They were held in jail for seven years while their case became a political cause célèbre. Sacco and Vanzetti protested their innocence to the end (as did the Rosenbergs), and they, like the Rosenbergs, wrote letters from prison that have since become part of the poetry of America and inspired Upton Sinclair to write his beautiful novel *Boston*.

It was apparent to most libertarians that Sacco and Vanzetti were to be put to death by the State not for their deeds but for their dangerous ideas. A most un-American way of doing State business.

The fate of those two Italian immigrants was to be very important in the pinnacle and nadir of Uncle Bob's political life. The free-thinking disciple of Christ that he was, as mayor he made Peabody an open city for free speech in the discussion of the case. In 1927, on the eve of the execution of the two anarchists, he invited Alfred Baker Lewis, Socialist, to address an outdoor meeting. It would be the only place in Massachusetts to allow a public gathering that night. It was *that* decision Uncle Bob had to make, and he made it with the help of Aunt June. He knew if he allowed the meeting and let the Socialist speak, his own career would be over and he could never run for mayor again or be in politics. And Uncle Bob loved being mayor.

He and Aunt June went up to New Hampshire to discuss it together in the privacy of "Home Nook," the tiny family estate. They stood under a young pine tree as they talked it over, and Aunt June (his college sweetheart, who had wanted to be a missionary in China, but instead, married to devote her entire life to him), quiet, strong Aunt June pushed him the way she knew he wanted to go but would not, without her insistence. They decided *yes.* Peabody would have a demonstration in the square the night Sacco and Vanzetti were killed in the electric chair. Uncle Bob and Aunt June called the tree they stood under "Decision Pine."

And so, thousands of people from all over New England and New York gathered that night in 1927 in Peabody, to hold a vigil. The Irish Chief of Police, who disapproved of the meeting, decided to break it up. Uncle Bob fired him on the spot and took over the meeting himself, guaranteeing by the authority of his office the right to freedom of speech. It was a scandal that remained about his name for years after—the mayor had taken the side of those two Italian anarchists, enemies of the state and country. But for Mama and Papa it placed Robert Bakeman on the side of the angels.

After his mayoral term was up, he ran again but was defeated, as he knew he would be. The town had had enough of his atypical political behavior. The Conservatives got back their influence. Uncle Bob had embarrassed them dreadfully. He was a most peculiar Yankee. He walked on the wrong side of the street and slept in the wrong beds. He was in love with those damned immigrants and Jews, all those "different" people who were demanding place and right and power they had not been born into.

After his political defeat, Uncle Bob left Peabody to start an experimental farm colony of picked prisoners from Norfolk Prison in Connecticut. His daughter, Pauline, remembers the "terrific atmosphere created for the inmates, at that time, a revolutionary concept for rehabilitation." She recalls being there herself, to play the violin in concerts her father set up for the prisoners who were not in jail, but living on the experimental farm. Uncle Bob didn't get along with the jailers running the prison, and so he left. He went to work for the Boston Civil Liberties Union, but was knocked down by a police horse in the Boston Common during a social protest march of some kind. A long and debilitating disease had by then found his body a willing host. He was suffering from gout. It was one of the most severe cases observed in years, according to medical experts who watched the illness rampage through his body. So Uncle Bob and Aunt June retired to his family seat in Alton, New Hampshire. There he talked and sang and preached and wrote and exhorted and influenced all who came to sit in his most unusual climate. And they did . . . come.

"He was quite a guy," his daughter, Pauline, says wryly; she, now, almost at the age at which I remember him. "It was like living with Jesus. Great for everyone else, but pretty tough on us, his children." (She meant herself and Young Bob, her brother.) "He wanted to be like Jesus the Prophet, not the Jesus of the Holy Trinity and the mumbo jumbo of the church. He never held much with the imposed ceremony. He was after the essence."

Uncle Bob's and Mama's and Papa's love for one another rubbed off on all of us, and so they were always marvelous, those weekends in New Hampshire. Aunt June, calm, wise Aunt June, was Uncle Bob's life-love. She cared for him with the patience of an attending angel. I have a sneaking suspicion he was also in love with Mama, and Mama's two daughters were certainly recipients of that glow. Visiting Aunt June and Uncle Bob was distinctly special. The atmosphere was astounding. It was a Beethoven concerto that ran for thirty-six hours without stopping.

What a marvelous thing to remember—only Love. I shall never forget it.

Papa's Pontiac would make the hill in first, up, up, to the top where "Home Nook" sat waiting behind a stone fence. Midmorning, the smell of hot wood in the sun, tiger lilies fighting for light amidst the long grasses—lilies, leaning

tipsily, drunken sentinels around the 175-year-old home-
stead. How cozily that tiny gray, saltbox cottage was sinking
into the earth, with the weight of eight generations in its
arms. Your eyes blinked as you ducked, entering. Built by
eighteenth-century men of smaller stature, the sun entered
low, out of politeness. "Home Nook" was just the right size
for twentieth-century children. You felt quite grown in its
scaled-down space.

"Bob, they're here!" Aunt June's voice would sing out.

The smell of old things, kerosene lamps, hand-hewn
boards, hundreds of old books and magazines, and the smell
of Aunt June's corn bread cooling for us. (They had received
a card we were coming. There was no telephone or electricity.) And the scents of Uncle Bob, consumed by gout,
hands and feet swollen out of proportion, scrubbed clean
by Aunt June. The smell of illness with old things, not sour,
but dusty, slightly sweet. Or was that, too, mixed with the
smell of fresh-picked blueberries and salt-pork grease, com-
bining with the grasses and hay smells sneaking through the
cracks from the New Hampshire hills? And was all of that
mixed with the meadows of Queen Anne's lace and the
subtle feces odor from the outhouse of Aunt June and Uncle
Bob, the fecal matter of nonmeat-eating animals, smelling
like the wet earth itself?

And there was Uncle Bob, in the earliest days I remember, sitting in a chair with book in lap, his swollen, gouty
feet in overlarge sneakers; his hands, joints distorted, waving hello in the air, hands eager to touch us in greeting,
young and old, his face glowing. In the later years of my
childhood, he greeted us from his bed, in a mound of mon-
strous flesh, eaten away yet still exalted; always, whether
from chair or bed, with the first sentence of the weekend on
his lips. In that greeting was always the word *love*, or *Jesus*,
or *friends*. It was embarrassing and beautiful. Uncle Bob
only talked about love. People were born only to seek love

and give it. What does love mean? How does it get lost?
How can one find it? In what myriads of ways can it be
trampled, yet rediscovered? What does it do to us when we
find it?

They were sexy as hell, those visits—so different from
the air at home. Why did Mama and Papa twinkle and ex-
pand in a way they never did at home? Uncle Bob threw
his arms about us, always lightly brushing my chest with his
distorted hands. Was it by accident, that brushing? As the
years went by, my growing breasts were there, and he still
touched my chest lightly, in greeting. Was he measuring my
femininity from summer to summer? If he was, he was the
only one. He was the first person I knew who called me
darling, the first man, to be exact. Aunt Pooney was the first
woman. It was a word never uttered at home, yet Mama
and Papa glowed under it in the context of "Home Nook."
Uncle Bob had a continuing affair with everything and everybody, but most of all with Christ. The forbidden words
at home—*Christ, God*—in New Hampshire, these words laced
the hours. The Bible, the forbidden book in the Marxist
household of Mama and Papa, was quoted constantly in New
Hampshire. Uncle Bob sang out the Scriptures to us like a
constant benediction. Mama and Papa listened because they
loved him, and in the evenings, when the children were put
to bed in little log cabins Uncle Bob had built down at the
lake, they would go back up the hill and talk way into the
night about the other things, history, war, local politics. The
next morning, Papa would give Uncle Bob a medical "going
over." They would discuss the dreadful progress of the crip-
pling case of gout that was invaliding him to chair and bed,
with no income coming in, no future, except the exercising
of a spirit that wouldn't give in. Those were the dark passages of the concerto, at which time Mama would take us
out for long walks in the blueberried hills—where it was a
different Mama, more relaxed, concerned, her face quiet,

lovely; her New Hampshire face, because of Bob. She even retained it in the car trip going home, when she would hold me in her lap, because I was the smaller, and sing me to sleep with e-lu-lu-lu-lu's as Papa drove back down Route One toward home in the blackness of a Sunday night. And as she sang, I would fall off, thinking how different it all was when we were in New Hampshire, sleeping in one cabin all together down by the lake, the whole family breathing in one room, waking in the same room, clothes scattered together, bathing before breakfast in the lake with common screams of delight. As her e-lu-lu's became fainter, I thought about how I had played the old pump organ the night before at "Home Nook" because Uncle Bob asked me to, how I played wild, crazy things, trying to please him with something that sounded like hymns. Yet the notes always came out Hebrew melodies with Spanish underpinnings, strange sounds indeed on a Yankee organ.

In some early year and on some morning of those weekends, sitting on the grass in front of the tiger lilies with Uncle Bob in his outside chair, he drew me close to him, opened a book to its last empty page, and drew a circle.

"Look, Doris, what I've made—the world! Now," he said, placing a dot on the circumference of the circle, "do you know what that is, that dot?"

I shook my head no.

"That's Doris."

We both sat looking at the circle and the dot.

"What would happen if I took that dot away from the circle?" he asked.

"There would be . . . a space," I answered tentatively.

"Splendid," he said. "The circle would be broken. The *circumference* of the world would be incomplete without you, darling. That's how important we all are. Never forget that. You are *indispensable* to the circle while you are on it." (He had just taught me two huge words.)

"And," he continued, "it is very comforting to me to know that . . ."—he pointed to the dot—"that you are there, completing my circle."

The orange of the tiger lilies blinded my eyes. It took me years to understand he was teaching me love and worth of self, that he knew I needed it, was not getting enough of it.

As I grew, he continued to write me letters, postcards, in his almost illegible handwriting, because of the gout. Through high school, college, and after I was married, the little scrawls of encouragement arrived.

On knowing I was lonely and lost, my first year away at school:

> . . . this is just a word to let you know where you stand with me, little comrade, and how much you mean to me. I sat by our lovely fire last night, and watched old, shapeless boughs, picked up around the yard, as they were transformed into colorful beams of flashing light—alive and creative, and I thought of you and created with you!

On a little postcard, received somewhere in the midst of my adolescence:

> . . . Doris, very precious, you are much in my thoughts and we are children together. How Time and Space do recede into their real place—as merely arbitrary signposts for those who need them—in the face of the great timeless and spaceless flow of awakened consciousness. And, isn't it great to be overcurious, spiritual explorers, and have someone like Doris as companion, to share the thrill of the new vistas, and the glimpse of far-off peaks still to conquer? I appreciate you keenly. Uncle Bob.

On my first trip to California, a New Englander crossing the Hudson River:

> . . . and long-distance journeys give vent for the feelings of bashful folks like me! It releases lots of Freudian re-

pressions, dynamites the logjams that prevent the free, creative flow to the bosom of Mother Ocean, and permits a climb into the fourth and fifth dimensions, where prose never leaves poetry, and vocabulary never lags. Amen. All of which means that I love you dearly—a love that has grown from the roots and included 30 years' experience with your tribe—a father with a depth of sentiment and loyalty that few people realize; and a mother who gave me the richest of friendships; and a big sister whom I have followed with the greatest interest and enthusiasm; and my shy, little pal, Doris, who at an early age seemed to be unduly conscious of being a second sister, who blossomed into a poetic, finely imaginative spirit, with splendid, if at times, rather mercurial moods. I am frankly and unashamedly in love with that Doris, and you can tell her—when you see her. Count me very close. Amen.
Uncle Bob

On the receiving of a present of lamps from my husband and me, after another admirer of Uncle Bob and Aunt June, Karl Lipsky, had arranged for electrification of the 175-year-old "Home Nook":

. . . all of which is just long-handed for saying, it was a splendid impulse to which you yielded (the sending of lamps), and it did cause celebration in the cardiac region. Dear old "Home Nook" will have to be introduced to itself when the lights are turned on, after 175 years of whale oil and kerosene! Wouldn't it be rich if a pageant could be held on the lawn, and each of the eight generations of children could appear in their own getup, and then, as a grand finale, have the coach light turned on the tiger lilies, and Doris, winding up on the little old organ with a Wagnerian "March of the Valkyries"? Amen . . .

A week after my marriage:

. . . this is just a word, dear, to send our blessing and

hopes for a rich experience. Remember, and tell your husband that your Uncle Bob says—marriage is a glorified friendship! I hope Jules realizes what a treasure he has annexed, and that he has, above all—UNDERSTANDING! Aunt June says "Amen." Love, eternally, dear. Uncle Bob.

Unabashed, romantic, supportive, wise. Uncle Bob Bakeman, long deceased, had been writing me love letters my whole life, and I never knew it. I received them, wherever I happened to be, reading them perfunctorily and putting them away, unfelt. But I never did throw them away. Some part of me saved them for future reference when *that* part knew I would be able to understand his spiritual spelunking and laying on of hands, his dogged insistence upon love in an insane world. He kept plucking me out of my vase, cutting off the "faultering" stem with words of love, and putting me back in the water of the world, in hope I would catch hold and rejoice.

Of course there was another side to this strange, vital man. I wish he were here to debate that other side with me, now that I am as old as my mother was when I sat at his feet in the grass amidst the tiger lilies of earliest days. He seemed so ancient then, but he was simply crippled, in the prime of life, struggling to remain alive as long and as richly as he could.

I would ask him . . . what about all that talk about "my Jewish friends, how I love them! I love them more than all—my Hebrews! I clasp my hands in yours. You are originators, the parents of Christ. I stretch my arms out to you, Harry and Mary. You keep me alive. Together we try to love as Man should love. There is nothing greater, nothing. If only all Gentiles and Hebrews could sit on the grass of 'Home-Nook.' What a glorious place it would be, the world in torment, lying down amidst the hills of New Hampshire." He ranted and raved and quieted himself, proselytizing his

Jewish radical intellectual friends coming up with their baskets of food.

What was the harm in his wanting to embrace us into the arms of Jesus? There was nothing wrong with Jesus, only with the world. Yet, was his delight with the friendship of Jews the inch-beneath-the-skin anti-Semitism of all Gentiles? Why did he never let us forget we were Jews and, therefore, special to him? I wish he were here to debate me and it, to shout me down that I do him an injustice. For he was the first one who taught me rhapsody, fervor, possession.

> The way he greeted us, or said good-bye to us—standing on the grass, legs spread wide, his feet bulging through his sneakers, cut open to make room for the ghastly gout-deformity, his arms raised high in the air, his plundered-by-disease-fingers pointed toward the sky—in praise of Being.

Ménage à Trois

DAMN it, if the Smiths are not getting ready to have another family. The love making, devotion, tender gestures are starting again. Or are they? They start and they stop. One day Pa is around. The next day he isn't.

> Will Spring bring courage with it? 'Lite on us . . . a breathless bird, with feathers sparkling in the sun? Will Spring remember us, glass and steel, unblemished by the shadow of a tree? How *will* we know it's Spring this year? A suburbanite will tell us, "The forsythia is out!" He might even bring us some. We will set the gangling branches in a marvelous blue bowl, underneath a mobile. They will press their yellow leaves against a window and whimper, like a child with homesickness.

One morning I look out, and there is Pa Smith with a blond, the only blond pigeon I've seen in all my months of pigeon watching. Mazie, the blond bombshell, had arrived in the corridor. It was far from coincidental that it was Spring. What a magnificent creature she is, young, tough, her feathers, indeed, sparkling in the sun. Where had she wintered, Florida? She goes right to the Smith ledge and begins to pace back and forth as though she is waiting for someone, as though she has a perfect right. Soon, she's joined by Pa, and he's all agog, pecking at her gently and making deep mating sounds. The ledge is exploding with spring light. Ma Smith is hunched nearby, in shadow, just watching all this carrying on.

My God, what's going on! Pa and Mazie are making love. Mazie is a caution. She has form, chic, sex appeal. The two spend hours flying in and out of the corridor, Mazie, teasing, hopping from ledge to ledge, Pa in hot pursuit, emitting sounds of delight. I don't believe Pa's taken a mistress, but he has. And Mazie is it!

Ma Smith just sits over on the parent ledge in bad shape. Her feathers seem to have lost their oil, and she looks plumb wore out, ruffled and scraggly. Pa looks great. Mazie doesn't know "from nothing." She is having a great time.

Mind boggling. Whenever I think I'm done with pigeon watching, something happens and glues me to the window. I cannot miss this new happening, because I don't believe my perception.

This situation went on for two days. Ma looked worse and worse. She was not even flying out to forage for food. Finally, on the third day, she couldn't stand it any longer, and what I thought she was going to do, she did. She challenged Mazie to a fight, on her own nursery ledge, where Plucky and Brownie and Ariel were born, the former grew, the latter died.

Ma challenged Mazie three times. It went on all day and was all-out war. Ma retreated to her ledge to recover after each battle, and she lost every one of them. The blond was younger and tougher and in better fighting shape. She obviously hadn't gone through a long winter of childbirth, Plucky, Brownie, snow, rain, hail, then Ariel and Ariel's death, like Ma had. All of that was enough to take the heart out of anyone, but Ma fought for her mate three times, and oh, did she fight, with Pa standing on the sidelines, just looking. The winner takes all. Him. I tried to remember that I was watching pigeons, and I tried not to hate Pa. Ma and Mazie were locked in ferocity, their wings almost tearing, as they pushed one another against the iron grillwork. But it was all too much for Ma. After her third challenge, late in the afternoon, she had to acknowledge her defeat. She repaired to the parent ledge and took up her loneliness there. It broke my heart to look at her trying to peck her injured feathers down while Pa joined Mazie on the nursery ledge and they cooed under her very eyes and beak. This was the coup de grace after the long, cold winter.

It was just as awesome as the best movie fight, just as frightening and disgusting. Mazie was an unbelievable type, a roller-skating-derby dame. Just for kicks, let's see the old lady fight and fall on her ass.

Then I noticed something weird as the days went by. A pattern was taking place. Mazie would disappear at night, after spending the day cooing with Pa, and he would join Ma on their parent ledge, snuggling tight to her, like in the old days. Pa was spending his days with the "new one" and his nights with his old mate. This went on for a week or so, but Ma continued to look terrible. The weather got bad, too, and her feathers never unruffled. On one of those particularly bad rainy spring days, I put food out for them and was able to get a close look at both as they flew over to feed. Pa looked sleek, although it was raining cats and dogs. But Ma had lost her ability to puff out and seemed to have lost all the oil in her feathers that would protect her from the cold and wet.

Now, had Pa looked for someone new because Ma was getting played out and he was doing a direct pigeon thing—

survival at any cost? Or had Mazie come along and "it" happened, and made Ma sick unto death? Was Ma Madame Butterfly or Carmen? I know if my husband left me, I'd lose my ability to puff out! There wouldn't be an air pump on earth that could inflate my spirit. The only antidote would be a lover, and they don't come so easy. Not good ones. And what lover worth his salt would want a bird who had lost her oil?

The situation was too loaded. Something had to give, and it did. Neither of the ménage à trois were around much. Ma still slept on the old parent ledge, and Pa was there occasionally. There seemed to be a slow disconnection, a casual passing, much as what happens with friends who have outgrown each other. You go to the old haunts, make a few attempts at dinner. You call a few times by telephone and, then, almost by mutual consent, you part, and a love or a friendship outgrown is over. So the Smiths did with me and our corridor after an almost six-month intense sojourn in their three-room apartment between the buildings on Eighty-third Street. They left me behind, and I missed them. I found myself turning my back on the west-facing windows so as not to feel the loss too much.

🍁

In the spring of 1975, as I recollect the passing of my Smiths, the long Asian war has come to an end (they tell us). At least the insanity of an American presence in Vietnam has come to an end. The American military, of which many of us are so ashamed, has tucked its expensive playthings under its arm and tried to saunter down the block toward home. But the bravado of the bully didn't work. The slobbery overgrown tough started to run, trip, dropping guns, tanks, helicopters on the way. Gold trickled from his pockets, lesser members of his gang picking it up and also running in all directions. It was a sorry sight as the runts of the block stood watching the leave-taking.

"Help, Ma!" the bully was crying, tears streaming from his eyes. "They're trying to beat me up. That's why I hit them."

"They were trying to beat you up?" his mother said in disbelief, as she stood on her doorstep watching her son's return.

"No one can beat you up, You're too strong, rich and handsome. You must have done something naughty."

"What's going on?" the bully's father asked, as he, too, came to the front door.

"Nothing, Father. I was trying to be the first and the best like you taught me, and they wouldn't let me," said the bully.

"Well, what do *they* know," said the father. "They're not very important."

"I'm not so sure, Father. They won!"

The bully was crying anew. "They called me terrible names. Fascist. Pig. Imperialist. Why, they made my own name seem like a swear word. 'Go home, Yankee!' they yelled at me. You told me guns were the best things to fight with. How come I didn't win? How come?"

Carrying Off
the Palm

PROMPTLY at seven in the evening, Papa's office hours began. When my sister and I were old enough to be responsible, we were allowed to run down the stairwell with the stained-glass window and open the door for the patients. Then we'd run upstairs and announce: "It's the man with the head! The man with the foot! The man with the heart! It's the woman with the bandage, the person with the ear! The little girl with the finger is here with her mother! It's the Polack, the Russian, the Greek, the Turk!"

The report had to be clear and no less importantly said than what was expected from The Messenger of a Greek Drama.

Anything could happen "downstairs," because those were the days of the true general practitioner. Papa did small operations, gave Freudian-oriented sessions to the disturbed. They were lucky he was an early student of psychoanalysis. Other doctors would have sent them to Danvers State Hospital, the red-brick looney bin on the hill. Papa was totally entwined in the mental and physical states of his patients. He worried constantly about both states. He studied medicine way into the night, after the office hours were over.

At times, when very serious things were taking place "downstairs," with the man with the head or with the heart, Mama would put on a clean white apron and disappear into his office. She was helping out as the nurse she had trained to be. Occasionally, the hush in the house was frightening, and a moan or a scream would pierce the upstairs. After it was over, Mama and Papa would talk in whispers. I know now that he performed abortions on many women and girls who needed them, for economic, psychic, or whatever reasons. Many scandals of the town ended in Papa's wastebasket. He was trusted.

One of Papa's more important patients was Mama. She suffered terribly from hay fever and allergies and had to be injected the year round with serum to lessen the blow of summer pollens. She would be overcome with such seizures of sneezing she would have to be led, gasping, to her room, the shades pulled down. There she would remain, while Papa had a very worried look and muttered "Jesus Christ" under his breath. There were other injections. The memory of them lies too deeply in my unconscious for me ever to pull them out, but Elizabeth, the older, remembers. Yes, there were other injections. Mama suffered from what the nineteenth century called "hysteria." When the tensions of a delicate nervous system took over, she would become unmanageable, cry, scream, crawl under her bed, with Papa running after her, a hypodermic needle in his hand. He would coax her out, inject her, and all would go quiet. The door to their bedroom would be closed for hours.

"Mama's resting."

Then she would emerge, faltering, eyes red from weeping, leaden with guilt, her face turned so inward she literally couldn't stand looking at me. I was sure it had to do with me, again, some naughty thing I had done that had thrown her into panic and made her die, temporarily. But it wasn't me alone that got under Mama's skin to make her sneeze and retch and cry out. She and her husband did their tricks on high-tension wires. They were constantly in debt. They harangued each other about bills and mortgages. Elizabeth and I were forever in private schools of dance and music. The punishment of being radicals in a conservative atmosphere must have been immense. She was a vain, proud, jealous woman who demanded perfection from herself and others. Money, money, money! The money they scorned as capitalistic sin, the lack of it, flayed them raw. For they both had an image to uphold, one of dignity, calm, well-being in the middle and upper class of a small town that only sensed but didn't know the extent of their inner radical life.

So it wasn't entirely my fault, not quite.

One of the things I did that made her angry was that I was a watcher, a mooner. I didn't care about achieving. I hung around and sniffed where I wasn't supposed to. I was a difficult child to push into a corner. I yelled and screamed, "No!" I dared her to give me love, and she dared me to ask for it. I had her spirit and was her child. I was a walking embodiment of the dark side of her, whereas Elizabeth was the light, an externalization of all that Mama dreamed and wanted to be, an artist, a dancer, in the hot white lights of center stage.

And I did nothing but grow, play jacks, skip rope, ride bicycles, moon, watch, improvise undisciplined melodies on the piano and until high school, curiously enough, bring home superior marks without trying. It was the without trying that drove Mama wild. I was directionless, and my languid body took up space in the armchairs when I should have been "doing something."

One sunny Sunday afternoon, with the usual symphony playing on the radio and me sitting in an armchair, half of me listening, the other half bemoaning my boredom and worthlessness, Mama looked at me in exasperation and exploded: "Stop sitting there! Do something! Go out into the

sun! If I hear you say once more you're bored, I'll scream!"
And she began to scream: "WHY DON'T YOU GO INTO
YOUR ROOM AND WRITE A POEM!"

"Leave her alone," Papa said quietly.

Write a poem? It was the furthest thing from my mind.
Write a poem? What embarrassment! She might as well have
told me to go fuck myself, which I knew as little about as
writing a poem. I was twelve. Masturbation, yes. Fucking,
no. Anyway, we were all here from the head of Zeus, weren't
we?

As for masturbation, I was quite certain I was the only
one in Peabody, Massachusetts, who practiced it, me and
the benighted, clinical cases of excess documented in the
volumes of Havelock Ellis's *Studies in the Psychology of Sex*
that Papa had tucked away in the glass bookcase in the sitting room. The Jung and Freud and *Peculiarities of Behavior*
by Wilhelm Stekel I didn't devour. They were grown-up
reading. The short, explicit case histories of Ellis were more
accessible essays of pornography for children to digest and
fall-down-dead-by. I was sure, if I had been alive when he
wrote them, I, too, would have been chronicled in Dr. Ellis's
tomes of sexual madness and aberration.

No one had ever breathed a word to me of the secrets
of the human body, even though one parent was a nurse and
the other a doctor. And yet to express oneself sensually
through poetry, dance, and music was not only condoned
but demanded.

I had a feeling, when Mama saw my languorous, bloom-
ing adolescence sitting in a chair doing nothing (and since
I invested her with the power of mind reading) that it
terrified her I would defile myself unless I was made to
"do something constructive."

I learned very early that sensuality was de rigueur, sexuality verboten. And yet, what were *The Well of Loneliness*
by Radclyffe Hall and all the privately and publicly pub-

lished editions of flaming literature of the twenties and thirties doing in Mama's bookcase, while she held to a priggish double standard? The schizophrenia of gentility was in practice in her sitting room and parlor while the bookcases exploded with forbidden words. When I was twelve, the words *pudendum, vagina, penis, clitoris* could start me shaking for hours. They were obviously the magic words of the devil, and Dr. Havelock Ellis, the devil's disciple. I couldn't find them anywhere else but in that book of evil.

The spirit? Yes. The body, its torments and delights? No.

The deep mystification of home was that Mama and Papa were straddling two centuries, as Enlightened Intellectuals of the nineteenth, and frightened students of the twentieth. It was all in their library, the new thoughts, the exposés, but only to be studied, not practiced. The peculiar thing was that they condoned birth control, free love for others, uncommon dress, breakaway behavior. Mama was an Isadora Duncan groupie, yet she informed Elizabeth she'd better be careful "down there" when she bathed, because it was "like glass." Me, she didn't tell anything. I grew like Topsy. I bled for the first time like an animal in the forest, without ritual or sacred rites. The twentieth-century personal freedoms from darkness were for others.

At home, it was still Tolstoian, Rousseauian delicacy—probe the torture and passions of the body discreetly, but the transcendence of the spirit was all and in spite of the body. James Joyce, Henry Miller, D. H. Lawrence were to be read but only as textbooks.

At twelve, I had it figured out. Up! with Marxism (that made my parents pariahs and scared the world more than sex). But sex, which everyone else seemed involved with, that was down! It was all very strange.

At twelve, I also knew something else was missing. I knew it had something to do with love—the kind that had reference to touching, fondling. But no one gave me a single intimation of the adolescent climacteric ahead of me. They must have been words reserved only for the wild, lost ones in the chronicles of Havelock Ellis.

My parents did have a deep love they expressed openly, besides their love for the world and its masses. Their deepest love was for the anchoritic state of one who decided he must describe, honor, invent and prophesy the beauty and preciousness of life—the artist.

There was no question about it. In the house in which I grew up, to be an artist was the ultima Thule.

Ergo, if I am an artist, I will be loved. Is not the artist the darling sport, the successful artist, that is. Although, in my family's defense, they drew to themselves all manner of artist, successful or not.

Mama ran a salon, an underground railway for artists going north to Gloucester and Rockport, Maine and Canada. Some of them needed rest and stayed many weeks. In the summertime, they came and went with their drawing boards and manuscripts, sleeping in the attic, with its two unfinished bedrooms and broken-down bedsteads, trunks and neglected toys, discarded flower pots and chipped objets d'art —a magic place of privacy. It was a kind of heaven for the young and not so young visitors, with their pale city skins and restless eyes. Their coming filled a void for isolated Mama and Papa in their small town. They brought with them the pulse of Boston, New York, and Paris, ate Mama's healthy menu, and talked late into the night about the world outside. They painted the small-town streets, the rocky coast of Marblehead, and read their poems and novels aloud to a hushed parlor of invited guests.

Very often, at the end of such a holy gathering, Elizabeth would be asked to dance barefoot on the Oriental rug in the parlor and I would be coaxed to go to the piano and "improvise something." From as early an age as I can remember, to create and give the gift was the most awesome and holy thing to do. That *giving* commanded total attention, brought tears to the eyes and sighs in the bosom. Evidently to be artistic was to elevate oneself a foot off the ground and attempt to fly. That's the way it felt when someone said: "Turn some lights off. Elizabeth is going to dance, and Doris will play."

"Ah," the guests would sigh, invitationally, and the parlor became a darkened theater, and we would show what we had learned, when the artists were visiting on summer nights. We were artists, too.

I've always been a bad memorizer. I could never remember my Bach or Mozart or Chopin or Satie or Bartok. So I would improvise little melodies of Oriental configuration. I wonder how much the Oriental rug had to do with it! The melodies would start like muezzin calls, grow into Hebraic plaints, and turn into loud Russian Jewish songs with Spanish rhythms underneath. Mama and Papa seemed pleased, but I never thought of myself as an embryonic musician. I hated to practice. But improvising? That was another matter. It was a way I could talk without talking; feel without exposure; express my love and receive it. (The room was full of Puritans.)

> Music is kinetic. It moves through space and leaves behind it an internal structure. Music is invisible architecture. It falls, note by note, like pearls on an alabaster floor newly laid. It rises, note by note, and, presto! with the speed of the unconscious . . . suddenly! a ladder here, a door there, a cantilevered terrace; trees, turns in a road, covered with fog rising. It makes skies, sunsets; ponders about fathers in love with daughters, dead mothers, dreamed of new love, tears, loss, joy. Music makes feeling palpable. Music is sneaky. You

see nothing, yet all is revealed. It is un-
matched in magic. It swirls the soul around
astringently, then disappears in thin air. Coming from a house of austerity, music was the
answer, the correct vehicle for secrets.

❧

Mama didn't approve of my improvising. She felt it was
too loose, too undisciplined. I'm told it had to be explained
to her that it was, on the contrary, a special gift and not to
be discouraged, even if it deflected energy from my prescribed studies of the "classics." I didn't know it, but I was
improvising "modern," making up my own chordal clusters
and sounds. By the time I was thirteen, I was accompanying
dance classes at the modern dance studio of Hans Wiener,
Boston's disciple of Mary Wigman, the German mother of
modern dance. I remember it as being an honor bestowed
on me, a heady experience, sitting at the grand piano, in
control of the sound and emotional tone of the shiny wooden
floor, the exercise barres, the dancers' ritual of exercise, sitting; exercise, standing. And then, ecstasy! Movements were
strung together to propel the dancers "across the floor" and
into space—and my fingers would fly with melodies and
rhythms, translating movement into sound. It was like being
on a roller coaster. It was like flying, improvising for modern
dance. A perfect outlet for an unruly, undisciplined, over-
emotional adolescent, filled with anger and unused love. And
it was obvious I had a gift of some kind, although a shady,
mystifying one, changeable as the weather, unfathomable as
the unconscious, from which it came and from which it received its energy. Improvising was talking through my
fingers on an ebony grand piano. It was driving a Rolls-
Royce with a special gear that made it airborne, while below

it danced the dancers, whirling, jumping, trying to catch the sound with their bodies.

I think I remember Mama sitting in a visitor's chair, observing. There was a slight smile on her lips, in spite of her deep disapproval of anything that lacked discipline. What she didn't know was that improvising for a dance class exacted great discipline. Each group of movements or exercises demanded a musical attitude. They dictated the length and kind of melody, the color of the chords and rhythms. They were riddles to be solved in given spaces of time. There were strict rules of the game to be observed. If the music was wrong, the timbre incorrect, the dance movements would turn to dross. If the music was right, the movements became noble ritual. It made one feel like a sorcerer incanting with the big, black ebony piano.

It was in those years between thirteen and fifteen that the instrument, the piano, became an extension of myself, an indispensable limb of my body. It is death to be in a house without one. And a closed piano is like a coffin.

❧

I have tried, many times, to recall those years between thirteen and fifteen. They were important and pivotal. I press and drive through past Time, trying to recollect, not with a *now* consciousness, but with my *then* consciousness. I end up always in a cul-de-sac, filled with misty angst and cancerous anger. Taste, smell, touch, objects—I can recall nothing of them. Only rebellion against the air of Mama and Papa's house. Unable to arouse anything in them but their rage. I was constantly in a state of mind of "What in hell are they up to? Do they read me? Do they 'see' me?" I can't recall ever looking at them. It was too fearful a sight. There was a dark, ominous thing to life they were keeping from me. Why else the heavy air? I felt I was marking time. Someday, soon, I'd fly away to college . . . if my grades were good enough.

As in kindergarten (with the hiatus of grammar school excellence) so in high school, there was always something wrong with my performance. Pleasing was not possible. If it was a B— in Algebra, then it should have been a B. They had stopped asking for A's. I practiced the piano but had to be forced to. That practice was to begin at four each afternoon. If I arrived five minutes late, I was slapped. But I still managed to be late. I lied. I was sloppy. I sweated, and it revolted Mama. She stood behind me as I played and smelled me and made me change my outdoor blouse. I met her anger with my own. When I didn't, I retired into depression and silence, the most effective weapon. Elizabeth was long gone, away at college. It was just them and me, a duel to the death. There was a silence between Mama and me that was like a cancer. The house, to me, was like death. There was no relief. Out of desperation, I would throw a bolt of anger in the air and be surprised no one died. Then I would turn it inward to myself, and it felt like death. I would spend hours looking in the mirror and hear it say, "Your eyes have secrets in them." And I would turn away. It was a face I didn't recognize. I threw the days away like cast-off ribbons from a birthday gift. Outside was a strange world of others. It didn't mean freedom to be out there. It meant lying about where I had been, why I was late, grasping those few hours with friends, free of guilt and duty. There was something wrong with me. I failed, was failing, would fail. Finally, the inevitable happened. I brought home the first C in Math either parent had ever seen. (Elizabeth graduated valedictorian of her senior high school class.)

Then came the D's and F's. I was guilty of first-degree murder. I was willfully lazy.

"Doris is not living up to her potential," said the notes from the principal.

Bang went the jail door of my cell. They weren't going to execute me. I would just have to remain forever in my own prison of worthlessness. And my jailer beat me.

I was getting too old to be hit on my "bottom," as Mama called it. So her anger lashed out on my face. There is nothing more mortifying and degrading than to be slapped in one's face. She did it constantly, swung at me sunny days and dark days. There was something wrong with Mama, I was sure of that. Was it her hay fever? But what was wrong with her in the winter? Her fatigue, her cooking dinner, then having to lie down from the exertion. It must be me. She was fine if they were going out to a political meeting in Boston, or their symphony concerts, or when the artists arrived from New York, or when she herself went to New York to visit Elizabeth who was, by then, at Barnard College.

No, it must be me, my fourteen-year-old mind told me. *I* was her illness, me and my inability to perform. *I was not bringing home the palm.* She couldn't use me to stretch beyond her own desires. I was hardly a modus operandi for her immortality. I was low normal, except for that crazy improvising I did on the piano.

My sister and I were brought up as only children. Nothing was ever done to make us friends. Elizabeth says she used to sing me to sleep when we shared a bedroom for a brief time. I don't remember. We were enemy ducalities, sworn to separateness, part of the greater nation, yet dedicated only to our own survival. We never shared the secrets of children, girls, young women. We lived together in such isolation it was only years later we learned we both hated cocoa for breakfast, both cooked it separately in separate pots before we went off to school, and both threw it down the sink, leaving the signs of having made it for Mama to see. If we had been friends, we could have cooked only one pot. At five, Elizabeth was performing in dance recitals. At eight or nine, she was choreographing dances. At fifteen, she was dancing solos on the stage of the Boston Symphony, one of Mama's temples, accompanied by the orchestra itself. At sixteen, she was a student at Radcliffe and at eighteen had transferred to Barnard so that she could study with Martha Graham and become a member of her dance company, which she did. Elizabeth was (and still is) a beautiful dancer and one of the lucky ones to perform and be a part of the creation of some of Graham's early masterpieces.

Elizabeth's life entwined with Martha Graham's was like going from the frying pan into the white heat of a crucible over intense laboratory flame. Mama and Martha resembled each other physically, to an astonishing degree. Mama's demand for excellence and quality, her rigidity and dedication to a doctrine (Mama's to communism, Martha's to her own vocabulary of movement and vision of theater, the most original in the twentieth century) was re-experienced by my sister when she flew into the orbit of Martha Graham's genius.

Strangely enough I, too, years later, was lucky enough to taste the punitive yet breathtaking beauty of that orbit. While attending the Juilliard School of Music, I ended up improvising for Martha's advanced class—the one she taught herself. It was at the same time, years before, that Mama had demanded I practice! From four o'clock to five-thirty, almost every day, I played in a room that seemed supported by Doric columns and that emanated the deep shadow and bright light of a Greek sky. I had eurekas imposed upon me I never counted on—what it meant to want to be an artist; the weight of that awareness; how difficult it was to become an artist and be born again, a child of the gods. I trembled with fear, played the piano, and learned more about the search for quality, form, line, song, dedication, ritual and the disciplines

—without which those in search of the divine would fail—than from any book, poem, or living artist. Perhaps Picasso could have equaled her presence; maybe Horowitz, through his fingers on his ebony piano, or Casals, with his cello between his knees.

But all of that was many years later than the time to which I have my ear. I had no idea I was to meet elements of Mama again in that New York studio on Fifth Avenue and Twelfth Street, in the old Macmillan Building.

I also had no idea when I was fourteen that Mama and I would have less than a year to live together.

Requiem

REMEMBERING . . . can be like swimming in shark-infested waters. You dive off
a rocky cliff into water that looks cool and in-
viting. There is a momentary exhilaration
until you sense shadows swimming beneath
you. The shock of shark fins, flags waving in
a dance of death, makes you wonder what
on earth prodded you to want to dive. You
pray you'll reach the rocky cliff again, that
your muscles and breath will become Olym-
pian caliber and you will make the safety of
the jagged shore; scratch your way to a place
from which you will not fall; turn and sit,
your skin wet with water beads, your brain
overheated. Wet and on fire you look down
at the Past from the safe perch of the Present
and contemplate the danger with impunity.

One day in the December of my fifteenth year, Mama,
unbeknownst to me, because we never talked of personal
things, consulted with Papa and later a Boston surgeon.
She then decided to have her appendix removed because

it bothered her. The occasional attacks of pain it gave her must have frightened her, although they weren't acute, and the thing of having something that wasn't functioning properly annoyed her sense of tidiness.

"Why let it kick up later, Harry," she said to Papa. "It worries me, so I'll take care of it."

"It's not an emergency. I don't believe in operating just like that."

"No, I've made up my mind. I'm going to do it."

"All right, all right, but I don't agree."

She said to a friend: "I'll look upon it as a kind of holiday. Take lots of books I haven't had the time to read. I'll lie in bed, be waited on, and luxuriate."

A week before she was to go into the hospital, she took me into Boston on a shopping spree, to buy a new bathrobe for herself for her recuperation. Thriftily, it would be chosen to fit me too, because I happened to need a new robe and would inherit it when she came home. The trip was one of our usual silent journeys, where I developed stomach pains, went into deep gloom, and had to sit down in every store, while Mama ran about like a girl. I felt so guilty sitting, and for reasons I didn't know, my heart was breaking as it always did when we were together. In retrospect, it was the symptom of a spurned lover. She found what she wanted, while I stared at a pearl-gray rugged floor and felt the air had been sucked out of the store. She made me try it on while I thought my gut would burst, my appendix, not hers. Thank God the shopping was over. We were on our way home in a bus from Boston. I had the window seat and went into a trance of telephone poles. I felt her looking at me from time to time, but we said nothing to each other. Just as we came to the outskirts of Peabody, a half hour later, we passed a cemetery. I noticed gravediggers leaning on their shovels, resting, and a newly dug grave ringed with hills of earth. I turned to Mama. She had seen it too.

Her blue eyes fixed on mine, and in a voice she had never used with me, an equal's voice, and with what I remember, and have tried not to remember, a face contorted with hatred and sadness, she said, "I bet you think that's for me."

"Oh, no, Mama! How could you say that!" And I hadn't lied.

There it was, finally out in the open in my fifteenth year. It hit me like a curse and felt like the stigmata of the devil. She had dumped her deepest fear on me and also legitimatized our incompatability. I went into mourning and forgot about it. I turned my face away from her, and we arrived home.

The next morning, Papa drove her into Boston for the operation while I was at school. He came home at night. The next day was the same; he left in the morning and came home in the evening. I felt free, went to school, and didn't practice the piano at four o'clock.

"How's Mama?"

"Mama's fine."

The third day, Elizabeth arrived from New York and was taken to see her. That evening I learned Mama's brother had come to Boston and was visiting Mama in the hospital. Why all the family? Mama was in the hospital reading books and wearing her new bathrobe. The rest is remembered like swimming in shark-infested waters. The evening of the fourth day, Uncles and Aunts in Peabody arrived at the house and just sat in the parlor. No one told me anything. I had been alone for four days, going to school, bicycling, visiting with friends. Great-Uncle Harris, sitting in the parlor, suddenly began to cry. He looked at me and moaned, "Mary, Mary, Mary." My heart stopped, and I ran to my room. Then someone drove me to Boston. I don't remember who. Suddenly life was peopled and unrestrained, helping hands, silent hands, everywhere. What in hell was going on? Elizabeth met me in the corridor outside a room.

She took me by the hand and led me in. There was Papa, gray from exhaustion. He looked like a stranger. And there was Mama, under an oxygen tent—no one had prepared me —pale, her hair loose, her mouth slightly open in distress. The shock of tears came so fast I thought I would faint. Mama tried to smile at me, and she nodded her head. She, too, seemed like a stranger. They were all strangers. Elizabeth, Mama, Papa. Something was very wrong. Almost as an afterthought I had been led into this room. They were not strangers. I was the stranger.

Elizabeth said, "She wanted to see you."

I saw a beautiful white hand extend from the opening of the oxygen tent.

"She wants you to kiss her hand."

I bent down, as though in the presence of a queen, blinded by a circle of gold, and I kissed her left hand. I can't remember whether I kissed her wedding ring or her skin. That moment has escaped me forever. Papa began to sob, and I was led out of the room.

Someone drove us home, Elizabeth and me. The next morning, I went to school as usual, made my own cocoa, as usual, and threw it down the sink, as usual.

At ten o'clock, the principal called me to his office. There was Elizabeth. My sister led me out without a word. On the steps of the school. I noticed it had started to snow and felt the principal looking at us from his window. As we stood in the winter air, Elizabeth put her arm around me and said, "Mama died early this morning." We both cried as we walked down the steps, and I remembered seeing tears in the principal's eyes. Why did it take so long? I sobbed, then went quiet, and we went home to a house that was an emptied ocean.

The whole town knew before I did. It was my French teacher, a friend of Mama's, who insisted I be taken home, that it was indecent for me to have gone to school in the

first place. But how was I to know? No one had told me
Mama died. They were probably in shock and busy with
grown-up arrangements. How to bury her? What place of
worship? For an atheist. It was all so swift and unexpected.
I simply got up, had breakfast, went to school, and with
the optimism of the young, sensed Mama was very sick,
but that all would be well. Papa would see to that.

Sometime that day, Mama was brought home, and she
was in the parlor in a coffin. I was in my room and never
left it. I developed a high fever and my French teacher sat
with me.

"Don't you want to say good-bye to your mother?"

"No, no, no. . . ."

The house was swarming with people, but I heard
Papa crying. I wouldn't leave my room. I wanted him to
come to me, but he didn't. I heard them say how beautiful
she looked with her hair down to her waist, that Papa was
sitting beside her, stroking it. I heard them all leave, and
only then, in the company of a boy cousin my own age, did
I stand in the bay windows of the parlor and watch a hearse
drive away from the house, with Mama's friends and hundreds of townspeople walking behind it, hidden under black
umbrellas, up the hill to the small Orthodox Jewish cemetery
at the end of our street, in a bad snowstorm. They had all
decided to walk, not ride, in her honor. She was that loved.

I wrote my first poem that winter, and it was for Mama,
about her lying there under the wet snow on Christmas
Day. How did she feel? Did she know I missed her? Would
forever miss her because we had not used the Time.

And when a famous Yiddish poet, Moshe Nadir, came
from New York to commiserate with Papa over the loss of
Mary, their Mary, Elizabeth's and my Mary, I was asked to
read aloud what I had written. The poet cried and said it
was a poem. I excused myself and went to bed.

I will always have a requiem ad infinitum

singing in my head for her. My ears hear *only* her meaning now, for I've long forgotten the sound of her voice. But sometimes I still walk in the snow that fell when she was buried, and think. . . . Oh, bastard day, embroidered with black umbrellas! How like a proud cat you brought me a dead mother and laid her at my feet.

❧

After Mama's death, Papa was wild, inconsolable. He shrank into himself and wizened. Somehow he maintained his medical practice on the outside and collapsed the moment he was inside. The house was a tomb in which she had been buried alive. Her smell was everywhere.

I was part of the inside. He was angry, aghast at what she had done to him, terrified of the responsibility she had left him—a female adolescent, who was beginning to resemble her. The two of us were locked up in grief and a house quivering with memories. We never spoke. His only words to me were uttered in high decibels. I didn't care. I had closed off too, picked up my fourteen-year-old life, and said, "To hell with you, you're a stranger!" Inside, I had begun to die for the lack of love. There was no one to confide in except my peers, who had not had the questionable taste or bad luck to lose someone yet—to have misplaced a mother and forgotten where they had put her. The situation was so inconceivable it didn't even warrant words with my friends, and so no one asked me, "How does it feel without a mother?"

Part of me watched Papa in horror. The other part was collapsing too, in spite of all my teen-age props. I bicycled under trees, riding wildly every afternoon (to this day, bicycling is freedom from grief), breaking every rule Mama had set up so carefully, the strict hours of learning, piano practice, early to bed, dancing lessons. They all continued but with only half of me, not scheduled, but haphazardly and without joy. Yet they saved me, the music and the dance, and the reading. . . . even if I experienced them with only half of me.

The other half was watching Papa, waiting for a sign, a coming together in our grief. It didn't come. I decided to forget her, and I did. To this day, I can't remember the sound of her voice or the contour of her face. When I ask for verification, I am looked at with amazement. "How could you forget her! She was unforgettable, the blazing blue eyes, high cheekbones, long hair wound round her head like a crown!"

I don't remember. Feeling, yes. Time, no.

Part of me was happy, because A. M. (after Mary) now, I could live my own life. My friends could come and visit for hours. I could fake study. They could even stay overnight. (Mama never allowed it.) I wondered how long this lasciviousness would go unnoticed. Then one day, my friend Gloria, whose family were fancy old Yankee leather people, came to study and spend the night. At home she drank wine before dinner and smoked cigarettes afterward. Why not in our home? It was the modern way. She bedded down and made her nest in one of the guest rooms in the attic, sipping her wine and smoking. I joined her, not in the sybaritic pleasures but in study for an exam. The next day, our housekeeper, an early American spinster hired after the funeral, told Papa about the Dionysian rites in the attic. He went into the kitchen, picked up a knife and, holding it high in the air, his face contorted with grief, threatened first to kill me, then to kill himself, because Gloria (subtext: "them," the "goy," the Jew-hater Yankee) in consort with me had "destroyed the sanctity of our house . . . with your mother not yet cold in her grave."

He broke down completely. After that, a silence, so deadly, was between us. Mama's dying had become such an act of attrition on her part, he could hardly look at me. We continued to die together, slowly; he, with the loss of his mate, and I, terrified of his grief, guilt-ridden that I felt freer without her, certain I had killed her and, like him, inconsolable with the loss.

If the earth had swallowed me up, it would have been better for both of us. His hand could not reach through space and touch me. My growing womanhood was the knife he brandished, symbol of his longing, my swinging skirts, my growing breasts. He had a compelling young woman on his hands.

Where was my sister Elizabeth? She was in New York, finishing her last year at Barnard, falling in love and marrying, to free herself from the loss and the love.

So, terrified of bursting, Papa and I turned the other way from each other. Our eyes never met. Not until I married!

Even then, he refused to look my husband in the eye, not till two years after our marriage. He had frozen me into his grief, kept me the age I was the moment Mama had died. It was impossible for me to have grown up, because Mary had *not* died, not really. How could I have grown up without her? If I was kept little, she was still alive, and his love for me, who looked like her, could not threaten him in his dream.

Those early years after Mama died, Papa and I lived in a pot, congealed with frost and snow, a dead body between us, and we didn't know how to throw it away, bury it— a macabre Georgia O'Keeffe painting, crackling, cold loneliness.

Was it any wonder I sat, the weight of my chin in my hand, gazing out the window for hours at little Ariel, wondering when and how Pa and Ma Smith could acknowledge the death. Papa and I had been as incapable of the act of burial as birds.

Years later, Papa told me, when he was driving Mama to Boston to enter the best hospital in the country to have her appendix removed by the best surgeon in Boston, she confessed to him that she had a slight sore throat. He said he drove the car off the road and stopped.

"In that case, forget about the operation," Papa told her. "It's not necessary, anyway. Forget it. We'll drive to Boston, since we're halfway, and I'll give you the money we would have spent on the appendix, and you'll buy yourself a new fur coat."

She insisted no, and Papa said he tried to argue her out of it. But she won, as she always did.

"You must tell the surgeon you have a sore throat," he told me he admonished her. "Let him decide."

She didn't, and Papa forgot to, as he had secretly planned. The operation went on as scheduled. Two days later, she developed peritonitis. She had had a strep throat. A day later, she developed pneumonia, was placed in an oxygen tent, and died of an embolism in her lung. Her body had become a comedy of errors. The best of Boston medicine consulted around the clock. They were in a state of mortification. Vibrant Mary, the wife of their colleague, was slipping away. They had no weapons to fight the infection. Sulfa drugs had no effect. It was before penicillin.

Even with his second wife of many years sitting in the room, Papa broke down in the retelling. Out of willfulness, she had as good as killed herself.

"What could I do? She was such a strong-willed girl . . . and I forgot to tell the surgeon. . . ."

How well I knew, along with him, how strong she was
—my beloved enemy.

There were so many unanswerable questions. Why had
Mama been so willful? Why did she play Russian roulette
with her life? How did Papa, a doctor, forget to talk to the
surgeon? We were discussing it in true Chekhov fashion,
just talking, talking, reliving, with no hope of learning anything or changing anything.

How could I press him for answers, as he sat there,
drinking the strong Manhattans of his later years. He still
missed her too much.

Miss Halpern,
Where Are You?

THE patterns were set. From now on, I was
on my own. Those who were afraid to love
me, or didn't love me, I loved. Those who
loved me I spurned. I was formidable. I
searched out the unattainables, made them
love me, then, faltering, they fell down backward, unable to tell me I couldn't have them,
because I was formidable. I was not unde-
sirable, but there were too many shadows
about me, and it scared other shadowy suitors.
Those with suns about them were unafraid.
But I didn't want suns! I wanted moons,
mirrors of myself, creatures strangling in their
own seaweed.

There were compensations in Mama's death. I was in
love with Gregory, a sinuous Scotsman of perhaps twenty
whom I met in my dance class. Mama had gotten wind of
it, because she appeared at class to watch more often than
usual. I sensed talk, but it was never directed to me. Then
she changed the day of my class to a time Gregory was not

attending. Then she died, and I was free to attend any class I wished. Papa didn't know the difference. Gregory was a black Scot, with white skin and green eyes. He wanted to be a professional modern dancer. In class, we were always contriving to be partners. We looked beautiful together, the teacher said. He was tall and muscular with his black and white handsomeness, and I, at fifteen, was tall, full-bosomed, with a tiny waist, and long hair I wore à la Veronica Lake bursting with excitement and premonitions of sexual power. I still thought a body was to walk to school, practice the piano, ride bicycles, roller skate, but *now* it was to dance with Gregory. I cajoled him into being my escort to my senior prom, and he came dressed in the most elegant tuxedo on the floor and his feet in black patent-leather dancing shoes. I wore a robin's egg-blue ball gown that was a French original from Filene's basement, with its tiny waist and Richard Straussian flowing skirt. I was the most sophisticatedly dressed member of the senior class. I think the gown was Elizabeth's, one she had worn to dances at Harvard while she was at Radcliffe. That's how grown-up it was. Oh, those were heady days, and only possible because Mama died and I was free . . . to kiss.

That spring, I wrote my first "piece" of music. It was for a group dance Gregory had choreographed and performed in a Hans Wiener dance concert in Boston at the Charles Street Theatre. It was my *Opus One*, and I played it "in the pit." I also danced a solo to some wild Spanish music. Before the group number, Hans Wiener came forward on the stage and announced there would be two Opus One's that night by a new young artist—I had danced and now they would hear my music. That performing was the beginning of my public exposure, the acting out of fright, joy, sex, terror, love needed and love given—in public.

There was no one to witness it. Mama was dead just a few months, and Papa did not attend. He was in mourning.

Why else would he not be there? Empty glory. If he had "seen" and "heard" me, he would have loved me.

It wasn't until years later when I'd written the score for the revival of *Marco Millions*, by Eugene O'Neill, directed by José Quintero for the first year of the Lincoln Center Repertory Theatre, that Papa looked at me a little differently; that perhaps I *had* grown up and was now my own spinning wheel with its whorl intact. Marriage didn't do it. Having a son didn't do it. It was in the signs of my becoming an artist that he read my independence, my right to speak and be listened to. Most of all, it was in my extraordinary luck to float into the atmosphere of O'Neill and Quintero that Papa grudgingly acknowledged respect for my "artistic soul." Until then, the songs and music I wrote for theater he called "piddling." "Folk music!" he scoffed. If one is a composer, one writes a symphony.

It seemed fated that my first important show would be linked with the name of Eugene O'Neill and the rockbound coast of New England (his last real home was in Marblehead, where we swam every day "in the Atlantic summers of our childhood," and his last hospital stay was at the Salem hospital, a mile or so away from Peabody and where Papa eventually died). Eugene O'Neill, New Englander, passionate, rhapsodic, victim of loss and too much love, maker of deep song from the stinging damp and cold of his inner and outer voyages. I understood his cry for clarification, and the sun in his throat; his wish for peace, knowing it did not exist, but that one must never stop looking for peace and beauty.

It also seemed a miracle that I was going to have the good fortune to work and learn from another great man of the theatre, José Quintero, the Panamanian of Spanish blood and temper, the only director to bring a neglected Eugene O'Neill back to the American theater, in full glory, with his

productions of *The Iceman Cometh, Long Day's Journey
into Night,* and *A Moon for the Misbegotten.*

It was a perfume so heady it made me reel but not fal-
ter. I was determined to work in comparable rhythms, commensurate with the importance of what I would learn from
Quintero about his visions of theater, and O'Neill in particular.

Marco Millions was written in 1923 and premiered in
1928 to mixed reviews, and O'Neill was disappointed. Lincoln Center's decision to revive it was courageous, because
it is a large, sprawling experiment filled with satire, social
comment, wit, show, and poetry and demands a full musical
score. In it, O'Neill created an extravagant lampoon of the
American businessman and a damnation of a vulgar society
in which beauty cannot survive.

In place of the ugly American, he set the play in thirteenth-century Italy and gave us the ugly Venetian, Marco
Polo, who spent years exploring China, bringing back to the
Western world none of its beauty, but only the material
things: firecrackers (gunpowder), spaghetti, and silkworms.
The poetry of the East and its spiritual wisdom escaped him
totally. *Marco* has been called "minor O'Neill" at various
times, but it is still the work of a giant playwright, visionary
in its comment on Babbittry and the lack of "soul" in a man
intent upon amassing "millions and millions and millions."

I had the time of my life watching José Quintero holding the O'Neill play high over his head like a sacred offering
to keep it from falling under the weight of the aborning
Lincoln Center. I watched the best stage managers (techni-
cally) in the business, who looked like bankers and distrusted
José for his poetry and demands. He needed to work in a
more intimate atmosphere. I watched his fight for rehearsal
time and the use of the actors in the newly formed repertory
company being hogged by Elia Kazan, who was directing
the new Arthur Miller play, *After the Fall.* I watched *that*

266

play in rehearsal, a play about a man playing all the roles of
victim, judge, and jury who brings himself to trial to relieve
himself of guilt; a man in search of personal and universal
morality. I watched Kazan work with the female star of that
play, who was being directed to look, walk, talk, and die
like Marilyn Monroe (in real life, Arthur Miller's second
wife). I watched Kazan, another great American director,
and felt privileged to watch, but couldn't help wondering
why he had cooperated with the House Un-American Activities Committee in the terrible fifties of the McCarthy era.
And I watched Arthur Miller watch Elia Kazan direct his
new play, the Arthur Miller who did *not* cooperate with the
Committee and was found guilty of contempt of Congress
because he refused to name friends and associates suspected
of being Communists. And I wondered how those two men
had made peace with themselves—enough to work together
on a play whose subject was guilt. Was it an object lesson
in maturity, civility, and humanity? I was repelled and bothered by the lesson. It had an unctuous, self-serving air about
it. And I did not like the Miller play. It had not transcended
self-pity, and the rehearsals reeked with overblown psychic
ritual.

The air was charged with negatives, assumed to be posi-
tives, because of who was doing the charging, Kazan and
Miller. I admit to bias. I was aware that José was fighting
for rehearsal time for Eugene O'Neill but losing out to a new
play by Arthur Miller until José put his foot down in a top-
level meeting. He said to Miller, "If my playwright were in
this room to protect *his* play, you, Arthur, would sit down!"
From then on, we had the rehearsal time *Marco* required.
I admit I'm gossiping, but it was all part of "I had the time
of my life" watching and smelling the blood in the bullring
of masters, learning that to be in it was to be hurt and wanting to be hurt. The price for the right to work in theater
was so high it could all but break your emotional bank, and

the tribute for the right to spill your guts and wait for the appreciative silence was astronomical.

I watched myself study and research, in preparation for composing, as I had never been motivated before. For weeks prior to writing down a note, I became both a sieve and a collector. I had to find themes for Marco Polo and his uncles traveling east from Italy of the thirteenth century to the China of a Great Khan. I had to find melodies for the Khan's granddaughter, a Princess alive and a Princess dead. I had to discover a theme for her funeral. I had to write a love song for Marco. I had to write a chorus for Chinese sailors going to Persia, clinging to the sails and rigging of a boat David Hays had so magnificently designed. I had to find sounds for the court of the Khan. I skulked about Asia House and the Oriental Room of the Public Library and discovered there was the sound of jade hitting jade in the opulent court of the Khan, the tinkle of unknowns, mysterious, exotic. The business manager of the production had a fit because he thought I was going to ask for curtains of jade to be struck by slaves (extras) to create the presence I wanted to build up for José. I explained to him it would be done with instruments. But the joke went around, and I was kidded that Local 802 of the Musicians Union didn't have sonorous stone players. I rummaged about for sounds of thirteenth-century royal funerals in China and made a decision to use a bagpipe and field drum for the ritual death of the Princess who was Beauty.

I watched myself reason that since O'Neill had written a poetic satire with political overtones in the twenties and was aware of Brecht's work overseas in Germany, I might find something in the paintings of George Grosz. Luckily, there was an exhibit of Grosz drawings, watercolors, and oils, "German period," and I ran, certain I would discover something. I did. The energy of the Grosz lines and colors, screaming comment and revolution, were exhilarating. The bitterness I could not use. Only the vitality of Grosz's renditions as they described the degenerate German upper classes of the twenties and their drowning blissfully in their own excrement. Somewhere here, there were colors I could use. The Germans of 1914–1926. The Venetians of Polo time. People in search of power. The Polo traveling melodies as they went east should have the clarity of a George Grosz line. And the Polo theme came: naive, witty, full of bravado, fluctuating between innocence and boorishness, without soul, satiric, flatulant, rhythmic. George Grosz showed me the way. I don't think I would have found it without him.

I watched myself decide, with José, that since O'Neill had set his play in the thirteenth century but had written a modern satire, I would write a modern score for ancient instruments. And so I used players from the New York Pro Musica, with their recorders, rebecs, vielles, sackbut, bagpipe, medieval trumpet, viola da gamba, bells, and percussive instruments. They would make, sometimes, the sound of a drunken medieval band, at other times something fragile, ancient; all, hopefully amusing to the modern ear.

I watched José shape a disparate cast, which was not prepared to act with music imbedded in the action, into a handsome production. I tried to approach his sensitivities and enhance them with sound.

I watched David Hays, the set designer, come up with breathtaking sets for *Marco*, and I watched Beni Montresor create incredibly beautiful, way-over-the-budget costumes. I watched David Hays turn away from me in jealousy, because the music was using up a great deal of José's time and interest, and I was but a newcomer in the Quintero galaxy. David's and José's careers had been linked gloriously for years. I watched David insist the orchestra be hidden, not visible, so he walled in the players on their balcony above the stage. I watched myself cry when, after having written a complicated accompaniment to a speech, it was decided by the producer, Robert Whitehead, and an actor that the music interfered. With tears on my cheeks, I explained the music was the satiric comment of O'Neill under the speech, and a tired Whitehead said, "Honey, what makes you think you are the voice of O'Neill?" José let me battle it out by myself, and he was right. *It* was learning. (Robert Whitehead is an illustrious producer. But there were so many important things that went wrong and needed fixing during the first year of Lincoln Center, that my tears were the least of them.) I watched them remove the music from the speech, and the audience did *not* clap after the actor's virtuoso turn. I watched them put the music back in, and the audience clapped after the speech for the manner in which the actor steered himself through the excitement of words and music. The music stayed.

I watched myself watch José Quintero fighting the demons inside himself and outside. And I watched myself learn from him, as I had from Martha Graham, about Quality, the personal and public fight for it, and how it can almost kill you if you let it, because it makes "others" feel inadequate and they would prefer your silence.

Papa didn't come to the opening of *Marco Millions* in New York. He spared himself lest the reviews were bad (I'm sure). Nor could he face the tumult of opening-night nerves and meeting new people. He let *Marco* run a month and then came; sat quietly through without coughing; met José afterward. They liked each other immediately, the dark Panamanian with the burning, black eyes and Papa, victim of his Yiddishkeit and reserve, uncomfortable anywhere out of his office, home, or hospital, unless the conversation transcended "niceness" and rose to meaningful exchange. They had things they could talk about. Both thought O'Neill a genius. Both led lives as commanded by dark spirits as had O'Neill. They were both, Papa and José, elegant men, consumed by their own pride and self-induced failings. They both were addicts.

José, at *that* time, to liquor that lessened the pain from the goring of the bulls in himself and gave courage to face the bulls in the theater, Papa to drugs (like many doctors) to steady his nerves in the goyish world and calm his asthma and emphysema.

Papa's only comment to me after the show was, "O'Neill would have been pleased. You did a good job." He didn't talk much about José, but I knew he had fallen in love with his spirit, as I had. In the next few years, I composed music for two more Quintero productions. On one of those December days, in a Japanese restaurant (of all places for a Panamanian, some Jews, and a Greek—José's friend Nick— to enjoy Christmas Day dinner), Papa helped José put on his coat at the end of dinner, as though José were his son. Papa smoothed down the collar as a parting gesture, and there were tears in José's eyes. He'd had terrible problems with his own father, and here was the touch of a father. I was amazed at Papa's gesture. I never saw him touch anyone else like that, except his grandsons, Chuck and Peter.

Papa adored artists of renown, the celebrated ones, children of the gods. In the gesture, too, I sensed a "thank you" —for me.

❧

Mama, at the end of her life, was a dedicated Stalin lover. Papa felt, prematurely, that the Russian brand was not "it," certainly not for what he had put his passion on the line. They had violent fights, privately and in public. Papa was rereading the writings of Trotsky out of intellectual curiosity, not realignment, but even the rereading was considered heresy.

The year Mama died was the same in which began the first public Russian trials, their purpose to isolate the so-called traitors against the Soviet. The beloved and honored names of early devoted revolutionaries were now being hissed as personae non gratae and the men behind those names were being sentenced to death or sent to Siberia. Mama went along with the party line. Papa would have none of it. Their voices screamed out night after night in argument and sometimes with friends, who were mostly on Mama's side. Papa would not accept the submerging of dissent.

One who *was* on Papa's side was Moshe Nadir, the poet. He and Papa were being called "Trotskyites." Nadir died a year or so after Mama, literally from a broken political heart. Because of his anti-Stalinist stance and a very early awareness there was something rotten in the Soviet dream, Nadir was drummed out of his poet laureate position on the big left-wing Yiddish newspaper in New York. He lost most of his lifelong friends, had a heart attack, and died.

I often wondered what would have happened if Mama had lived through more years of political history, whether she would have agreed, eventually, with Papa. The year she died, the atmosphere in the house was so fraught it could well have led to divorce because of ideological incompatibility.

On those violent evenings of verbal combat, Papa, after a few drinks, would become eloquent and scream that communism was not the salvation of the human race. Anyway it was anarchism! Not anarchy! Anarchism! The divine state in which everyone would be so good, so disciplined, people would not need controls; the controls would have to have come slowly, through education not with trials and deaths and exile; that Stalin was a killer, that the dream they had hoped for was not going to happen in Russia. "They were peeing in the soup in Russia"—it would have to happen somewhere else.

And so ended the atmosphere of a special house, the end of their real laughter, the politics, the artists, the singing, the good stories and the dancing barefoot in the parlor, the end of the Yiddish Bloomsbury Bunch in Peabody, Massachusetts, and the rare individualism they exuded. Rightly or wrongly they lived it in the best traditions of America, "New Englandly." And certainly in the spirit of Uncle Bob Bakeman's "My Creed," jotted down probably before 1920:

> I believe that the wisest man in all the world is not wise enough to act as conscience for me. I believe in being true to my conscience, in the face of conventions and reputation and laws and friends and job and family.
>
> I believe in the holy quality of the pain that comes to anyone as a consequence of my being true to my conscience, and I want to be big enough to want every man to be true to his, even if it must mean pain for me.
>
> I believe—whoever you are, whether you are black or white, in prison, or on a throne, whether you are called good or bad, whatever you have done in the past or shall do in the future, I believe in You.
>
> And I believe supremely that the time for me to begin to practice these beliefs is not at the elusive moment when I shall have greater influence—but Now.

❧

When Elizabeth walked me down the steps of the high school, telling me Mama had died, I did say one thing to her before I sobbed and went quiet. What I said was, "She won't be able to see me go through college!"

For many years later, in search of education, as was expected of me, I did my best to make good on that cry. I was the most dreadful student come along to plague the dean of a college. It wasn't that I failed from dumbness. I just wouldn't appear in class. Formal education bored me. I was unable to apply myself without Mama's insistence and control of the spokes. The regulator of speed, the whorl of the spinning wheel had been broken, and I spun into my late adolescent years, not promiscuous, but just in search of love and elegantly out of control. After all, I *had* been fashioned, albeit with great difficulty, into a New England shape; to be of use, tireless in my search for balance; to be thrifty, make things; to be contained within my form, to make a pleasant sound when I moved.

I looked like a wheel, I felt like a wheel, but when rolled, went crazy. My only mistake was that I was a wheel without its whorl!

I was sixteen my first year at college and much too unready for the loneliness away from home and familiar things. As unpleasant as they were, they were familiar. Papa, not wanting me to be too far away, enrolled me at the Boston University College of Music. My marks were not good enough to attend an Ivy League college as Elizabeth had done. So the family flag of education was fluttering sadly halfway down its pole. I moved out of the house and took up residence, eighteen miles from Peabody, in a dorm on Beacon Hill. From there, I continued my dancing lessons, made friends I never in my life saw again, learned to chain smoke, discovered every moviehouse in the downtown district of Boston, and one day joined a theater group, conveniently one block away from the dorm on Beacon Hill.

My mailbox was filled with letters and postcards from the dean, "Please appear at my office" . . . "Miss Halpern, where are you?" I answered none of them. I was too busy becoming the composer in residence of the theater and writing my first musical called, *Nor All Thy Tears*. It was reviewed admirably. I was petrified lest anyone in the family see my name, because the question would have been posed, "When did you have the time!" So my second Opus was also unattended by those who, if they had been different people, might have been delighted. It never occurred to me that I should sit down and level with Papa, tell him to stop wasting his money on formal education for me, that I was one of those unruly ones who could only learn by experimentation, never by the rules.

By the Spring, Boston University made it known I had received F's in all subjects because of nonattendance. Papa had a tantrum fit for a king, that raised the roof in one of the attic bedrooms where I was crying. Elizabeth was called home from New York for the scene, and I heard Papa screaming downstairs, "Why didn't she tell me what she was up to? I would have taken the money and flushed it down the toilet! What does she want? [He had heard me sobbing my heart out upstairs.] What does she want? [He was frantic for my happiness.] I'll do anything she wants."

What I really wanted was to sit in my pot all the live-long day and not fly at all—like Bozo. I had no wish to achieve, only to rest and ruminate, become closer with Papa (which was impossible), and try to sort out the madness of my days. I didn't want to *be* anybody. I just wanted to *be*. Instead, I ran to the head of the stairs and yelled down to the judge and jury, "I want to live in New York and go to the Juilliard School of Music."

Much to my surprise, I was accepted at Juilliard. Sight reading, transposition, ear training, it was all in my bloodstream because of the early training at the Faelton School. I became a member of a freshman class again, but this time in what was considered an Ivy League school of music. I was bored to death. The letters and postcards from the dean began to arrive again. "Miss Halpern, where are you?"

🍁

With the dumbness of a lower creature, in late adolescence, under a green moon, pump-primed as I was for the stone well of me to run dry, crumbling, so were the walls giving in to the dry rot of angst, I rushed to Maine to retrieve my lover, master of my fate, captain of my body. How in love was I with him, all of twenty, or was he nineteen? And his letters had ceased. Why the silence? I flew to Maine like a wild goose off-season to find out if that tree where I had chosen to nest was there. I flew with my heart in my mouth, in the car of a roommate at college. The greenness of Maine appeared. Whatever was myself became the motor. We flew toward the answer. A male child would tell me whether I lived or died. We drove up a long dirt road; finally, a bracelet of pines, a strange sky, a new place harboring a body and mind I had decided I couldn't live without. What was I? Seventeen?

"Where might I find Victor K.?"

"He's in the theater building."

Naturally. Where else would he be, the stage-struck, white-faced, burning, selfish young boy that he was, father of my first unborn child. Was there a rival? We had driven nonstop from New York to Maine, under a sky filled with chicken lickens threatening to fall earthward. Had we not spent a year of college in the nuptial bed? Were we not eternally sealed? Why had the letters stopped? Oh, I loved too hard. It was all too hot, too white, too premature.

"You can't mean it!"

"You're upsetting me. I have a job to do here," he said.

"You must be kidding."

"No, I'm not kidding. Go home," he said. "They're all looking at us."

"Go home? Where? We're home, you and me."

"You and I," he corrected me. "I'll see you in the fall, when school starts."

He didn't say that, but it was something like that. It was some unidentifiable flying object he was riding in my direction; some round cool, smooth, metal rejection he was propelling in the green air of a pine-splitting headache night, and the moon was green and adolescent. Behind me were eight hours of driving. Ahead was the trip home to Papa's house in Massachusetts—and the same kind of love.

❧

On April Fool's Day of the previous spring, Papa had taken himself a second wife, not out of attraction or as a challenge, but for survival alone—to have a woman in the house. He married Diana, an old family friend, herself a new widow with a young son, Robert. It seemed like a natural move, without upheaval. They were horrendously mismatched. It was a disastrous relationship that lasted for the rest of their lives. They lived longer together than either of them had with their first loves. Mama's presence never left the house. Diana couldn't expunge it. She never tried, and if she had wanted to, Papa wouldn't have let her. It remained to the end a house lacking, a house in mourning. Someone was always missing, and when Papa died, many years later, the last word on his lips was "Mary."

❧

The most amazing thing happened after Papa died. As though programmed by a hypnotist, unbeknownst to myself, I went out in search of a killer to love.

A German boys' choir sang Gregorian masses all through the night, while we lay side by side, trying to sleep, until it was time for my enemy to leave. There was no foundation, nothing experienced but pain wearing its masquerade-love costume, so tattered, I should have recognized the ruse, but didn't.

Gravitating toward the most opposite I could find, a "revenge fuckeur," the black cupid slipped from the bed before dawn, leaving me with an aching pelvis. Alone, in a borrowed apartment. I had allowed myself to be sniffed out, tracked, caught by a Doberman pinscher trained to kill. Then, curiously, he changed his mind. Another thought took its place, copulation. With the foreplay of a killer, not rough, devilishly beguiling, slowly, slowly, he played me into submission. Played me into the guise of an extinct dodo bird, left me with a hooked bill, ridiculously short legs, and wings useless for flying. He was off to Europe, and it all meant nothing in the long run.

Looking backward, it meant everything. I had allowed him to be my water witch, allowed his divining rod to find old, underground springs, still bubbling, looking for forbidden streams, looking for forbidden rivers, looking for forbidden seas.

It was later that I thought in terms of streams, rivers, seas. When he left, it was really more like a sewer. I remember I groaned and the water was polluted. I was wet with sweat and fear in a loaned bed. It wasn't something I had done lightly. He had sought me out, convinced me attraction was all, that love was not the issue or important. That's all I needed to hear. I set out to convince him otherwise. I tried and banged myself against the Oedipal wall, again, again, again, loving, giving of myself, flushed, glowed, manic in the conquest. God damn it! You invited me, I'm your guest. Love me! It was just like the old days, with Papa and me, close, passing each other at all times of the day, yet no love. I would make him. Force him to show, to say. It didn't work then. It didn't work now. But ah, later my enemy came back from Europe, loving. It was too late. I turned my back.

I don't think I'll ever love a killer again. But who knows the darkness of the well with its underground springs, still looking for larger bodies of water in which to empty and release energies. The open-endedness of the "who knows" is frightening.

Perhaps, if it's remembered that to seek the spirit of a dead father, in the corpus of a lover, is an act reeking of necrophilia . . . perhaps *that* image will still the underground springs. Perhaps. My God, it should!

❦

The real end of the first nest.

A year after Papa died, his second wife, Diana, also died, and the house on Central Street was sold. I was awaiting remnants of my original loves and life that would arrive in a moving van. Papa's truly dead, Mama, long ago. Now their cherished things would speed through a dark, wet night, with Mama and Papa sitting in the back of the van on their horsehair sofa, holding hands like two mad angels running away from heaven. Come home they are, indeed, to test my hospitality. Mama, with her hair unpinned; Papa, his moustache still blond and uncertain. How young they look. And how old I felt waiting to receive them.

I think about that receiving of furniture seven years ago, as I look out on a rainy, empty pigeon ledge. Empty of nest, mother, father, children, family. A time was over. It will never *be* again. A cello is playing an accompaniment in my head and high above that instrument is a medieval melody. Spanish? Moorish? The melody weaves its way on a lyre, accompanying the travel of a van filled with artifacts from Papa's house, newly sold. The van speeds through the heart of New England, past the sea, field, fences, doorways of my childhood. Rushing past the ghosts of witches, past the elms, the McIntyre fluted fireplaces and vestibules, past the L-shaped farmhouses, past the clapboard-white and barn-wine shadows, past tobacco vineyards and apple orchards where new immigrants with dark skins work and sigh and turn in their sleep. The van comes hurtling into New York, where I wait for it to shock me into recognition that a time is over. Like a young aborigine receives the ritual mask from his elder, so I shall polish the furniture that was once theirs. The Time locked into their cherry wood will shine now in my house—until I don't need the mask and pass it on.

Endings

MY Diary says it was late May, 1973. The Smith family had been long gone. I looked out the window and saw White-Tail, the medieval Prince of Evil, the one who tried to push Brownie and Plucky off their ledge; the one who fought with Pa Khrushchev and lost; the one who tortured Bozo as he sat in his pot, unable to fly, and finally did push him off and make him fly. There was WhiteTail, the enemy, the gangster, the taker of what wasn't his, but who had always been vanquished, each repulsion a glorious war: the Battle of Agincourt, Waterloo, Bunker Hill, when the Greeks defeated the Persians at Marathon. The Smiths and the Khrushchevs had won them all against WhiteTail. Here he was again. And I was glad to see him! There hadn't been a pigeon around for weeks. What was he doing? He and a mate were taking possession of the prized nursery ledge that once belonged to the Smiths. Victory at last. It was almost summer.

WhiteTail and his mate were billing and cooing and carrying on. Twigs and sticks and new grass began to appear on the bare ledge, with no pots. I groaned. Not again! My animus for WhiteTail was disappearing. How could I be so fickle to the memory of the Smiths! WhiteTail was starting a family, that's why. How could I turn my back on a family? Well, I would not become so directly involved this time. Life would be easier, anyway, and they won't need me.

I look out a few days later and the nest is half built. My human neighbor appears at the window, pushes away the *half*-built nest. It falls down four stories. My stomach turns and I go about my business. I don't look out for almost a week.

Damn it, if there isn't a new nest almost fully realized. A hefty nest this time, almost ready for a new creature. I am working at the typewriter, my back is to the window. I hear scraping. Willie, the cat, runs to the window and looks out, but I don't turn. I hear more scraping. I turn around and see my neighbor, female and pregnant (the *first* full view I'd had of her in all the months of pigeon watching), and I see her sweeping off the new nest. I hear it fall.

A surge of hatred. I am actually crying. WhiteTail and mate return to see the nest gone. Confusion, like the confusion of Ma and Pa Smith when Ariel died. I can't work anymore, and, although midafternoon, I pull the window shade down in the watching room.

The next day was a day that made one think of summer, curiously, not the summers of recent past, but the summers of one's childhood. It was a day in May that surprised me into thinking it was June, with June's full convening of branches at the garden's edge. One wanted to be young like the green of it, calm as the shade of it, where leaves, entwining, managed to be gentle. A convening of branches, where the sparrow and the robin democratize under the auspices of two lilac bushes. A day in June, when I wished I were a delegate with wings.

I look out the window. There are three slick, shiny black pigeons, the like of which I had not seen in the corridor from the beginning to the end of my watching. They are perched about the iron grillwork of the Smith nursery like an honor guard. Suddenly, they fly against the neighbor's window and break it! They observe their deed and fly away.

When I saw those three pigeons, dressed in black leather, I called for Jules to join me. So I fantasize or exaggerate none of it. I had a witness.

It was obvious. Those birds were crack militia sent to do retribution. Someone had to let humans know they had no right to destroy the nests of others.

The pigeon population of the neighborhood came to see the "happening." WhiteTail and his mate hovered about what was to have been their home. Then, almost on signal, they all left. Not one pigeon has been back to our corridor since.

Yom Kippur of '73 was a fabulous, Indian summer weekend. We looked at each other in our house and wanted to "take off." Several suggestions were made. Each one was wrong, somehow. We were tired, and engagement with people had to be special. We went over the list of friends living out of town who had been saying, "Come," But there was personal trouble in each of their houses. We felt like being selfish and did not go. We figured an inn would be the answer, but it was short notice to try to make a reservation. We wanted warmth, quiet. It would have been good to be with friends unencumbered with tensions, but there were none. How about just going up to the Cloisters to mosey around in another century for the afternoon? No. We needed to "take off" and fly.

The radio was on while we were debating the subject. It was a glorious blue morning on the East Coast of the United States. Suddenly the bulletin came over the radio: "Israel, attacked by Arabs on Yom Kippur, the holiest and most somber of high holidays for the Jews." The tiny country was reeling and pulling itself together. My heart rolled in its cavity, as did most of the world's, all except the Jew haters. Tears came. It was war for the Jews again. Could Jews never stop eating the bitter herb, one year in symbol, the next year in reality?

Now, let's really get away.

"Let's go home."

"Home?" My husband looked at me strangely. "There is no home. Everyone's dead," he reminded me.

"Let's go home anyway."

The air was quickly cut with questions and figurings.

"Yes, let's fly to New England! There are still good cousins there. They'll be amazed to see us."

We hadn't been back since Papa's death, those seven years ago. Yes. Let's be with the family. The cousins will meet us at the airport. It would be a reunion of Jews, my Jews, in the face of everything that was bitter. Let's fly into the vortex. We wanted a quiet weekend? Hell, let's go right into the hurricane of beginnings, memory, blood relations.

For the first time in my life, I felt I could shoot a gun, walk onto a battlefield and destroy myself for an idea—the survival of Jews.

It was an irresistible feeling. I wanted to be with my own while Israel was fighting for her life. Even Jules, my German-Jewish, sixth-generation-American husband, felt that way. So we took the air shuttle to Boston and were met by Cousin Benjie, now a man of seventy, who grew up around Mary and Harry, and for whom Papa was a surrogate father and friend; and Cousin Dorothy Richmond, Great-Uncle Sam's daughter and her husband, Mac. It was good to be with them. They were my own. Benjie, the atheist, or at most, agnostic, had just come from "temple." That was a shocker. But, why not? He, too, was worried about Israel. We drove north, chatting madly, and then fell silent. It felt good driving through the darkness toward Peabody with my own. We didn't have to talk. We knew who we were. Benjie had diapered me and baby-sat for me and watched me grow. He knew the childhood pleasures and storms and every minute configuration of the past Time of the reign of Mama and Papa in Peabody. He had studied his dentistry books at our dining room table and matured under the tutelage of Harry, and had become the second Jewish dentist of Peabody. Benjie was my last link to the anecdotes and richness of the house on Central Street. Dorothy was the cousin who admonished me about a Jew having to spit nine times when he saw a cross.

As we drove north, we each knew we didn't have to speak, about how strange it was that Papa wasn't there anymore. Still, it was going home.

In my lexicon, there is no such thing as "You can't go home again." We grow. We clarify ourselves, but our computers have forever stashed away the original imprints. The brain throws nothing away until the heart stoppage finishes the imput of energy. Then, and only then, do our encyclopedias become obsolete, stop recording, storing, imprinting.

The next day, Benjie, Jules and I were out raking up leaves that rose ankle high over my cousin's lawn. For me, it was an act of combing the hair of the Past into neat piles, collecting the fallen-out, placing it in black plastic bags, a neat and healthy burial under the dazzling blue of a New England fall sky. The Past was beautiful yellow, reds, mauves, and orange, disintegrating gently to our touch, with a stoicism born and bred in New England.

I asked to be driven to the town square, and then up Central Street to look at the house I had not seen for seven years and which we had sold after Papa's death.

What happened? Central Street, once the quiet, tree-lined offshoot of Main Street, was so changed I didn't even know I was on it. It was like coming out of anesthesia. For a dreadful moment, I couldn't recognize anything.

The shape of the place had been remolded, pushed about into car washes, pizza parlors. The South Congregational Church, which had stood in the square in one form or another since 1711, had been torn down and the land bought by the American Oil Company! In its place was a huge gas station. I expected a nurse to tap me on the shoulder, "Hello, honey, wake up. It's all over." But we kept on driving. I said, "Go slow. I want to stop in front of Papa's house." I didn't know when to expect it. Didn't I know it would be like this? Didn't I know the old centers of Revolutionary towns were disappearing, while their outskirts were becoming their new centers, and their shopping marts, with mile-long parking areas, were now the churches of the suburbs? Of course I knew, and I didn't care. To hell with it. I had other images in my computer, and they were indestructible.

There it was, Papa's house, shamefaced. I had caught it lying with its shoes off, encrusted feet showing through gaping holes in its socks, a booze bottle abandoned a foot away from where it fell, a tender, fallen look on its face, the eyes pale blue and still modest in spite of what it had been through. "How could you have let this happen to me?" it said.

How could I have let it happen? I tried to explain. Stop the highways? Stop the free enterprise system and the bourgeois panting into the suburbs to get away from the ghettos? Stop their shopping centers with unlimited choices for gluttons? Stop *all that* from oozing like larva into the rolling woods and hills of what used to be my New England?

Poor house. We could barely meet each other's eyes. I mumbled something polite, like, "Your stained-glass window is still on the stairway." And it answered with a great sigh. There was no energy for loud complaint. Too much had happened. People had left, the people who polished old wood and planted willow trees. They were up there, a mile away, in the cemetery. The house was down here. There was no one to give it comfort. It lay like an old prostitute, its legs spread wide, in the same position the last customer had left it. Now, animals were nestling in its crotch and weeds growing into its ears. The white-clapboard, black-shuttered yesterday was sinking into silly putty, black and blue, leaning into itself, spent.

Benjie and Jules wanted to drive on, but I made them wait, got out of the car, and walked to the back yard, to see what the maple tree, planted on my twelfth birthday, was doing. It had reached above the roof of the house. Glorious. But pigs had hammered a circular bench into it, and jammed a basketball net under one of its arms. I caught a sense of old iron bedsteads and broken wheels flung about the brown fall grass. And that was the end of that. I had seen what I came for.

I knew Jules expected me to be crying when I got back into the car but I surprised him.

"On to the cemetery!" I said cheerfully and we drove up to the end of Central Street, onto a side road, to a gentle, hilly place, where everyone would be. Benjie, being a trustee of the cemetery, had its key. He opened the gate. We were the only ones there. I ran to find familiar names in stone. Everyone Papa had ever treated and healed was there, every Jew, that is. My Past, my Jews, my childhood. There was Great-Uncle Harris and his wife, and Papa's mother, Grandmother Pearl from the fields of her father in the Ukraine, and Papa's sisters, and Mama, next to Papa. There was Mrs. So and So with the heart, and Mr. X. with the head, and Mrs. Y. who kept plaguing Papa in her old age about whether she could eat carrots. There was the mother of one of my classmates, who fainted in the bathtub and had to be lifted out nude and everyone saw her pubic hair. And there was the rich leather manufacturer who snubbed Papa because he was a Socialist. There they all were, the all-rightnicks and the strange ones, and the poor.

Benjie began to enjoy it with me, and recalling, laughing, he filled me in on this one and that one. We turned over the stone pages of Jewish history in Peabody with the glee of flipping through the family album. I felt Jules standing back, observing me, wondering when he would put his arm around me (because he knew me so well), to help me put my pieces together. Jules didn't need to be told by Uncle Bob that marriage was a glorified friendship.

But it wasn't necessary. I was euphoric as a village gossip, just learning at a wedding that the bride is pregnant.

I turned to Jules. "It's all mine. Crazy as it is, it's all mine, my lovely, mad, immigrant Jews." Only then, did the crisping, late afternoon October air catch me in my throat.

Then I ran my hand over the gravestones of Mama and Papa and we turned away and left.

Coda

"ONLY then, did the crisping, late afternoon October air catch me in my throat." (It was like the repeating of a phrase of music.)

Jules and Benjie walked to the gate of the cemetery and waited for me. That's what happened. And I search for the quality of that moment before I touched the headstones and "turned away and left."

The first thought to end that sentence was, "and Jews are dying again in Israel."

The second thought was: I'm standing here, different, not the child, not the growing girl, not even the woman Papa knew in his old age. I'm standing here with one breast. I'm different, and yet strangely, whole, more whole than I've ever been. I was on my own, yet theirs.

I took Time in my hand and threw it up in the air like a primary-colored rubber ball and placed Mama and Papa at the dinner table. But it was all different. I would tell them how I felt, who I was, particularly Mama (she had left so early). And even Papa. Some of it would be new to him, even though he sensed so much, though we talked so little.

287

We would sit over wine and talk and talk, and I would tell them what happened to me, that I did become "an artist," their heart's desire; that it took years of being pickled in brine, and was not easy; that part of me wished I had been born a pigeon, a creature with feathers, or no clothes at all, like a horse, always naked and always beautiful; but that I had made peace being human; that I was essentially an optimist and have always tried to breathe life into dead things, with a stubbornness that defies explaining, even tulips; that with the hindsight and armor of scar tissue, I could see why I never did become a composer of symphonies, as Papa had hoped (that he would sit in Symphony Hall and hear my novels in sound); that it never could have happened to me. I was too concerned with the female part of me, the content and inner space of myself. That magic blending of male and female, form and content—the sine qua non of every great artist—had not happened to me, but it might yet; that there were so many unanswered questions, and my need for love as a woman was so great, there was little energy to allow for the masculine part to be exercised, the part that cleaves out forms and creates shapes, moves recklessly and with virility into situations that demand large architecture; that I thanked them for their inheritance and forgave them their sins of omission. I wanted them to know I felt alive through the use of Time, and a woman who had come from their nest; that I no longer needed the ritual mask; and I had embraced its essence and would pass it on; and that I would never stop searching for a sense of Order within and *beyond* the circumference of our wounds, theirs and mine.

Standing there in the bright Indian summer sun, I laughed out loud.